THE
EVERYTHING
TIME
MANAGEMENT
BOOK

How to get it all done and
still have time for you!

Bob Adams

Adams Media Corporation

Avon, Massachusetts

An Everything® Series Book.
Everything® is a registered trademark of Adams Media Corporation.

Published by Adams Media Corporation
57 Littlefield Street, Avon, MA 02322. U.S.A.
adamsmedia.com

ISBN: 1-58062-492-8

Printed in the United States of America.

J I H G F E D C B

Library of Congress Cataloging-in-Publication Data
Adams, Bob
    The everything time management book / by Bob Adams
        p. cm.
    Includes index.
    ISBN 1-58062-492-8
    1. Time management. I. Title.
    HD69.T54 A4 2001
    640'.43—dc21   2001022042

Illustrations by Barry Littmann, Kathie Kelleher
and Eulala Connor/Portfolio Solutions.

This book is available at quantity discounts for bulk purchases.
For information, call 1-800-872-5627.

Visit the entire Everything™ series at everything.com

Contents

Preface
Jason and Andrea's Story vii

The Case vii
The Verdict ix

Introduction
Time Is Not Money xi

Part I
The Basics

Chapter One
**Your Love/Hate Relationship
with Time** 3

What Is Time? 4
External Time 5
Internal Time 6
Why Most Popular Time Management
Systems Don't Work 8
What Is Your Attitude Toward Time? 9
Why Time Passes You By 13
Tracking Use of Time 16
Factoring in Reality 18
Jason and Andrea's Time Relations 20

Chapter Two
Mastering Your Mess 23

Learn to Prioritize 24
Important versus Urgent 26
Accepting a Shift of Focus 28
Setting Goals 29
The Almighty To-Do List 32
Scheduling 36
Recognizing and Respecting Your Limitations . . 39
Maintaining Management 41
Jason and Andrea Take Control 42

Chapter Three
The Art of Organizing 47

Let Simplicity Be Your Savior 48
Organization 48
Simplification 50
Elimination 51
Avoid Lists of Lists of Lists 53
Organizational Tools 55
Jason and Andrea Together in Organization . . . 60

Chapter Four
Accomplishing More in Less Time . . . 65

The 80/20 Rule 66
Multitasking: Pros and Cons 69
Trick of the Trade 71
Making the Most of Every Moment 73
Stick with What You Start 74
Do It Right the First Time! 75
The Importance of Listening 77
Eliminate/Control Distractions 79
Interruptions 82
Don't Be Afraid to Delegate 87
Hiring Help 91
Jason and Andrea Keep on Learnin' 93

Chapter Five
Using the Internet to Save Time 97

Time-Consuming Traps on the Internet 98
Finding Information with Ease 99
E-mail 101
Personalizing a Search Engine 105
One-Stop Shopping 108
Travel Made Simple 109
Other Plans to Make 111
Online Education 112
Using the Internet to Find a Job 115
Jason and Andrea Become Internet Savvy . . . 119

Part II
Pyschological Setbacks in Time Management

Chapter Six
Unveiling Motivation 125

Who Has Control? 126
Excuse Me? 128
Parkinson's Law 131
Taking Breaks 132
Put Off Procrastination 134
The Pains of Perfectionism 140
Reap the Rewards! 142
Jason and Andrea Get Motivated 145

Chapter Seven
Do You Suffer Sensory Overload? . . . 149

Slay the Giant! 150
Make a Trade 152
Emotions 154
Pounce on the Paper Problem 156
Making Wise Decisions 158
Fear 164
Jason and Andrea Unload Their Overload . . . 165

Chapter Eight
Struggling with Self-Esteem 169

What Is Self-Esteem? 170
Low Self-Esteem 173
High Self-Esteem 176
Good Self-Esteem 178
Improving Self-Esteem 178

Positive Self-Talk 182
Handling Criticism 184
Jason and Andrea Take Time for Reflection . . 187

Chapter Nine
Is Your Stress Level Skyrocketing? . . 191

Stressless—Is That Even a Word? 192
Identifying the Source 196
Taking Inventory 197
Adjusting to Achieve Balance 199
Maintaining Methods of Healthy Living 200
Setting Up a Routine 201
Learn to Say No 204
The Luxury of Leisure 206
Jason and Andrea Battle Stress 208

Part III
Applying the Basics to Your Life

Chapter Ten
Your House on Your Time 215

Practicing What You've Learned 216
Cleaning the House 219
Furnishing Food 225
Organizing the Home 227
The Moving Mess 231
A Circus of Household Chores 235
Time Management Maintenance 239

Chapter Eleven
Your Work Space on Your Time 243

You've Heard It All Before 244
Organizing Your Work Space 247
Multitasking in the Office 252
Delegating in the Workplace 253
How to Make the Most of Your Commute 255
Maintain Control of Your Work Space 259

Chapter Twelve
Your Personal Life on Your Time . . . 263

Put It into Play 264
Keep in Touch 267
Relationships 269
Education 271
Health 273
Hosting Parties 276
How to Use Your Vacation Wisely 278
Creating Quiet Time 280
Keeping Up with Your Personal Life 282

Index 285

Jason and Andrea's Story

The Case

Jason rushes into the house to escape the rain. He tosses his keys on the table by the door, not noticing as they slide onto the floor. He doesn't bother to take his shoes off, because he will need to leave right after dinner anyway. Instead he tracks water and mud through the living room, thinking he will have time to clean up the mess later.

He walks sheepishly into the dining room expecting to see his wife, Andrea, and their son, Matthew, already eating. He is late getting home from work and didn't have a chance to call. But no one is there. The table hasn't even been set.

Their dog, Barney, nearly knocks him over in greeting. He barks several times—his way of letting Jason know he has yet to be fed. Jason, trying hard to ignore Barney, seeks out his wife.

He finds Andrea in the kitchen, stirring with one hand, pulling a dish from the oven with the other, all the while balancing the phone between her ear and shoulder. She glances up and mouths the word "hello." He smiles, knowing he isn't in the doghouse. But his irritation flares as he realizes a late dinner means getting back to work later and less sleep tonight. He sighs as he plops into a chair. He drums his fingers impatiently on the countertop. Knowing he isn't helping the situation, he gets up to pull out the lettuce for a salad. At least he can help speed things along.

But Andrea shoos him away with a spoon. She can't stand it when anyone invades her work space. Jason would be in the way and would break her concentration. She is already backed up as it is. She scribbles a note to herself on a sticky note and affixes it to the refrigerator door. She is running late for the class she teaches

on Wednesday nights, and she still needs to do a load of laundry so her family can have clean clothes for tomorrow.

Jason feeds Barney and then walks back into the living room, resolving to wait patiently. He begins to compose a list in his mind of what still needs to be completed before he can go to sleep. Just thinking about it makes him tired, but he allows his eyes to wander around the room. The plants need to be watered pretty badly; most are on the verge of death. The television screen has a coat of dust at least an inch thick. A stack of unopened mail lies on the coffee table. Books are scattered all over the floor, most of which belong to him. Also, the clumps of mud he tracked in seem to be spreading around the house of their own accord.

While Jason is taking mental notes of everything that needs to be done, Andrea continues to prepare dinner in the kitchen. Still on the phone, she desperately searches for the pen she just had a minute ago. She reaches into the junk drawer to find another one and is stabbed by a safety pin. Sucking on her pricked thumb, she decides to give up her search and just memorize the phone number. Once she gets the information she needs, she impatiently cuts the conversation short. She loads her arms with dishes, drinks, and food, and hurries into the dining room. She drops a plate along the way. It shatters, and she scoots the glass out of the way with the toe of her tennis shoe.

"Dinner's ready," she calls.

Jason jogs in from the living room, tripping over one of Barney's toys. He sits down immediately and has a biscuit in his mouth before he even grabs a plate. Andrea also grabs a biscuit and calls upstairs, "Matthew, dinner!" Then she turns to her husband and says, "Jason, will you have Matthew clean up that glass? I'm late for class."

Jason nods, thinking of what he should start on first after he eats. He debates just taking the meal to go as his wife leaves the room to call their son by the stairway. A couple of minutes later she walks back into the dining room with her keys dangling from her pinky finger and crumpled papers sticking out of her book bag.

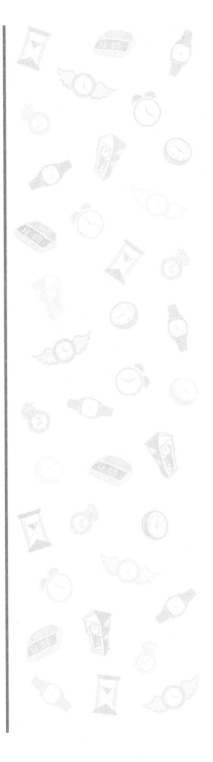

"Did Matthew go to a friend's house?" she asks.

"I don't know. I haven't seen him all day," Jason replies.

"What do you mean you haven't seen him all day? You were supposed to pick him up from soccer practice!"

Jason's eyes widen. "I thought you were picking him up today."

"You know I don't have the time—" they both begin in unison. The slamming of the front door halts their argument. Matthew, completely drenched, walks into the dining room, dragging his gym bag behind him. He drops into a chair looking quite irate and grabs a plate, refusing to look at either of his parents.

The Verdict

Jason and Andrea have lost touch with their lives and each other. Both work full time, volunteer in the community, have many domestic responsibilities, and raise their son. They consider their family life to be a happy one, but the truth is that they simply don't take the time to discern whether or not that is really so. The same applies to their working lives. Both work hard and take great pride in their work. However, neither Jason nor Andrea really knows what satisfaction, if any, he or she gets from his or her job. They have the model family, but no time for its upkeep.

This couple is in desperate need of time management skills. Their hearts and ideals are in the right place, they just don't know how to go about getting everything accomplished effectively and efficiently without sacrificing what they hold dear. Their stress levels are soaring, their relationships are slowly breaking down, and time is passing them by—never to be recaptured.

It may seem as though these two are a lost cause, but as disorganized as they appear to be, they have traits in common with most of us. Because none of us is a lost cause, it is possible for Jason and Andrea to restore their values and happiness by honing their time management skills. Forgetting to pick up their son was the straw that broke the camel's back. They realize their need for time management cannot be put off any longer.

This book will follow Jason and Andrea as they work to gain control of the time they spend and the time they waste. Their progress will be noted at the end of each chapter. They will be taken step-by-step through the process of making time for the important things in life. Though they will encounter their own individual hang-ups, they will trudge on through. The end result will be a close-knit family with its priorities and values intact, and all three will ultimately lead healthier and more relaxed lives.

INTRODUCTION

Time Is Not Money

Welcome to the wonderful world of time management, where interruptions are a thing of the past, nothing is ever overbooked, deadlines don't exist, you never feel pulled in two separate directions at once, and leisure time is the only time. Unfortunately, if that is what you had in mind, you are deceiving yourself. You cannot escape the needs and urgencies of your everyday life. However, you can learn to manage your time wisely, and this book is going to give you a realistic view on how to do just that.

First, congratulate yourself on taking the first step toward a well-rounded and happy life. There will be lots of pats on the back throughout, so you might as well get used to it.

Let's get one thing straight right off the bat—time is not money. That cliché is a thing of the past. Time these days is far more valuable than money. You can earn more money, you can steal money, you can even mass-produce money if you have the right equipment. You cannot do any of these things with time. We are allotted 24 hours a day, seven days a week, and that's it. When it's gone, it's gone.

This is why time management is so important. By learning to manage your time effectively and efficiently, you will have more time for the important things in your life—family, fun, yourself, and so on. Your stress level will even out. Relationships will improve. Goals will be reached. Overall satisfaction will be standard.

This book will help guide you through the basics and help you to apply them to the different aspects of your life. However, it cannot do the work for you. You must create a time management system that is tailored to your needs and that fits into your lifestyle.

A time management system can be maintained only if it works with you, not against you. If you have to completely turn your life upside down, you are doing something wrong. A complementary system will bring organization and awareness into the life you are already living.

If you are determined to bring a balance into your life that will create harmony between your work, home, and personal lives, then by all means continue reading. You are up to the challenge. If you are unsure of your abilities to gain control, read on. You will find the confidence you need to take hold of those reins. If you think you are a hopeless case, give this book a chance to prove you wrong. You are not alone in those feelings, and you are a perfect candidate for the opportunities offered ahead.

This book is divided into three parts. The first part is designed to guide you through the basics of time management. The second part will help you face and deal with those emotional issues that inevitably affect your management of time. And the third part will pull it all together and guide you through applying your newly created time management system to your life.

The information you will find in the following pages is for everyone. Regardless of whether you are a Wall Street tycoon, a work-at-home parent, a child, or whatever your situation may be, the guidelines in this book can be applied to your life. Accept the challenge you have presented to yourself by reading on, and learn to live your life to its greatest potential.

PART ONE

The Basics

I n this part you will learn the skills you need to create a time management system that will work for you. You must use these skills as the foundation for your approach, for without them, disorder and instability can rule your life.

First, you'll find out how to discern your attitude toward time. Then, you will discover how to create a plan of action. Read part one carefully. While it is obvious you do not have a lot of time on your hands as it is—or else you would not have picked up this book—you will not regret spending the time it takes to read attentively. Don't think that you can just skip past the basics and head straight into applying time management to your life. This route will just be a waste of your time. You cannot sign up for a class and immediately take the final exam without having studied the subject, can you? The odds are you would fail the test. The same principle holds true here.

Time management will allow you to lead a well rounded and balanced life if you let it. However, be prepared: It will take a lot of work. But with your happiness waiting for you at the end, why wouldn't you put a little sweat into it? This isn't to say you are not going to have any fun with this. As long as the basics are set as the foundation, you can twist and turn your system into whatever works for you. Part one sets the stage by:

- Defining the different types of time
- Helping you discover your attitude toward and relationship with time
- Teaching you how to recognize and focus on the important things in your life
- Showing you how to set up a system of organization
- Informing you of ways to accomplish more in less time
- Offering ways in which the Internet can be a useful tool or a major distraction in your time management system

Your Love/Hate Relationship with Time

Whether you realize it or not, you have a relationship with time, and a rather intimate one at that. As in any relationship, you have your ups and downs, but we are going to work on building a healthy and stable relationship that brings you continuous pleasure and peace. No, this is not some crazed, ethereal, how-to book—but it will take a slightly different approach to time management than what is considered conventional. Don't worry, the schedules, priorities, and organizing are still included, but the unique element of discovering your relationship with time is added to the mix. In fact, this is the special ingredient that sets this time management guide apart from the rest.

What Is Time?

Before you can begin to manage your time, you must define it. Time is one of the most versatile words in the English language. Consider all the different ways in which we use it: hard time, keep time, it's about time, on time, closing time, time of year, double time, overtime, what time is it? etc. The list could go on until the end of time, but you get the point. Because time is not concretely defined, it is important to create your own definition in terms of your attitude and feelings toward it. This will take a great deal of reflection on your part, but you cannot take a step forward until you do.

Establishing your relationship with time—the thoughts, feelings, and actions involved—is an essential part of learning to use your time wisely. Everyone's relationship with time will be different; therefore, all strategies for managing time will be different. It's not unlike buying a new pair of glasses. You must have an examination to determine your individual prescription. Your brother's glasses aren't going to work well for you because they weren't created to meet your needs. Although you may be able to see fairly clearly with borrowed glasses, your vision is not at the optimal level it could be. The same is true with time. If you are to reach your optimal level of time management, it must be tailored to your individuality.

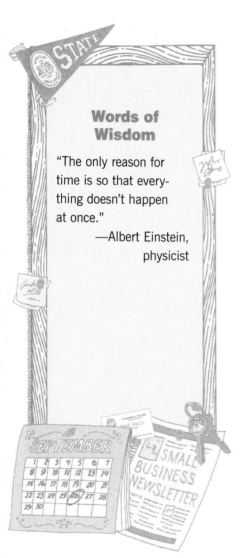

Words of Wisdom

"The only reason for time is so that everything doesn't happen at once."

—Albert Einstein, physicist

For instance, a person who fears time will need to create a time management system different from that of someone who challenges time. The system of someone with a spouse and children will differ from that of a person who has no dependents. Organizational systems, goals, and priorities will vary according to your personal tastes and mindset. Your strengths, weaknesses, commitments, lifestyle, and responsibilities all play a role in the conception of a time management strategy. Therefore, with each variance, the basic time management system will have to be altered slightly to accommodate your individual needs.

External Time

There are two different types of time in direct relation to everyone's perception: external time and internal time.

External time is the time we are all aware of. It measures the duration of events, allows us to coordinate our activities with those of others, and is structured and constant. It is measured in hours, days, and years. It is the standard by which we live our lives. Because it is a physical reality, it is beyond our control. Our only hope for harmony is to learn to adjust our ways of living to accommodate external time.

How often do you look at your watch? We are constantly aware of the time. We have to be, in today's society. We have meetings, appointments, schedules, and deadlines to meet. You could very well lose your job, damage relationships, and miss opportunities if you disregard the clock. However, it is not always in your best interests to allow external time to govern your actions.

It is external time that sets limits on our productivity, creativity, and well-being. Because this time is structured and unchanging, we feel the need to accomplish all we can within the time constraints, lest we allow even a fraction of time to slip past us. We make schedules revolving around these rigid measurements. We estimate how long we need to accomplish a task and try our best to make it fit within a specified number of minutes, hours, or days. This

creates a lot of tension, anxiety, worry, and frustration—all for the sake of external time.

External time is comprised of a past, a present, and a future. The past is behind us, forever gone. The present is the moment we live in now and is all we have to work with. The future is an ideal, something we constantly strive for. With the perception of external time, the future is always coming at us. We can do nothing to slow or speed its advance. Because of this knowledge, our thoughts are divided between the present and the future, occasionally reaching for the past. To always have an eye on the clock disrupts our natural flow. We are unable to reach that ultimate level of productivity because we are always grounded by time.

The future represents possibility. If we do not enjoy our present time, we imagine the future. The grass is always greener on the other side. Even if we do enjoy our present time, we know because of the steadfastness of external time, it will come to an end. That knowledge forces us to look to the future for upcoming happy events so we may escape the impending disappointment. Though we are physically rooted in the present, mentally we are never in one place. This opens the avenues of poor time management.

External time is not something we can disregard. It is always pressing against us, urging us on. We live within its bonds and abide by its rules. Without it our lives would be chaotic. It is a necessary evil. While we cannot change external time, we can learn to effectively adapt our ways of life to complement it.

Internal Time

Internal time is not nearly as concrete as external time. In fact, it is best described as a sense of time. Internal time is not measurable. It is not comprised of minutes or days. It is different for every person and fluctuates with every activity. Because it is an abstract concept, it is difficult to give you a clear-cut definition. However, know that internal time changes. Its foundation lies in your thoughts, feelings, and actions; therefore, you do have control over this type of time.

Have you ever found yourself to be so engrossed in a project that you simply lost track of time? Did you feel a sense of time-lessness? This is your internal time. In this realm we don't feel the limits or pressure set by external time. That freedom allows us to accomplish tasks that may otherwise be labeled "unable to be completed on time." Surely there have been times in which you were absolutely sure you would never be able to make dead-line, but by some miracle you did. Your feeling of hopelessness allowed you to let go of external time and thereby work solely on internal time.

Because we are limited by external time, we have a tendency to ignore internal time. However, it is in the realm of internal time that you are the most productive and creative. Here, nothing matters but what you are working on—goals, priorities, and standards all fall to the wayside. You become so absorbed in the project that external time does not exist, and, therefore, you "lose track of time." You may find that this will happen quite often when you are enjoying yourself. A feeling of timelessness arises and allows the activity to become even more gratifying. However, you lose that sense when you acknowledge that the activity must come to an end (recognizing external time). Then, all of a sudden, outside influences rush in and bring you back to reality.

Of course, we can't live on internal time only. In our world that just isn't possible. We coordinate our lives with those of others on the basis of external time. However, it is possible to work on internal time often. The key to summoning internal time is involve-ment. Gradual involvement will lead to engrossment, which will lead to a sense of timelessness. Have you ever noticed how your degree of involvement in a project directly relates to the efficiency and quality of its completion? The more involved you are, the more likely you are to do a good job. That is because with your degree of involvement, the project becomes more important to you. Involvement is the golden secret.

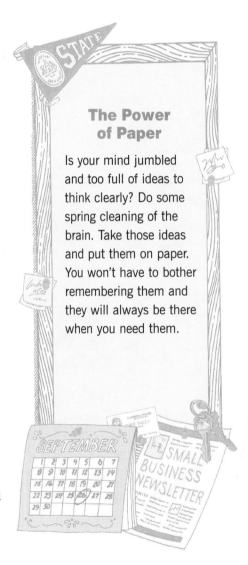

The Power of Paper

Is your mind jumbled and too full of ideas to think clearly? Do some spring cleaning of the brain. Take those ideas and put them on paper. You won't have to bother remembering them and they will always be there when you need them.

Tapping into your internal time reaps all kinds of benefits. Not only do you reach that optimal level of productivity and creativity, but also your stress level lowers. The timelessness gives you the freedom to escape the pressures and bonds of reality. Your overall quality of work will improve, your relationships will strengthen, and, in essence, you will find greater peace in your life.

Why Most Popular Time Management Systems Don't Work

Time management systems are like diets in several ways. First of all, they are both common items on New Year's resolution lists. Second, people often dive into both with the greatest of intentions, only to slowly lose interest until the goal is entirely forgotten. Lastly, both work for a little while, but eventually the weight and the chaos slowly creep back into your life.

So how do we create a time management system that works once and for all? What makes this system any better than all the others available? The secret lies in the balance between the two types of perceptual time. Most time management systems focus on only external time. They don't offer the possibility that time awareness can ever leave the psyche. There are also a few that focus on only internal time. These simply won't work because it is a fact that our lives are affected by external time.

It is necessary to discover how we relate to time as well as learn and apply new skills to achieve the best possible time management system. If you are unaware of how you view time, your feelings toward it, and the preconceived notions you have regarding it, your skills may work for a while, but eventually you may find that you have fallen back into your old patterns. The time management system discussed in this book involves the reconstruction of not only your time habits, but also your overall relation to time. This will allow you access to higher levels of performance, satisfaction, and peace.

Because discovering your relationship with time must be done with self-reflection, there is little to do but try to get you started. This first chapter is devoted to doing just that. Try to keep these first few sections in mind while reading the rest of this book, because from here on out we will deal with only external time. To make your time management system work at its optimum level, you will need to incorporate both types of time.

What Is Your Attitude Toward Time?

Even though time is set and cannot be changed, our individual perceptions of time vary greatly. Before you can move forward with honing your time management skills, you first have to use a bit of that time for self-reflection. Ask yourself the following questions:

- What time constraints did I experience growing up?
- How do I handle situations in which I am running late?
- Does it seem as though time is always working against me?
- What was my family's overall attitude toward time?
- Do I feel lost without my watch?
- Do I have leisure time?
- How well do I handle leisure time?
- Does time control me?
- How do I define "on time"? Early? To the second? Half an hour late is just fine?
- Is managing time a desperate act for me?

By answering these questions truthfully, you will be able to discover the underlying influences that have shaped your time awareness. For example, if you grew up in a very organized and time efficient atmosphere, your attitude toward time will be significantly different from someone who grew up in a random and disorganized environment. Or perhaps your preconceived notions of time led you to create your own perception.

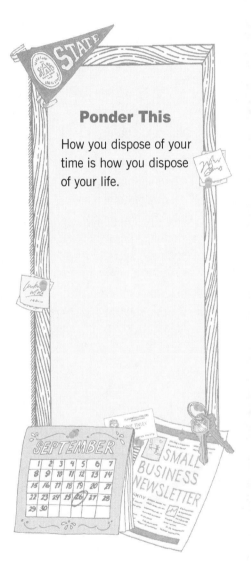

Ponder This

How you dispose of your time is how you dispose of your life.

Though there are several attitudes you can take toward time, this section will identify some of the most popular. Your transition into effective time management will be a lot smoother if you first determine why it is you feel you need more control.

The Enemy

When a person is asked what relationship he or she has with time, more often than not, "Time is my enemy" will be the answer. Most of us feel that time is working against us; that no matter how hard we try to get it under control, we are always bested. Time is the executioner. Of course, this is a self-defeating and unrealistic attitude. Time is neither an enemy nor an ally. Time is simply there. It is a constant that we use as a scapegoat to blame our problems on. Because it will not and cannot bend to your will, you may think you are powerless in its grasp.

However, if you really thought that were the case, you wouldn't have bought this book. Could it be that subconsciously you know that the "time is my enemy" maxim is merely a cover-up? Time cannot be an enemy, for if it were, it would have to make an effort to create misery in your life. Time does nothing but keep pace. It is impersonal and disinterested. Your first step toward time efficiency needs to be an adjustment of attitude. Take the blame for your ineffectual time management and then take control.

Use It, Don't Abuse It

Some people value their leisure time but abuse it. Work time and leisure time might as well be measured by two entirely different standards. Quite often these people will have a solid handle on their time management while working, but when it comes to play, they just aren't sure what to do with themselves. Time for them is not a constant; instead it changes from a well-known and comfortable friend to a stranger that has invaded their privacy. Leisure time can cause a well-organized and structured worker to panic.

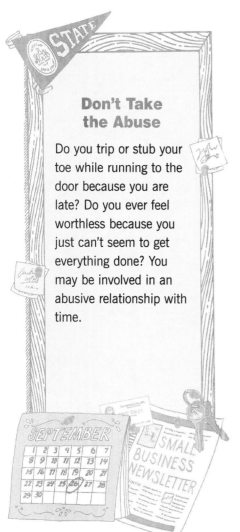

Don't Take the Abuse

Do you trip or stub your toe while running to the door because you are late? Do you ever feel worthless because you just can't seem to get everything done? You may be involved in an abusive relationship with time.

However, it is not time that is creating this tension, it is a lack of value recognition. For those who fear leisure time, it may simply be that they are afraid of wasting that time. Ultimately these people will do one of two things—either overflow their days and nights with work or do absolutely nothing during their leisure time. Because they believe they won't have as much control with their leisure time, they don't make an effort to use it wisely for fear of failure. Or perhaps it is simply because they don't know how to spend their leisure time sensibly.

If you fall into this line of thinking, cheer up; there is a quick fix to your dilemma. Those same principles you use at work can be applied to your leisure time. First, you must realize that time does not change, regardless of whether you are at work or play. If you manage your time well at work, you obviously have a value system set up pertaining to the demands of your work. You have prioritized, set goals, and found a balance between what is important and what is urgent. Now all you have to do is simply apply those same standards to your leisure time.

A Fear of Work Time

Some people take the opposite approach with time. Their leisure time is highly valued and work time is a thing to be feared. These people also consider time to take on different standards of measurement. Quite often they aren't happy with their jobs or feel as though work is something that is forced on them. They will subconsciously, or sometimes blatantly, create a resistance. Their leisure time is spent in a fulfilling manner while their work time is spent in chaos, accomplishing very little. They consider time spent working to be time taken away from their lives, which leads to the belief that they are rejecting their values.

With this outlook, time will pass quickly when spent in leisure activities but stand still while at work. Again, an adjustment of attitude needs to be made. You can still enjoy your leisure more than working time, but if you have a better outlook toward your work, time won't seem to take on such different proportions. Analyze

what it is that enables you to make the most of your leisure time and apply that to your work time. For example, perhaps your goals are more clearly defined in your leisure time than they are in your work time. This can make a world of difference when perceiving the amount and quality of time spent in each.

Granted, the situation, values, and goals will be different within each area, but if you employ the basics, you will have a good foundation to work with. As your working time management skills strengthen, you may find that you get just as much satisfaction from your work time as you do from your leisure time, albeit a different kind of satisfaction.

Perpetually Late

There are some people who make a habit of being late to everything—social functions, work, appointments, etcetera. For these people, time is a brick wall they are always running up against. Most will have developed a reputation for being late. While they may be displeased with this reputation, it does serve as an excuse, and others may come to accept this excuse. However, this can backfire. Those who are continually late may find themselves stuck in a rut of constant tardiness because it becomes expected and accepted of them.

There are also those who are late only in certain aspects of their lives. For example, someone may be consistently on time for work (sometimes even early) but always late for social and family functions, or vice versa. Quite often it can be the sense of responsibility or fear that determines arrival time. Regarding the above example, this person may feel a stronger sense of responsibility toward his employer as far as time is concerned and is therefore driven to be punctual. Family and friends will likely be more accepting of his tardiness, so the repercussions will not be as severe.

While it may be expected, and even in some cases accepted, consistent tardiness shows disrespect for other people. You may also miss out on opportunities to take on responsibilities as others may not feel that they can rely on you.

For those of you who are perpetually late, whether in every-thing or just one aspect of your life, there are a few things you can do to try to curb your habit. For instance, you can trick yourself by setting your clocks forward a bit. Or you may just plan to be at your destination 15 minutes before you are expected. If you are nor-mally 15 minutes late, this should get you there right on time. You may also try scheduling at least 10 minutes of downtime between activities. While these tactics may help, your determination and development of an effective time management system will carry you even further.

Disregarding Time

Finally, there are some people out there who simply have no regard for time. You may think this is an ideal way to live your life, but this can create just as many problems as believing time is your enemy. If you have no sense of time, you have no guidelines to use to accomplish things. "Goal" is a foreign word to you, and dead-lines don't exist. Basically, you have set yourself apart from the motivators of the world. You may believe that you are free of time, but doesn't your lifestyle indicate that you are just as obsessed with time as everyone else? If you constantly resist the idea of time, you are giving it continuous play. Considering that you have to acknowl-edge that it exists, you cannot escape it entirely. Time is not some-thing that can be ignored for long. This is not to say that you should obsess about it, but at least try to recognize its effects on you and take control.

Why Time Passes You By

Do you often feel as though you've been stranded on the time highway, only to be passed by again and again by those who have their lives in order and are in control? Most of us feel that way at least some of the time. But if you are reading this book and are serious about strengthening your time management skills, then you will soon be in the driver's seat.

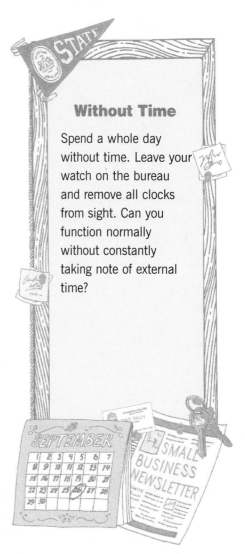

Without Time

Spend a whole day without time. Leave your watch on the bureau and remove all clocks from sight. Can you function normally without constantly taking note of external time?

First, you need to determine why it is you feel you don't have the time you need. If you were given more time, how would you use it? Pretend you will be granted an extra eight hours tomorrow and write down all the activities you would get to within that time span. Now go back over the list and rank each one. Take a look at the first few items that have the greatest importance. Have these items been pushed aside for a while? Even though they are important to you, do you feel they aren't important enough to deal with right away? Are these the reasons behind your desiring more time? If so, you may be stalled in the emergency lane.

What Are the Setbacks?

What is holding you back and what is working against you? Take a step back and try to look at your life objectively. Are there recurring factors in your life that won't allow you to get ahead? If you are like most, there are several small details that can add up to big problems. You may or may not realize what these setbacks are. Ask yourself the following questions:

- Do you try to fit a double workload into a single day more than once a week?
- Do you have difficulty saying no to a request for your time?
- Are your goals and aspirations unrealistic?
- Do you have a tendency to procrastinate?
- Do you daydream often?
- Do you own a wide variety of personal organizers? Or none at all?
- Do you take pleasure in your work?
- Is your day filled with matters that must be attended to right away?
- Do you show symptoms of perfectionism?
- Are you swimming in sticky notes?
- Do you rush around the house while your family enjoys their leisure time?
- Do you often have more than two things going on at once?

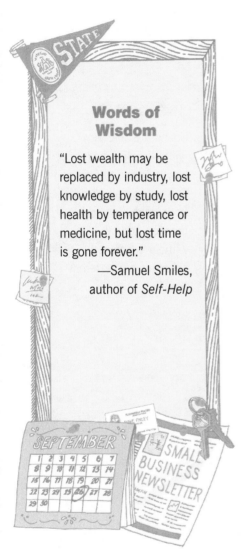

Words of Wisdom

"Lost wealth may be replaced by industry, lost knowledge by study, lost health by temperance or medicine, but lost time is gone forever."

—Samuel Smiles, author of *Self-Help*

- Do you have a tendency to lose things?
- Do you enjoy starting projects, but have difficulty completing them?

Discover the Root of the Problem

Chances are, you will have answered yes to at least one of the above questions, maybe even several. The answers aren't important here; what is important is the degree of awareness you have achieved. Consider the reasons behind the yes answers. This is key. Take a moment to analyze why it is you feel you daydream, or why you lose things. It is the reasons behind the actions that we should concern ourselves with. Don't feel you have to be fluent in psycho-analytical babble to accomplish this. The reasons themselves can be very basic and do not necessarily have to be traced back to your childhood. The point is that you cannot defeat a problem without first getting to its root.

If you answered no to all questions, don't assume you are in the clear. If you are concerned about your time management skills, there must be a problem somewhere. It may be necessary to dig deeper into your daily schedule and nit-pick all details before you are able to discover what has been tripping you up. Perhaps you have formed habits you weren't even aware of. Again, take a look at those important activities you cannot get to without the aid of a time genie. Consider why you have chosen these items to push aside for later. What sorts of things stand in the way of your accomplishing the important? Try to be as specific as possible.

Know Where to Begin

Keep in mind, this exercise isn't designed to help you place blame. Rather, it is intended to help you give reason to your hectic life. Once you discover the areas that need the most attention, you will be able to work efficiently on your time management skills. Don't feel bad if it seems as though your entire life needs to be worked on; that feeling is actually quite common.

Time is not the issue here, our use of time is. We have to take control and adapt our lives to complement the time we are allotted. Depending on your degree of desperation, it may take a couple of hours or a couple of months to fix all of your time management concerns. Regardless of how much time it may cost you up front, developing good time management skills will make it seem as though time is finally at your command.

Tracking Use of Time

We have established that time is constant; it cannot be changed to fit your needs or anyone else's. We all have a certain amount of time allotted to us, but how we choose to use that time varies widely. To be successful in time management, you must first take a look at how you presently use the time you have.

Time Log

Keep a record of each activity you participate in within a 24-hour period of time. Yes, this will take away from the time you have, and you may even feel it is necessary to record how much time you spent recording activities. But this is a relatively easy way to get a good look at your time habits and how many of those are wasteful.

Create three columns on a piece of paper. Title the first column "Time Began." You will record, to the minute, what time you begin an activity. The second column will simply be "Activity." It is a good idea to add detail to your entries in this column. For instance, instead of simply saying, "exercised," you could specify jogging and give the total distance you ran. The third column will be, of course, "Time Ended." Again, you need to record the time exactly. An optional fourth column is titled "Completed." This is useful for those tasks that are part of your to-do list. However, since this exercise is meant only to track your time, this column may or may not be of use to you.

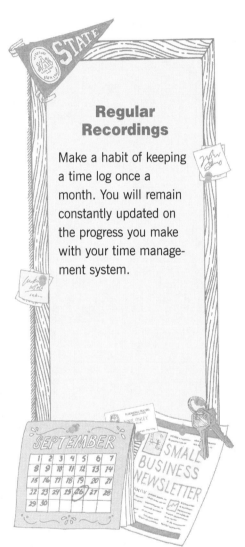

Regular Recordings

Make a habit of keeping a time log once a month. You will remain constantly updated on the progress you make with your time management system.

Keep in mind that every minute needs to be accounted for. Try to be as specific as possible. The more specific, the better you will be able to calculate how your time is spent. For example, be more specific than just recording "work." Break it down into specific tasks, even if they aren't completed. Also take note of all interruptions, distractions, and breaks. At the end of the day, calculate how much time was productive and how much was wasted. (Breaks do not count as a waste of time.)

Record Your Findings

Grouping your findings into categories such as "Productive" and "Wasteful" will work just fine. However, you may want to break them down even further into subcategories such as "Interruptions," "Breaks," "Family Time," "Work Time," "Complete Waste of Time," and so forth. You get the picture. Divide them up into areas that are important to you. You may be surprised to find that you accomplish more than you thought. On the other hand, you may find that you waste more time than you make use of.

	TIME LOG	
Time Began	**Activity**	**Time Ended**
5:45 a.m.	Alarm clock goes off—15 minutes of snooze time	6:00 a.m.
6:00 a.m.	Dress, start coffee, stretch	6:20 a.m.
6:20 a.m.	Jogging	7:05 a.m.
7:05 a.m.	Shower	7:20 a.m.
7:20 a.m.	Dress, hair, makeup, etc.	8:00 a.m.
8:00 a.m.	Coffee, breakfast, morning paper	8:30 a.m.
8:30 a.m.	Commute to work 9:00 a.m.	9:00 a.m.
9:00 a.m.	* Greet fellow employees * Answer voice mail and e-mail * Check planner for daily schedule	9:30 a.m.
9:30 a.m.	Organize desk, final preparation for meeting	9:40 a.m.
9:40 a.m.	Personal phone call	9:50 a.m.
9:50 a.m.	Use restroom, refill coffee, head to conference room	10:00 a.m.
10:00 a.m.	Meeting with VP and marketing	11:30 a.m.
11:30 a.m.	Down time—talk with fellow employees, refresh in restroom, relax	12:00 p.m.
12:00 p.m.	Walk to deli	12:10 p.m.
12:10 p.m.	Lunch and gossip with coworkers	12:50 p.m.
12:50 p.m.	Walk back to work	1:00 p.m.
1:00 p.m.	Paperwork/research	1:50 p.m.
1:50 p.m.	Chat with coworker	2:05 p.m.
2:05 p.m.	Paperwork/research	2:45 p.m.
2:45 p.m.	Outline proposal	3:00 p.m.
3:00 p.m.	Write proposal	3:05 p.m.
3:05 p.m.	Personal phone call	3:15 p.m.
3:15 p.m.	Coffee, restroom break, chat with coworkers	3:35 p.m.
3:35 p.m.	Write proposal	4:40 p.m.
4:40 p.m.	Break	4:50 p.m.
4:50 p.m.	Clean desk, organize things for tomorrow	5:05 p.m.
5:05 p.m.	Commute	5:30 p.m.
5:30 p.m.	Post office	5:45 p.m.
5:45 p.m.	Driving	6:00 p.m.

(continued on page 18)

TIME LOG *(continued)*		
Time Began	**Activity**	**Time Ended**
6:00 p.m.	Grocery shopping	6:35 p.m.
6:35 p.m.	Drive home	6:50 p.m.
6:50 p.m.	Unwind, relax with drink	7:10 p.m.
7:10 p.m.	Prepare/eat/clean up dinner	8:00 p.m.
8:00 p.m.	Phone calls to friends	8:30 p.m.
8:30 p.m.	Drive to Laundromat	8:40 p.m.
8:40 p.m.	Laundry, read magazine	9:40 p.m.
9:40 p.m.	Drive home	9:50 p.m.
9:50 p.m.	Drop laundry—collapse on couch in front of TV	11:00 p.m.
11:00 p.m.	Wash up, go to bed	

Now that you have an idea of where your time is going, you can begin to plan your strategy. Hopefully, this exercise will have shown you what areas are in desperate need of attention and what areas seem to work well for you.

Don't throw your log away. Hold on to it. In a few weeks, you may want to repeat this exercise and take a look at how the two compare. By then, you should be showing some progress. If not, you will want to reevaluate your strategy.

Factoring in Reality

Let's face it, our dreams of time management aren't always going to end up with a happily-ever-after ending. We live in the real world and must take that into consideration. Reality has a way of altering even the most carefully laid plans. The best way to curb the destruction this may cause is to be as prepared as possible.

Granted, you can be prepared for only so much. However, as long as you accept the possibility of a setback, you are further ahead than you may think. As you begin to analyze your use of time and how to make the most of it, pencil in interruptions to your plan. By allowing for these interruptions, whether it be an emergency situation or a brain freeze, your schedule will not be as affected.

Time Estimations

Reality hits full force when you pretend you are superhuman and expect to get things done in less time than they should take. Not only are you going to do a poor job, but because you only scheduled a short amount of time, the rest of your list of to-dos is going to get backed up and may lead to even more delays due to a lack of confidence. Preparing a realistic time frame for the completion of tasks is essential for good time management. Actually, now that we are down to earth, why not schedule a little extra time in case your pencil lead breaks and you don't have a sharpener handy.

Some people even recommend scheduling twice the amount of time a task should take. Then you will almost always come out ahead. If this plan of action appeals to you, by all means set it in motion. However, consider that this strategy could also backfire. What happens when you finish the report in less than half the time you anticipated? The next item on your list is a lunch date that won't take place for another hour. What are you going to do now? Of course there are always other things to be done, but what if you are so in awe of the spare time you have that you simply do nothing? That time could have been put to good use but, instead, was wasted.

Life's Surprises

There are some things you simply cannot anticipate. Life is full of little surprises! But don't let it get you down. Your plan for time management is just that: a plan. It isn't a strict code you must obey at all times, nor is it the ruling force for your life. It is simply a guideline to help you accomplish what you want and need to accomplish without losing your life's essence. As long as you keep one foot on the ground at all times, you are free to move about in the wonderful world of time tranquility.

A Simple Definition

Time management is essentially doing the right activity at the right moment.

Jason and Andrea's Time Relations

When we left them, Jason and Andrea had recognized their need for time management skills. We will now follow them through the steps they take to gain control over their use of time.

On close examination and reflection on the past, Jason and Andrea discover their relationships with and attitudes toward time. Neither of them had ever really considered the idea that they have a relationship with time. Time was just an integral part of their lives that had little to do with them personally. However, they now realize that how they view time has a significant impact on the way they spend it.

Jason

Jason discovers that his relationship with and attitude toward time is based on fear. Jason grew up in a very time-conscious family. His parents weren't necessarily organized or time efficient, but everything revolved around the clock. Dinner was always served at exactly 6:00 P.M. sharp, snooze buttons were disabled on alarm clocks, and being late was considered a deadly sin. The idea of internal time was thought of as a fairy tale, not at all evident in reality. Jason grew up with the clock as a strict guardian that never left his side.

He realizes that this foundation holds a strong base in his life today. Because his job revolves around the clock, he is more comfortable with this aspect of his life than any other. Meetings, deadlines, and fixed hours are a comfort to him. He can work well when time is clearly defined. For this reason, he often brings his work home or stays late at the office. Time at home and in his personal life is much too unregulated for Jason's tastes, and he is therefore terrified of it. Because time at home and in his personal life are scary areas for him to confront, he subconsciously tries to avoid them by stretching out his work life to spill over into everything he does.

Jason's fear of time governs his actions. Chaos and disorganization feed off this fear.

By recognizing his attitude toward time, Jason can now take the first steps toward successful time management. He realizes what he must face and is eager to dispel that fear.

After reading this chapter, Jason started to keep a time log to find out where his time was spent during the day. As expected, most of it was spent on work-related activities. Time at home was spent mostly searching for lost items, taking care of urgencies that were created because of procrastination, and sleep (though just a small fraction). He found that there was a total of two hours of time spent that he cannot account for. This time is wasted time that could have easily been assigned to his priorities.

Andrea

Andrea's background is slightly different from Jason's. Her family constantly raced against time. Time was considered to be the enemy. They weren't afraid of it, rather they considered it to be a challenge to defy any and all time constraints. Therefore, they filled their lives with constant activity, trying to fit everything they possibly could into every single day.

Andrea's life now reflects that same attitude. She fills her days with as many tasks as she can. These tasks don't always relate to the important things in her life, and each is given equal priority. Because she considers everything to be important, she has difficulty deciding what to do and when. For example, she considers teaching class and washing clothes to be of the same importance. Instead of taking time to prioritize her tasks, she does several things at once, never allowing her focus to remain on just one thing. Even the different aspects of her life all blend together. One thing is always overlapping another.

Her constant battle with time holds her back. She now realizes that her view of time has actually become one of the time constraints she so vehemently fights against. Because of this knowledge, she has come to the conclusion that she has been self-defeating and using time as an excuse. She can now sign a peace treaty with time and learn to let her priorities and goals in life take precedence over other aspects. No longer will she let her "enemy" stand in the way of her self-control.

Andrea also kept a time log. Her log reflects that she is constantly on the run. There isn't time left over at the end that is not accounted for. Activities were back-to-back, and breaks were not a part of her day. Even though this may seem as though she has a good grasp on her management of time, it actually shows the opposite. The activities Andrea completed were all considered urgent to her, and none of them were done well. The activities overlapped one another continuously. She did not devote her full attention to even one. (There wasn't time enough to do so if she wanted to get them all done.) Andrea's day is geared toward quantity, not quality, and this one day was a good example of how she spends her life.

The End Result

Now that Jason and Andrea have defined their attitudes and relationships with time and discovered how their time is spent during the day, they are able to make that shift in focus that will make a world of difference as they attempt to manage time. Granted, this will take some work, but they are determined to make the best of their lives. They have accepted the challenge. Have you?

**Mastering
Your Mess**

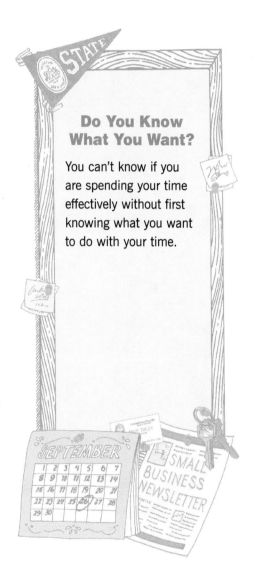

You should now understand some of the psychological factors that are involved in your current management of time. You have kept a time log and know where your time is spent, how much is wasted, and which aspects of your life are of greatest importance to you. Knowledge is a fabulous thing, but it isn't enough to get your time under control. The next step is to take action.

In this next chapter, you are going to create a strategic attack. You will learn to prioritize, acknowledge the difference between important and urgent, set in motion a shift of focus, master the to-do list, create a schedule, recognize your limitations, and maintain management of your time. It sounds like a lot, but once you get in the groove of things, your time management system will take over. You just need to get it started, and this chapter will help you do just that. Are you prepared to become master of your mess?

Learn to Prioritize

So now that you are all geared up and ready to dive headfirst into the time management mélange you call your life, where do you start? Before you do anything else, you need to set your priorities. What do you need? What do you want? Where do you want to go? Where do you want to be? There are a thousand questions you can ask yourself, but what it all boils down to is finding out what is most important to you.

Time management is spending your time appropriately and effectively. Unless you have a list of priorities, you will never be able to assess how far and how well you have progressed. Therefore, it is essential that you take time with this first step and get it right.

Priorities can be classified in several different ways. For example, you will have a different set of priorities at work than you will at home. However, for the time being, look at your life in general. Encompassing all of these different divisions, brainstorm everything that is important to you. Your list may be long or have only a few key items on it. Either way is fine, just remember to be honest with yourself.

Once you have a list compiled, pull out the top ten items that have the most significance to you. However, don't toss the rest. You may want to use them later for other lists or to reevaluate this one. Then rank these ten accordingly, with number one being the highest priority. Don't worry, this is for your eyes only, so no one else is going to see that you rate your dog as having a higher value than your friends. If you have difficulty ranking one item over another, don't fret about it now. This list is by no means set in stone. In fact, it is necessary to continually reevaluate and restructure as you proceed throughout life.

WEEKLY PRIORITY LIST

Home	Work	Personal
1. Laundry	1. Outline proposal	1. Write thank-you notes
2. Clean	2. Research	2. Get haircut
3. Call plumber	3. Check competition	3. Renew gym membership
4. Wash/Detail cars	4. Meet with Marketing	4. Call Grandma
5. Fix entertainment center	5. Rework proposal	5. Buy Sarah's birthday gift
6. Frame posters	6. Run everything by client	6. Plan spring break with Nikki
7. Buy new futon cover	7. Meet with Advertising	7. Schedule manicure
8. Wash windows	8. Run proposal by Mr. Klein	8. Plan next month's "girls night"
9. Call contractor about garage	9. Compose detailed presentation	9. Check holiday airfare
10. Pack up stuff for charitable donation	10. Schedule meeting with VP	10. Spa

Now that you have a tangible list of what you hold dear, refer to it often. Keep it within reach at all times so that when a question of how you will spend your time arises, you will have a guide pointing you in the right direction. Don't hesitate to make changes; it is to be expected.

This is not the only time you will be asked to prioritize. Establishing priorities is the key to effective time management and will come into play in nearly every aspect. So, it is essential that you learn to do it well this first go-round and form a good basis for the future. Later, we will prioritize within the different divisions of your life, but keep in mind this master list holds the greatest importance.

Important versus Urgent

Several people use the words "important" and "urgent" interchangeably. However, these words do have different meanings and they hold great consequence in terms of time management. "Important" means that something has value or significance. "Urgent" means that something calls for immediate attention. To be able to prioritize correctly requires your knowing the difference between the two.

Too often people—usually poor managers of time—consider nearly everything to be urgent. It is impossible to make decisions regarding what and when tasks should be done if everything demands attention right away. While struggling with the decision-making process, you waste time, not to mention delay those urgencies even longer. The cell phone is ringing, the computer is shouting that you have mail, you are late taking your child to school, and the dog is whining to be let out. What do you handle first? Granted, it is hard to ignore the beeps, rings, and shouts of technology today, but are these really urgent? Because they cater to our senses, it may seem so. Even though you know that if you don't let the dog out, you will have a not-so-pretty mess to clean up—which will, in turn, cause you to be even later in dropping off your child at school—you reach for the phone first because it is the most demanding to your senses. You don't think; you react.

Important matters are often pushed to the side in favor of urgent ones, even though it is the important things that will have the greatest influence on your life. Important matters include your family, health, future, values, security, and so forth. The list will vary from person to person, but it all comes down to what you personally consider meaningful. It is the important matters that you are in control of, but how much time do you really spend exercising that control? Because you are in control, they don't take precedence. Instead, you would rather deal with those issues that aren't so much in your control, so as to get them out of the way. In the back of your mind remains the idea that once you deal with the urgencies, you will have all the time you need to handle the important issues, but are we ever free of urgency?

Too many urgencies will leave you constantly on the defensive, never getting to experience the offensive. They demand your time, even though they may not be important. You must weed out the truly urgent matters from those that just sound urgent. Disregard the latter for just a moment and take a close look at the truly urgent matters. Is it possible that some of those matters might have been resolved if they had been handled before they reached the urgency point? If you are realistic, the answer will be yes. We often get caught up in the urgency mode and disregard all other tasks to be completed. This becomes a vicious cycle of chaos because those tasks that have been disregarded will eventually work their way into the urgent category. You may as well forget about the important items. They have just become dreams at this point.

Make Your Own Demands

Don't give away your time just because someone is shouting out demands. Make your own demands and give your time to those who deserve it—this includes you.

Breaking the Cycle

So how do you break the cycle? First, you need to categorize your activities. Divide them into four categories to get a good look at what emphasis you place on each.

The first category will include those activities that are both urgent and important. These should take precedence over everything else. Some items that may fit into this category include: taking your child to the doctor if there are signs of an allergic reaction to a medication; finishing a report that may influence whether or not you get a promotion; getting your squeaky brakes checked before embarking on that mountain drive; and catching the next flight out to attend a relative's funeral. These actions require very little thought and are quite often simply reacted on.

The second category is comprised of those activities that are important but not urgent. Examples of these include: getting a regular physical exam; discussing upcoming vacation time with your family; sorting and paying bills; and returning your mother-in-law's phone call.

The third category includes the activities that are urgent but not important. This can be the troublesome classification. Urgency wants to scream importance, but on careful examination, most of these urgent matters hold very little long-term value. Speeding for fear of being late, answering some phone calls, and running to the nearest pay phone to answer a page from someone you don't even know are some examples of urgent but not important activities.

The final category is the not urgent and not important division. These activities are often just for fun. This category is comprised of such activities as watching television, catching up on hometown news/gossip, sorting though junk mail, and spending hours trying to beat the latest video game.

Once you have classified each of your activities, hold on to this documentation for a little while. You will be using these categories and their components to evaluate and reorganize your schedule. The trick will be to try to find a balance between those actions that are urgent and those that are important. If you feel overwhelmed with the urgencies, try avoiding those activities in the last category for a couple of days to free up some time and take care of the urgencies. Keep in mind that the important activities will eventually become urgent if they aren't handled in a timely manner.

Accepting a Shift of Focus

You have your list of priorities in hand and you know what is important to you, so how do you apply these ideals to your life? It's all about focus. Right now you are probably so focused on the completion of tasks that you are allowing your life to slip right by you. Granted, picking up this book was a nice step in the direction of gaining control, but without the proper focal point, it isn't going to get you very far. You could have the sharpest time management skills around, but if you don't use them to zero in on what is important and valuable in your life, they aren't worth the time it took to learn them.

If you are having time troubles, chances are that you lost your focus somewhere along the line. Perhaps you can still see what is important, but it is just a bit blurred. What we want to do here is learn to shift our focus away from the urgent and concentrate on the important. Sometimes this is a difficult thing to do when your life is seemingly ruled by the urgent. This is not to say that you should disregard those actions you need to take immediately—you simply cannot do that in life. But don't allow the urgent to hold great significance. Once the task is completed, that's it. Any further thought of it can go right out the window. Too often people concentrate on the immediate tasks that need to be completed and brush aside everything else, including their families, their goals, their health, and many other valuable things.

If you want to make the most of your time, keep referring to your list of priorities. Don't let it slip from your mind. As soon as you lose focus on the important things in life, you lose the ability to make calculated decisions, to achieve goals, and to enjoy yourself overall.

Shifting focus is not an easy thing to do. You first have to realize what it is that you tend to focus on. What stands in the way of your priorities? Be willing and determined to make that change. Once you make the shift, you may not accomplish as many tasks as you did beforehand, but keep in mind that it isn't the quantity but the quality that matters. This is not to be used as an excuse to get rid of all those odd jobs you dislike so much. Rather, it should just take away from the significance you place on the task, as well as the stress you place on yourself.

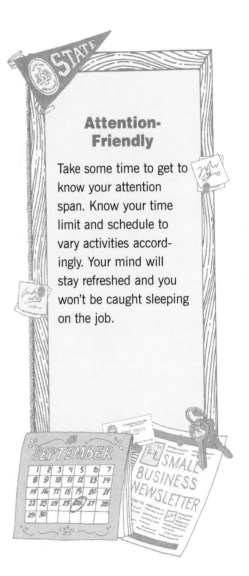

Attention-Friendly

Take some time to get to know your attention span. Know your time limit and schedule to vary activities accordingly. Your mind will stay refreshed and you won't be caught sleeping on the job.

Setting Goals

You've had the importance of goals drilled into your head since you were in elementary school, but who would have thought you should have paid attention to it? Now that you are older and set in your ways, it's time to uproot and regress. Actually, whether you realize it or not, you have been setting goals your entire life. Even when you were a baby, there was probably at least one point in time when you decided you wanted that forbidden pacifier and neither hell nor high water was going to stand in your way of getting it. You knew even then that only action on your part would satisfy your wants. Times haven't changed that much.

You want to take control, and goals are part of your offensive strategy. Setting goals is important. There's simply no way of getting around it if you are serious about managing your time.

Once this task is completed, the rest of the ride is comparatively smooth. You should have your life's priorities set out before you. To know what is important to you gives you a good feeling, but you can only stare at the list for so long. You must take action to ensure that those priorities maintain their status and that you live your life accordingly. So how do you do that?

The Task at Hand

First, consider the divisions in your life. For instance, you will most likely have different ideas of what you need to accomplish at work than what you need to accomplish at home. Separate the different areas of your life that you feel deserve their own set of goals. For each classification, brainstorm immediate tasks as well as long-term projects or aspirations. Take some time with this; it will be the foundation for your schedule.

Once you have a healthy list, apply your newfound prioritization skills. Although it isn't really essential that you prioritize, it always helps to clearly define what is most important to you.

Next, label four sheets of paper "Daily," "Monthly" or "Weekly," "Annually," and "Lifetime." You will transfer the ideas onto the proper sheets according to when you feel they should be accomplished. So far so good? Okay, so now comes the fun part.

Defining Your Goals

For each idea, you will need to come up with a statement that clearly defines your intentions and leaves no room for misinterpretation. If you decide you want to buy a house, what are the specifications for this house? How big should it be? Number of bedrooms? Bathrooms? Where is the house going to be? Do you want to live in the city? In the country? How much do you want to spend? How much can you spend? What are the amenities you desire? There are several questions you can ask yourself. The point is to get as specific as possible. Don't worry, you always have the option of changing your goals as you go along.

Defining Time Limits

Set time limits. This is just as important as the goal itself. Without time limits you have no way of knowing when you should work on the project or when it should be completed. For immediate tasks, try to set the time limit to the hour or even minute if possible. For longer-term goals, you may need to be a bit more vague. But always try to get as close as you can. Though there may be motivation to complete the project, if there isn't a deadline, it is easy to push it aside to make room for something else. Don't allow this to happen. Be as strict with yourself as possible when it comes to your goals.

Define the Steps

Once you have a precisely defined goal in front of you, break it down. There are steps you must take to reach the end goal. What are they? Again, be specific. Set time limits to these as well and you will find that the journey to the end goes by rather smoothly and quickly. These mini goals are the stepping stones that also act as stimulants. If you have tasks on your schedule that often directly relate to your goal, encouragement will follow the completion of each task. The light at the end of the tunnel will shine brighter and brighter with each step taken. The further you are able to break down the goal, the easier it will seem to achieve.

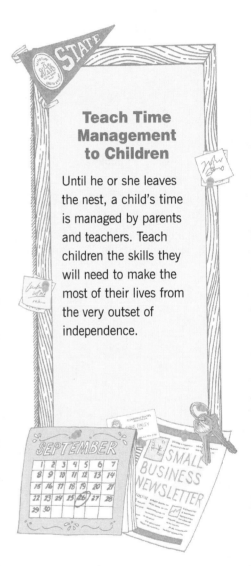

Teach Time Management to Children

Until he or she leaves the nest, a child's time is managed by parents and teachers. Teach children the skills they will need to make the most of their lives from the very outset of independence.

Remain Realistic

All the thought and preparation you put into setting your goals will be of no use if you are not realistic. That house you want to buy may simply be out of reach. Yet if you set it as a goal, you will end up not only with disappointment but, quite possibly, with a load of debt as well. Your mini goals should help you determine the accessibility of your goals. Keep in mind that there are always repercussions if your goals are not based in reality. This is not to say that you shouldn't dream. Set your standards high, just not out of reach.

Now that you have your goals and mini goals written down, you are ready to get to work on them. Like your priorities, your goals should always be within reach. They will help you to maintain focus and motivation. However, it isn't good enough to just keep them close by. You have to incorporate the mini goals into your schedule.

The Almighty To-Do List

Yes, even this version of time management incorporates a to-do list. You simply can't get by without it. Sounds pretty self-explanatory, right? Just write down what you have to do. Unfortunately, many people create to-do lists that actually work against them instead of for them. The key to a successful to-do list lies in three little words: "simple," "realistic," and "accessible."

The Benefits of a To-Do List

Creating a list of what needs to be done has many benefits. It allows you to plan ahead. Creating a day's to-do list first thing in the morning or before you retire every night creates a sense of order in your life. You are able to eagerly, not anxiously, anticipate the day ahead of you and rest easy. With your handy list, you will have a feeling of security and confidence.

The list does not permit you to forget things. This in itself is a principal reason for many to keep a to-do list. Let's face it, in the

One Activity at a Time

Allowing an activity to swim around in your head will pull at your concentration. Decide when to do it and forget about it until then.

hustle and bustle of our everyday lives, it is easy to overlook an important task. However, the consequences of forgetting that task may not be so easy to overlook.

The decision-making process is easier with a to-do list. Also, the list may serve to motivate you. An added bonus of a to-do list is that you get to cross off all you accomplish. This leaves you with a feeling of success, and who doesn't want that?

The Consequences of a Poorly Prepared To-Do List

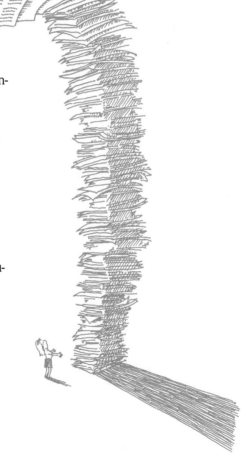

Now for the ugly side of the to-do list. Keep in mind that the following issues are only the consequences of not creating a healthy and sound to-do list. A bad to-do list has the power to destroy your self-esteem. If you are unable to complete even a fraction of the items found on your list, you may become so upset with yourself that you begin to believe that you are a failure. It can make your life even more hectic than it was before. You may find yourself constantly scampering about trying to complete everything on your list. Your stress level could rise. You may neglect the important things in favor of the small urgencies. Your list could deny you the proper eating and sleeping habits. You may miss opportunities by focusing only on your list. It can affect your mood and mindset. In short, the list could very well make you its slave.

This is why it is so important that you are careful in preparing your to-do list. The consequences of poor preparation can be appalling. However, do not fear. Once you finish with this section you will be master of the list, in control, and ready to conquer.

GOOD VERSUS BAD			
Daily To-Do List		**Daily To-Do List**	
Call Lesley	✕	End world hunger	
Schedule meeting with Cheryl		Start a business	
Call insurance agent	✕	Run a coast-to-coast race	
Work on resume		Hand wash all laundry	
Get a haircut		Rebuild the car engine	
Return mother-in-law's phone call		Write a book	
Pick up fresh fruit at the market		Put in a new lawn	
Drop off clothes at dry cleaners	✕	Climb Mount Everest	
Schedule doctor's appointment		Lose 50 pounds	
		Walk the length of the Great Wall of China	
		Invent something	
		Get a new job	
		Start antiwar campaign	
		Redecorate the entire house	
		Become fluent in a new language	
		Run for president	
		Be a hero	

Are You Ready to Take Control?

First, you need to relax. This exercise is not going to hurt you. Don't allow your brain to overload with ideas of what needs to be done. Clear your mind of any future activities aside from those belonging to the day ahead. Focus only on what needs to be accomplished today.

Begin by writing down the urgencies. These are probably foremost in your mind anyway. Next are the important items. Consider also the want-to-do items. A day filled with constant need-tos and should-dos will exhaust you pretty quickly. However, you do not want to go overboard with items added. Once you are pleased with the list you've created, estimate a time allowance for each. It is a good idea to overestimate a bit. This will give you a cushion.

Now you need to put your prioritization skills to the test. Rank each item according to the precedence it should take. Don't stress yourself out over this. Keep it simple. There is no need for additional comments or justifications. The list shouldn't itemize too many activities. But it also shouldn't itemize too few activities. Simple does not equate slacking. Simple means clear and precise. If you have to question the list regularly, it isn't doing you much good. But also bear in mind that this list is not set in stone. It has the ability and probability to change. It is simply a list of ideas and possibilities for a run of the day's activities. It will be difficult to change a list that is complicated and full of intricate detail. Simplicity will take you a long way.

Your list should reflect reality. Those consequences mentioned above are mostly due to the refusal to incorporate a reality base in the list. Do not overburden yourself with a thousand activities that need to be completed. Do not rank everything number one. Also, don't plan to cram activities back-to-back. You will need a break, and not everything will go as planned—that is guaranteed.

Estimating time is another area people have difficulty basing in reality. We like to think we are superhuman at times. What would normally take someone an hour will take you only a half hour because you know a shortcut or you expect a surge of energy to hit about that time. Be realistic about your expectations.

Above all else, the list needs to be accessible. Even if you are prudent in your list preparation, taking the time to carefully evaluate every item in terms of importance and being realistic to the point of tears, your list will not do you a bit of good if you leave it lying on the kitchen counter. Now you may think this goes without saying, but more often than you think, lists are composed on a scrap of paper only to be thrown away minutes later by an unaware passerby. Or perhaps you are so absorbed in your list that you forget to write down "carry list on person at all times."

These things do happen. That's why it is important to write your list somewhere easily accessible. For instance, most paper and electronic planners have a place designated specifically for to-do lists. Or you may have your own system that works better. Regardless of where you choose to keep it, it needs to be with you at all times.

The to-do list is the foundation for a perfect schedule, and scheduling is the next step in getting your life in order. Although many believe the schedule to be the forefather of time management, until you master the to-do list, you will be unable to complete your transition from a time captive to a time commander.

Scheduling

Now that you are satisfied with the goals you have made, it's time to merge them into your life. This is accomplished through scheduling. Take note that there is a difference between scheduling and planning. You can plan to go to your cousin's friend's sister's wedding, but until you actually schedule it, what are the chances of your really making it there? Planning is the thought process you must undergo to decide how your time is to be spent. Scheduling is the act of assigning a designated time to execute an activity.

The Necessities

Scheduling shouldn't be scary. If you think about it, several things are already scheduled for you. For example, sleep is a given. That already blocks out a big portion of your day. But remember to be realistic. If you require eight hours of sleep a night, don't schedule only six because that is what you wish you could get away with. Wishful thinking has no place on a schedule.

To get the hang of successful scheduling, start out specific. On a sheet of paper, create a table that shows every hour of the day. Go ahead and write in sleep. Now, consider the other daily rituals you must carry out. Shower? Let's hope so. Assign showering to a half hour block. Eating? Though you should eat three times a day, most of us don't, so assign realistic and appropriate time slots. Exercise? Commuting? A television program you just can't bear to

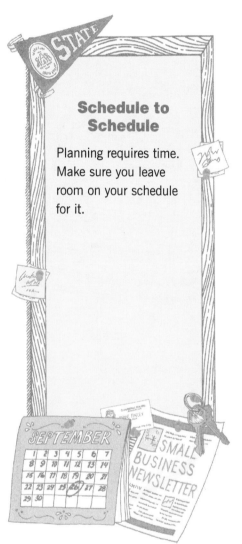

Schedule to Schedule

Planning requires time. Make sure you leave room on your schedule for it.

miss? Assign the activities that you take part in every day to their particular time slots.

Once you have the necessities out of the way, take a look at what you have left. Not really a whole lot in comparison to the empty sheet you started with, is there? Think about whether there are any activities already planned for the day. Does your son have a soccer game? Is there a company meeting at work? Do you need to give your spouse a ride to the airport? Schedule these things as well.

The Importants

Now that you have all the tedious things out of the way, whip out the handy dandy goals you set. Start with the dailies. Look at the mini goals, if any, for each goal. Pick a time that will correspond effectively with each activity. But don't overdo it. If you see that you have time left on your schedule, don't start penciling in tasks that aren't planned for today quite yet. Leave approximately two hours of time (it doesn't have to be in one block) open on your schedule. You will undoubtedly come across urgent tasks that you had not planned on. That unscheduled time is perfect for playing catch up, taking care of unexpected business, or regrouping. Also, don't forget to schedule breaks. These are very important and, quite often, aren't taken if not scheduled. Use the following schedule as a rough outline to help get you started.

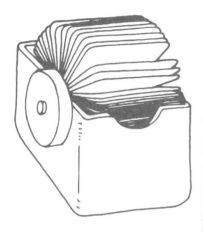

	Mon.	Tues.	Wed.	Thurs.	Fri.	Sat.	Sun.
5–6:00	5:30 Aerobics		5:30 Aerobics		5:30 Aerobics		
6–7:00							
7–8:00				Stratton Project			
8–9:00	Write up Proposals	Meeting with Bruce					
9–10:00			Call Harry Goldstein		Interview for Assistant		
10–11:00	Meeting with Marketing		Interview for Assistant				
11–12:00		Call Luke Holden					
12–1:00	Lunch						
1–2:00		Staff Meeting					
2–3:00			Prospectus Meeting				Wedding shower
3–4:00			Prepare for Stratton Project		Marketing Meeting		
4–5:00	4:30 Doctors Appt.						
5–6:00							
6–7:00		6:30 Haircut	Dinner Meeting			Ladies Night	
7–8:00		Aerobics		Aerobics			
8–9:00	Dinner with Joe	Call Sandy and Nikki		Laundry!	Dinner/ Theater with Joe		
9–10:00			Movie night				
10–11:00							
11–12:00							

The Results

So your schedule has made room for the essential, the tedious, and the important. Is there a nice balance there? Have you devoted too much time to the tedious and hardly any to the important? Make sure your priorities get just as much play as the rest. Are you satisfied with the results?

As your scheduling skills strengthen, you might find you do not need to break the day into half-hour slots, nor do you need to write down sleep and a shower. That's fine as long as you recognize that time is devoted to these things and not try to overbook yourself. Find a scheduling pattern that works well for you and stick with it.

It is a good idea to schedule ahead of time. Don't try to sit down hour by hour and figure out what you need to do. As tasks cross you, write them down and then forget about them until their time comes. It is recommended you use a pencil for scheduling. Changes will have to be made from time to time, and being able to erase things makes the job much easier.

Look over your schedule the night before to make any necessary changes and to basically prepare yourself for the day ahead. Schedule what you can for activities in the future. Don't forget that you still have to administer to the monthly, annual, and lifetime goals.

Recognizing and Respecting Your Limitations

Even though you may feel superhuman from time to time, you still have your limitations. It's nothing to be ashamed of. In fact, you should be thankful for your limitations. However, they can benefit your life only if you recognize, accept, and work within them.

Recognizing your limitations shouldn't be too hard. We all know the things we can't and shouldn't do. For example, you cannot go without sleep for two days in a row and still function properly. That is a limitation. Because each person has a different physical and mental makeup, each person will have different limitations. Though there are some limitations that are universal, such as time and health, others are specific to the individual. Recognizing these will often come about through trial and error. If you are having difficulty recognizing your limitations, see if any of the following serve to hold you back:

- Physical attributes—a bad back, poor hearing, poor eyesight, height, a broken limb, etc.
- Temperament—nervousness, irritability, shyness, anger, etc.
- Ability—skill level, education, experience, etc.

Accepting your limitations is the hard part. Too often, people refuse to accept the fact that they can't do everything all the time. So they push themselves harder and harder to defy this limitation. Eventually they will crack. Whether it is due to a resulting health problem or a serious intervention from a loved one, their supposed time in the sun will come to an end. On reflection, they will find that what they pushed themselves for really held very little overall meaning in their lives. If you have difficulty accepting your limits, keep an eye on your priorities. By focusing on what is important to you, it will be easier to disregard all the outside nonsense and work within your boundaries. Your best is the best.

Limitations are good for you. Yes, it seems as though they are nothing but a hindrance, but without them many would easily work themselves into an early grave. Limitations force you to ease up on yourself. However, if you do not respect your limits, your world may easily be an angry one in which you compete with everything around you, even yourself. When you are in constant competition, your preferences don't have meaning. They are lost to you, and to replace them, you focus on the preferences of others. Limitations allow you an excuse—although you don't need one—to maintain focus on your own priorities. Accept it: You are human and therefore have limitations. The sooner you realize this and learn to work within those boundaries, the better off you will be.

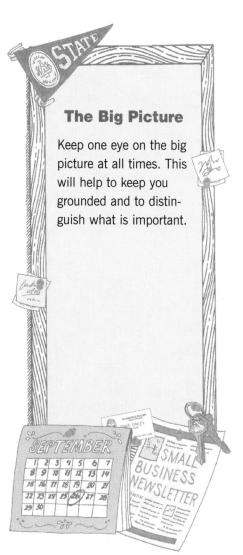

The Big Picture

Keep one eye on the big picture at all times. This will help to keep you grounded and to distinguish what is important.

Maintaining Management

All of your hard work thus far will have been for naught if you don't maintain management. It is easy enough to do, plus it will save you time in the long run. However, you must not fall behind. If you get too far behind, you might as well start all over, and no one wants to do that. Keep up and you will come out ahead.

Now that you have prioritized, set goals, and perfected a schedule, you are well on your way to gaining control of your time. That is all well and good, but keep in mind you aren't finished, nor will you ever be. Good time management requires constant maintenance. You will have to reorganize your priorities, reevaluate your goals, and update your schedule. All this needs to be done on a regular basis. Don't give up now. You've come so far already. Maintenance is rather easy, as long as you keep up with it.

Maintaining Priorities

Keep a steady focus on your priorities. The list will always be within reach if you begin to question yourself. Because priorities are those things that you hold most dear, it should be quite clear when a new priority arises. Perhaps you have a child reaching school age. All of a sudden the list changes. All you have to do is pull out the list and make the adjustments. This is not to say that you will forget your child if he or she is not written down, but it helps to see that when you add a priority, the others will be affected. Take a little time with the list and determine which area will have to give a little in order to make room for the addition. Because it is all set before you, you don't run the risk of leaving something out. There doesn't even have to be an addition or subtraction to call for reworking. It could be that as you've moved along in life, the level of importance you placed on things has changed slightly. Maybe number three will move to the number one position. You may find that you don't need to set a specific time to go over your priorities because they will be examined regularly anyway.

Maintaining Goals

Goals will need constant reevaluation. Your daily goals are obvious. Either you achieve them or you don't; they will always be in front of you. However, the monthly, annual, and lifetime goals have a way of fading from the picture for long periods of time and then sneaking up on you suddenly. Don't let this happen. Stay on top of them so they don't get out of control. You will know best how often to check on your goals. Perhaps you can form a habit of going over your goals at the beginning of each week and checking their progress. Or maybe you feel confident enough that those you set will remain as is and do not need to be evaluated that often. Again, it is what you are comfortable with, but do not put off looking over them until they are right on top of you. Besides, keeping an eye on your goals will help you to stay on track with what is important.

Maintaining a Schedule

Your schedule speaks for itself and will undoubtedly change often. Items will be bumped off and added on a daily basis. But don't get too caught up in the daily activities. Remember that you have scheduled items in advance as well. Consider whether or not your daily changes will affect your future schedule. It is always a good idea to keep an eye on your schedule anyway so you know what is ahead of you and can physically and mentally prepare yourself.

Jason and Andrea Take Control

Jason and Andrea use the knowledge they discovered in the first chapter to help them create an objective view toward how they make use of their time. By using such a solid foundation, they are able to dive headfirst into the attack. Both use different strategies and are on their own in the battle. However, they both come out ahead and are able to reunite their lives, creating a stable and healthy family life. They know their work is not done, but they are taking the first steps toward balance and happiness.

Jason

Jason has difficulty right off the bat. His list of priorities is easy enough to write, although it is rather long. But once he finishes, he realizes that he hasn't even begun. All of his priorities are work related. They reflect his authoritative position, the level he wants to reach with his job, and what his coworkers and boss expect of him. There is no mention of family and personal life, even though he holds both of these in high regard. His mind is geared toward work and that realization stops him in his tracks.

So, Jason takes a deep breath, scraps all he has previously written, and begins anew. This time he thinks first of his family, which he considers to be the most important thing in his life. He lists all he can think of and then begins on his personal life. He finds it is rather easy to keep going once he gets started; he simply had to make that shift in focus first. Finally, he ends with his work life.

The list of priorities brings him down to earth. He realizes that most of the things at the beginning of the list—which hold the greatest value—are what he has a tendency to ignore. Now this could easily bring Jason's self-esteem level down, but instead it spurs him to become even more determined to set things right and gain control over his use of time.

He is eager to begin setting goals and finds that he has quite a knack for it. Setting the goals is fun and easy; finding the time to achieve them is a different story.

Jason already has a habit of keeping a to-do list, although sometimes it is only a mental list. He likes to know what needs to be done and is constantly on the lookout for things that need his attention. Needless to say, his to-do list is probably ten times longer than one you would ever create. He separates the urgencies from the rest of the items listed and, with a heavy sigh, takes out his schedule.

Since his schedule is already filled with work-related activities, Jason knows it is going to take some serious reworking to make everything fit. By taking the time to carefully examine the importance of each item, he finds that he is able (and willing) to delete

Patience Is a Virtue

Time management requires patience and persistence. It won't happen overnight.

quite a few items. He then pencils in the urgent activities that demand his attention. Next, he makes room for priorities and goals. Some things on his schedule he winces at having to remove, but he now realizes the importance of the importants.

Jason is well on his way to creating a time-effective and efficient schedule. He knows his limitations and also his weaknesses. He is going to have to work hard to maintain his new clear focus; old habits are hard to break, after all. But with his list of priorities and goals with him at all times, he has the incentive he needs to make it work.

Andrea

Andrea has no trouble creating a list of priorities. Her priorities encompass nearly everything she does. Her list goes on and on. However, once her hand cramps from writing, Andrea stops to take a look at all that she has written. She again considers the difference between importants and urgencies. Both are intermingled and given the same value on her list. Accepting the difference is a difficult thing for Andrea to do, but she sets her jaw and gets to work.

Quite a while and several internal battles later, Andrea has a list of priorities she is very proud of. She had to make a shift in focus while creating it. Her time use has always been governed by the quantity of work instead of the quality of work. Her list of priorities helps her to see the pitfalls of this type of focus. She resolves to remember that not everything is important and to keep her focus on what is important.

The to-do list and scheduling are other problem areas for Andrea. Andrea is the queen of multitasking. She never makes a list of what needs to be done. Instead, she just does it. Even when she is doing something else at the time, if an urgency arises, she takes care of it as well. She just does not stop. One task is always backed by another, and overlapping is the norm.

Therefore, the idea of having down in writing what needs to be done is a scary thought. But she figures if she is going to make an attempt at successfully managing her time, she might as well go all the way.

Scheduling is difficult. Assigning specific times to activities is a rather foreign concept. So, she starts out slowly and very detailed. The day is divided into 15-minute slots. She first pencils in those activities that are a part of her routine—showering, sleeping, and so forth. Once she has those slots filled, she breathes a little easier. Because she can't write one thing on top of another, her instinct to multitask is curbed at every turn. After careful deliberation, Andrea finally has a schedule. She has lived her entire life without one, so this is a defining moment.

The End Result

Andrea still thinks of herself as superhuman at times, and Jason still has difficulty keeping his work in the workplace. But both of them now have the skills they need to overcome these tendencies. They also have their priorities and goals to keep them in check when they feel as though they are regressing. Even though they haven't yet perfected the strategy, they are ready to move on to the next step: organizing.

**The Art of
Organizing**

Up to this point, you have done a lot of mind work. You have discovered your perception of time, created a list of priorities and goals, shifted your focus, and determined the difference between important and urgent. That's quite a bit of exercise for the brain. Now it's time to do a little legwork.

Organization is an essential element in your time management system. Though it will require physical activity, don't believe that you can stop using your mind. You are going to have to figure out how to make an organizational system work to its greatest potential, while tailoring it to your needs. Organizing is truly an art. You won't necessarily have to invest a lot of blood, sweat, and tears, but you will need to work hard and work smart to get this accomplished.

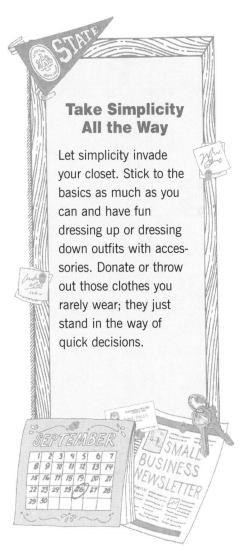

Take Simplicity All the Way

Let simplicity invade your closet. Stick to the basics as much as you can and have fun dressing up or dressing down outfits with accessories. Donate or throw out those clothes you rarely wear; they just stand in the way of quick decisions.

Let Simplicity Be Your Savior

Organization. Simplification. Elimination. Relaxation. All these "-ation" words sound like a fantasy, don't they? Well, you should be pleased to know that they are all within your reach. The basic idea behind organization is to live more simply. Living more simply requires eliminating clutter. Eliminating clutter reduces stress. Reducing stress creates a peaceful and relaxed atmosphere. But before nirvana can be reached, you have to start at the beginning.

Organization

Some of you may think that organizing is way out of your league. You have nowhere to start and wouldn't know where to go once you did. Let's get one thing straight: Organizing is not labeling and color coding every item you own, nor does it even require you to own a filing cabinet. Organization is a system—any system—that works for you. It allows you to locate items and to work efficiently and effectively. Organizing is personal. What works for you may seem like utter chaos to someone else. Don't bother making comparisons—our ultimate goal here is to simplify your life, and that is not an idea you can just borrow. Some organizational tools may work in the same manner for two different people, but the systems themselves must be customized. Though there are several tools out there designed to make organizing easier (some of the more popular ones will be discussed later in the chapter), not all are going to pertain to your lifestyle. In fact, if not used correctly, they can just add to the clutter you are trying to eliminate.

Take a look at everything around you and decide if you have any systems that are currently working. If so, you will want to expand on these since they probably came about naturally and without prior thought. Even something as simple as hanging up a wet towel every day in a particular spot is its own system. Don't overlook the simple things; it is exactly those things that we are reaching out to. Use this system to spiral outward. Start small with other household items, and then see if the system can be applied to other areas of your life. Can it be used at work? In your personal life? If not, don't worry; other systems can be created.

Housing the Homeless

Do your keys grow legs and run away from you every morning? Do you ever threaten to throw your son's shoes right out the window if you trip over them one more time? Does your secretary or assistant ever complain that he or she simply cannot find a single thing in your office? If you can answer yes to these and similar questions, you may have a homeless problem.

A good way to start organizing is to house the homeless. Think about all those items you are consistently losing and searching for. Items you use every day deserve their own space. For instance, keys are a popular object to lose. Why not give them their very own hook next to the door? Or a specified pocket in your purse? Get into a routine of placing items in their homes. You'll be glad you did when you don't have to get down on your hands and knees and search every dark corner of the house.

Bills and receipts also merit a designated space. You may choose to use a simple filing system, an organizer made specifically for the payment of bills, or a basic paper tray. Whatever you

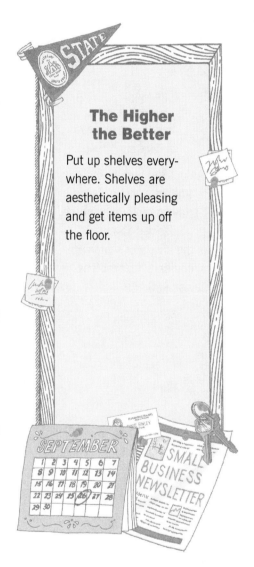

The Higher the Better

Put up shelves everywhere. Shelves are aesthetically pleasing and get items up off the floor.

choose, just make sure to use it. Keep all your bills together in one place; the same goes for your receipts. Another suggestion is to keep a pen, stamps, and return address labels in the same area as your bills. This will make the dreaded chore of dishing out money less of a headache.

Dozens of household and office items can be given their very own homes. Pens, paper, utensils, phone numbers, addresses, books, hair accessories, medication, jewelry—the list could go on and on. The important thing to remember is that every time you have to look for something, time is wasted. It doesn't have to be nice and neat to be organized. As long as you know where to find a particular item, you have done your job. Those items that seem to evade you will be under your control when given a home.

Simplification

Simplification is the act of reducing disorder, confusion, and stress. We all say we wish we lived simple lives, but is that really the truth? Yes, certain areas of our lives would flow much smoother if simplified. But don't we sometimes enjoy the madness of it all? There's nothing wrong with that. You just need to decide which areas of your life could use some simplification.

Hopefully you have now initiated an organizational plan of action. During all this organizing, did you happen to notice how much stuff you have? Did you perhaps question its worth or whether or not it even belonged to you? Or maybe you just stepped over it and didn't even glance back. If you really want to simplify your life, start sorting.

All that stuff you own in one way or another takes up your time. Whether you are repairing a zipper on slacks you rarely wear or continuously tripping over that doll your daughter doesn't even play with, stuff will get in your way. Think about all you own and what kind of upkeep you must maintain, how much money is spent on luxuries, and whether or not it is even worth it. We like stuff. Stuff signifies success. But really now, how much can you take?

Save Time with Smaller Accessories

Consider purchasing a smaller wallet or purse. Having room only for the necessities saves you the hassle of searching endlessly for that long-lost $20 bill.

Look again at your list of priorities. Whatever you own that didn't make it to that list is up for questioning. By no means should you ditch your comforts and live on the streets. Rather, just take stock of what you own and how it may or may not clutter your life.

Stuff is not the only thing that stands in the way of simplification. The following are some other ideas that may help you to live more simply:

- Your family does not need an elaborate meal every night. Grilled cheese and tomato soup will feed them just fine once in a while. Don't forget the splendor of takeout!
- Telephone calls and correspondence need not go on forever. If you are brief and to the point in a conversation, an e-mail, or a letter, you will get your ideas across more clearly. An important idea may be lost amid excessive detail and require yet another chat session to reiterate.
- Constant worry leads to complications in life. Try not to worry about those things that you have no control over. If this is a difficult thing to do, reason with yourself. Talk it out and make yourself believe that worry will not help anything; it will only harm. The fewer worries you have, the simpler life will seem.

Elimination

Now that you know what stands in the way of simplification, what will you do about it? This is where elimination plays a role. For those of you who are pack rats or create a special relationship with everything in your life, this may be a very frightening concept. But have no fear, you, too, can eliminate items with ease.

Label a good-sized box "Uncertainties" and go through your house room by room. Set the box in the center of each room and carefully go over everything you own. If an item is unrecognizable, sticks out like a sore thumb, has no earthly use you can think of,

Make a Party of Those Old Papers

Gather all those old paper products you want to get rid of. Collect them for a couple of weeks and then throw a party. Use them to make a bonfire and host a marsh-mallow roast! (Check your local laws beforehand, and use good judgment for safety.)

or is something you haven't thought about, much less touched, in the last six months, place it in the box. Don't worry, it isn't going to the trash—yet.

When the box is filled to the rim or you have completed your round of the room, the elimination begins. First, separate all paper from the pile. This will probably reduce its size by half. If the print is too faded to read, it automatically goes—no ifs, ands, or buts. Newspapers, magazines, newsletters, and anything dated prior to the previous month goes. Those items that have dates within the previous or current month can be rifled through to see if there are any articles you want to read. If so, clip the article and throw out the bulk. There will probably be some papers you feel you should keep, whether for tax purposes, sentimental reasons, or just plain gut instinct. Use good judgment here. If it is something that you aren't going to see until next time you go into an organizing frenzy, seriously consider its disposal; it's probably not that important. If tears come to your eyes upon its leaving your hand, keep it; it's not worth the emotional pain.

Once you figure out the paper puzzle, you will probably feel much better about tackling the rest. However, the rest is a lot of stuff. Make sure you're up for it. The items in this pile made the cut because they were unrecognizable, did not fit properly anywhere else, needed to be fixed, or had not been used in the last six months. Some of you will have no problem just bulldozing the entire pile out the back door into the trash, but others will suffer from postpartum depression if the situation isn't handled gently. However you choose to address the pile, keep in mind that whatever you don't get rid of will have to find a place to rest, meaning more time and thought on your part.

Elimination does not automatically mean it goes to the garbage. There are other ways of eliminating clutter that may in fact make you feel better about letting go. For instance, you can sell those items you will no longer need. This way you will at least be getting a little something out of them. Just be careful not to turn around and use that money to buy even more useless things. You can ask your friends and family if they would have any use for the items.

Remember, one person's trash is another's treasure. Or you can donate the items to a charitable institution.

The time spent eliminating depends on the size of the space you have decided to tackle, as well as how many items you have to sort. If it looks as though this project may take you quite a while, break it down. Don't feel as though you must attack the entire house in one afternoon. Do one room at a time if that is what your schedule allows. Though this is an important project, don't sacrifice your priorities to make room for it.

Once you are able to organize, simplify, and eliminate, it is time to relax. No longer do you have to listen to the cries of clutter surrounding you. Nor will half your life be spent on the hunt, searching for keys, glasses, shoes, your brain. It's reward time. Throw yourself a party welcoming you into the world of simplicity.

Avoid Lists of Lists of Lists

How many lists do we compose in a year? Let's see, we have grocery lists, mailing lists, Christmas lists, people-to-thank lists, books-to-read lists, movies-to-watch lists, home-improvements-to-be-made lists, invitation lists, wish lists, and so forth. The list of lists is endless. But do we really need all these lists?

Lists are a great way to lay out before you things that need to be done. You need lists only when you wish to get a firm grasp on your management of time. However, consider also that composing lists takes time, thought, and energy. Since you are striving to use your time efficiently and effectively, lists may not always be the best use of time. Too many lists can confuse and torment you, forcing you to actually lose time in the long run.

For instance, if you are an eager time manager, it is likely you have pencil and paper in hand at all times, ready to organize and execute any task. Lists are your friends, and you enjoy the security of their companionship. At your son's first soccer practice, you diligently write down the names and positions of all teammates. You are prepared to later research their phone numbers and parents' names. You do the same at your daughter's volleyball practice.

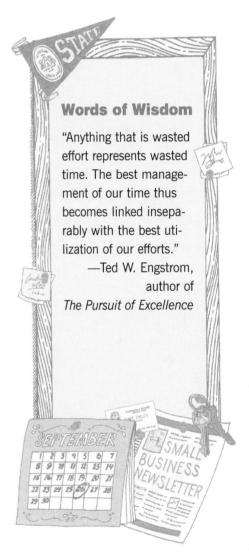

Words of Wisdom

"Anything that is wasted effort represents wasted time. The best management of our time thus becomes linked inseparably with the best utilization of our efforts."
—Ted W. Engstrom, author of *The Pursuit of Excellence*

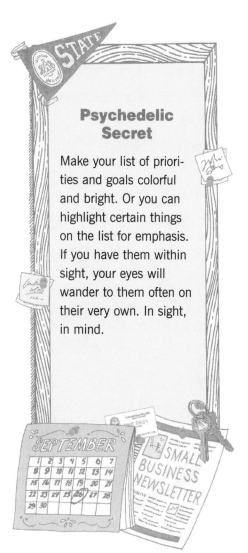

Psychedelic Secret

Make your list of priorities and goals colorful and bright. Or you can highlight certain things on the list for emphasis. If you have them within sight, your eyes will wander to them often on their very own. In sight, in mind.

On the drive back home, you notice men outdoors mowing lawns and trimming hedges. You hardly wait to get in the door before you begin to compose a list of things your husband needs to get done around the house. Because you are kind and value the equality of the relationship, you compose a list for yourself as well.

This is just the beginning. By the end of the day, you have so many lists, you don't know where to keep them all. They all have their own importance and should be easily accessible. You have fifteen sheets of paper and spend 10 minutes trying to arrange them all on the refrigerator door. Meanwhile, you've lost your list of meals to prepare and therefore have no idea what to fix for dinner. You are running behind schedule. Or at least you think so—you really haven't had the time to look at your schedule all day. You did manage to find your to-do list and realize that you need to call Mary about the fundraiser tomorrow. Knowing you have her phone number written down on the "Fund Raiser Committee" list, you head for the refrigerator. It takes you at least a full minute to scan all the lists before finding the right one. By the time you find what you are looking for, you have forgotten who it is you are supposed to call and why, so you head back to your to-do list to refresh yourself.

Does this sound even vaguely familiar? If so, you may be a list junkie. There's nothing wrong with creating lists. In fact, they are necessary at times. You need to have a list of priorities, a to-do list, and a list of goals, to name a few. But it is when you create lists that have very little value and only possess the possibility of future use that you begin to waste time. If you need to make a list of the lists you have, it's time to get some help. An overabundance of lists will trip you up. You will spend time rifling through the different lists to find a particular item. The mere sight of several lists can make you feel extreme pressure and anxiety that is irrelevant. They can make you feel rushed constantly, and you may lose sight of what is important amid all the itemized papers.

Use lists to help you remember, to plan ahead, and to keep your priorities in line. Lists will make your life easier and more organized, if used effectively. Take a look at the lists you have now.

Are there any that could be combined? For instance, if making a phone call is on your to-do list for today, write the phone number of the person you are calling on that same list. You have the information you need right in front of you and won't waste any time searching.

Use your best judgment when it comes to making lists. Weigh their importance and how much they will benefit you in the future. Don't spend time on making lists for mere possibilities. Remember, you are in control here, so make list making work for you!

Organizational Tools

Before you grab your credit card and start ordering every organizer you can find, take stock of your current systems and figure out which ones, if any, you really need. Quite often people believe organizational tools will be a quick fix for their time management problems, but in several cases, the tools fix nothing and serve only to cause even more problems. Remember to let simplicity be your savior.

There are some very handy tools on the market these days, and with technology steadily trying to outdo itself, more and more items are appearing that seem to make your time management efforts effortless. However, keep in mind that it takes time to learn how to use a new device and not everything you try is going to be all that useful. The key is to find a system of tools that saves time, not takes up more of it. Take a look at what type of system works for you and find tools to complement that system.

The Basics

There are some basic tools that nearly all time managers will want to have. First of all, you will need a calendar. But what kind? With the wide assortment of calendars out there, it's difficult to choose. But consider your needs. Do you need it just to show the date, or are you planning to mark appointments on it? Do you want a big one that you can see across the room, or a small one to fit

in your purse? You should also consider where you want to place it. You will probably want a different calendar for the office than the one you will want for your home.

Though you may find that you need more than one calendar, don't plan on utilizing more than one for your appointments. If you have appointments scattered on various calendars, it's almost a surefire bet that you will miss something.

A calendar used for the entire family can be a very efficient tool in time management. Keep it in the kitchen or some other high-traffic zone. Encourage members to mark down all upcoming activities and appointments. This is a good way to keep tabs on your family and allow everyone to know what is going on in each other's lives. If you choose to utilize a family calendar, also mark significant events in your own personal planning system, in order to reduce the chances of your missing something.

A good way to keep yourself on track at all times is to invest in another basic tool of time management—a daily planner. These hot items make it seem as though your entire life can be recorded in one small portable book. Go into any office supply store and you will find shelves upon shelves of daily planners. They come in an assortment of sizes, colors, styles, and bindings. Now the hard part is finding the one that suits your needs.

Again, you need to know what you want to use it for before even thinking of making a purchase. Don't let the fancy ones suck you in if you will use it only as an appointment book. Consider the convenience of the sections offered. For example, several planners come equipped with blank pages for notes; pages for shopping lists, to-do lists, and check lists; an address book; a telephone book; a personal budget; a month-by-month calendar; weekly spreads; maps; emergency information; and even calculators. If you will use all this stuff, that is fantastic.

If not, weed out sections you won't use. Get your planner and be happy. But if you already have working systems set up, don't feel as though you need to transfer everything into your planner. Use what works for you.

You may also want to consider creating your own planner. Since you know what will work best for you, why not? It can be as simple as a spiral-bound notebook or as elaborate as a customized leather-bound book with a table of contents leading to color-coded sections. The choice is yours. But do keep in mind that for this to work effectively, it must be portable, updated frequently, and organized.

The Frills

The basics are a given. Now it's time for the frills. While your time management system should be practical and efficient, that doesn't mean you can't have fun and take advantage of the ever-changing technology out there.

Electronic organizers such as PalmPilot, Sharp Wizard, and BlackBerry Handheld can be seen in the hands of just about every third person you come across. These handy little contraptions bring the power of your computer to the palm of your hand. You can organize; set appointments; store addresses, phone numbers, and to-do lists; track your time; and make changes quickly and easily. What isn't to love?

However, be sure you want to take the plunge into the trek of technology. If you aren't familiar with the products, it will take a bit of time to research and find what best suits your needs, not to mention the time it will take to learn the programs. Keep in mind that electronic organizers can be expensive and can break. Also, all the neat features they offer may become a distraction.

However, if you are eager to jump in there, you will find a world full of quick solutions and seemingly effortless organization. Feel free to try your hand at it, but above all else, find something that works well and stick with it.

Tools for the Home

There are some organizational tools that just seem to suit every home. This section will give you a couple of the more commonly used. However, do a little shopping and compare items to get an idea of what would work best for your home.

- Hooks. These tiny little angels are heaven-sent for your time management needs. Consider all you can do with hooks. Keys adore hooks and are comfortable making their home there. Hats, leashes, bathrobes, bags, umbrellas—these are all things that love hooks. Think about what it is you lose most often. Can hooks come to the rescue?

- Containers can work wonders all over your house, though they are most often preferred in the closets. You can use plastic bins, baskets, or even bags, just as long as you add your own personal flair. Why make this a dull sight and boring job? Containers make it easy to organize items. For example, you can store sweaters and winter clothing in plastic bins during the summer. Then they will be out of the way, neatly nestled, and free from moths, mildew, and mold. You can group items together in containers for easy access and less confusion. A container is the love child of organization and aesthetic appearance. Take advantage of its innate need to coordinate pleasurably.

- Literature sorters are handy items that help you to curb the paper problem. You can invest in a magazine rack, a catalog binder, a carousel divider, or a state-of-the-art literature center. Depending on the literature that accumulates within your home, you may have a need for several different types of literature sorters. Though convenient and orderly, don't allow these sorters to tempt you to keep unnecessary and useless literature.

- Shelving. Your choice of shelves within the home can help you to use and organize the space available at an optimum level. Use wall shelves to get items up and out of the way, saving floor space. Corner shelves fit nicely and make for good displays.

There are all kinds of organizational tools out there that you can use around the house. Some are beautiful items that will enhance the overall appearance of your home, and others are simply practical applications designed only for order. Do some brainstorming and shopping around. Perhaps you will even be able to come up with an organizational use for something not otherwise used for that purpose. Make it fun and personal. Remember to complement your time management system; otherwise, you may run into problems down the road.

Tools for the Office

Unlike the home, the office is stricter in its organizational needs. Like the home, the office needs a bit of flair and personality. Because organization just looks good, many people try to get their office in shape before creating order in the rest of their lives. Also, because the office is often more tense and stressful, it cries out for organization.

Some basic tools that have become staples around the office include filing cabinets, paper trays, bulletin boards or dry erase boards, and maybe the occasional rubber band ball. But there is a wide assortment of tools to choose from:

- You may consider adding a shelf or small bookcase to make access to objects easier and to give the space a more sophisticated feel.
- Desktop organizers are available to take care of all your common supplies such as pens, paper clips, staplers, staples, sticky notes, scissors, and calculators.
- Quite often you can find matching storage units for computer disks, CDs, message slips, phone numbers, and just your basic odds and ends.

Color Coding

Use bright colors to liven a dull planner. Colors also come in handy for prioritizing or sorting items. Stickers, collages, anything that makes you smile will bring a hint of fun to an otherwise wearisome organizer.

Take stock of your time management hang-ups in the office and try to match them with an organizational tool. With everything that is out there, you will surely be able to find something that matches not only your needs but your taste as well. These tools are a good way to add a bit of personality to your office without turning it into your second bedroom. The office is definitely a place that can use some personality. By making it your own, you will be more motivated and inspired while at your desk. It won't seem so dull and won't work to drag you down. Also, it may just inspire others to do the same, which will create a more relaxed and comfortable office area. Take advantage of the wonderful features of organizational tools and use them to their full potential.

Jason and Andrea Together in Organization

Organization and simplicity appeal to both Jason and Andrea. However, they are at a loss as to where to begin. Creating an organizational system that works for two people is obviously a little more difficult than creating one for an individual. Everyone is different, and if an organizational system is supposed to be tailored to a person's individual needs, how on earth can you create one that will cater to two people?

Jason and Andrea find a way to make it work. Because we know the two of them are rather strong-willed and determined people, organization is a battle hard fought, but won.

Jason and Andrea realize that an organizational system for their home life is going to have to be a combined effort—with their son, Matthew, included. For this reason, they choose to warm up with their personal and work lives first. This way, they can create their own individual systems before determining how to bring them together.

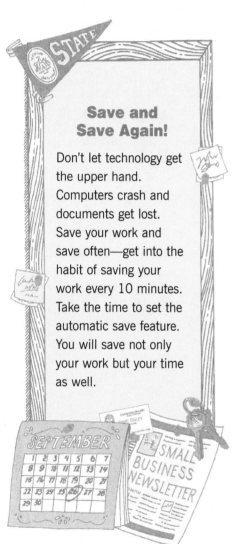

Save and Save Again!

Don't let technology get the upper hand. Computers crash and documents get lost. Save your work and save often—get into the habit of saving your work every 10 minutes. Take the time to set the automatic save feature. You will save not only your work but your time as well.

Jason

Jason begins with his work life. Here, he already has an organizational system in place. However, it is not something he purposely installed. The organization of items is just a natural setup for him. Upon close examination, Jason finds that his system is based on convenience. Because he is so busy, he arranges things in groups of like items. Books are arranged according to subject, not alphabetically. Extra supplies are not placed all together, but next to the work area they pertain to. For example, printer cartridges are not placed in the same location as extra pens and pencils. They are placed in a drawer next to the printer, along with extra paper. Some people would be driven mad by this system, but it complements Jason's line of thinking. The most important part is that it works well and will stick.

Jason spends an afternoon carefully taking stock of everything in his office. Not all items are secure within the system. He finds that most of these items are those that he spends countless minutes searching for time and time again. He decides to arrange everything so that it fits within the organizational system. Of course, he will have to get used to consciously thinking about the system, but because it has already proven itself to work well, he should have little trouble maintaining it.

Andrea

Andrea wants to give up before she even starts. Finding an already-established system in her mess of a schedule is a difficult thing to do. She chooses to begin with her personal life and is surprised at what she finds. Because her personal life is all her own, she doesn't have to worry about the systems laid on her by other people. She allows others to have a hand in setting her schedule and systems for the other areas of her life, but her personal life is all up to her. Here she finds that she is actually an inherently organized person.

Simplicity is the key to Andrea's organizational system. Whereas in the other areas of her life she is bombarded with activities, ideas, and tangible items, in her personal life she keeps things quiet and uncomplicated. She has very few tangible items involved with her personal life, but those that are involved are very basic and to the point.

For example, Andrea keeps one book that contains phone numbers, addresses, dates of special occasions, random thoughts, and ideas that she comes across; stationery and stamps; and other frequently used items. She doesn't have to think about where she last left so-and-so's number or if she missed a birthday. Everything is right there in one place. Note that there isn't anything that is not used frequently; no random papers or business cards of people she doesn't remember. Everything in the book is neatly settled and necessary—no frills, no complications.

Andrea is eager to bring simplicity to the home, and Jason is eager to bring convenience to the home. Even though this may sound like a nice blend of qualities, their systems aren't always going to work well with one another.

The Dilemma

Jason likes *stuff*. This isn't to say he is terribly materialistic. He just likes to be surrounded by items that bring him joy, even if he doesn't get around to paying attention to them. His mind is stimulated by the eye, and objects around him are used to that end. Andrea's system of simplicity begs to get rid of the "clutter," as she views it. Her system is hard-pressed to work well if there is a lot of stuff lying around in the way.

Andrea is comfortable in the areas of the house where she spends the most time. For instance, she refuses to allow anyone else near the kitchen while she is cooking. She finds peace in the familiarity of the arrangement of items. Granted, they are all located in rather inconvenient areas, but she knows where to find things. They have their own home and to uproot and move these items seems rather cruel to Andrea. Granted, she isn't the only one to work in the kitchen. Both Jason and Matthew fix dinner from time to time as well. Jason's system of convenience could really stretch its legs in the kitchen, making it an organizational wonderland. But Andrea would be greatly displeased with this improvement.

The Compromise

Trying to find a common ground when both Jason and Andrea are excited about their own systems is going to take a lot of compromise. But it can be done. If both systems are installed and given a chance to flourish, they will eventually fall into the patterns set by each. However, they first have to figure out where and how much of each system to incorporate.

They quickly see that arguing isn't going to get them anywhere, so they both concede to give a little. Jason agrees to allow some of his stuff to be placed in storage. When he tires of the decor, he needs only to rotate items from the house to storage, and from storage to the house. This way, the house has a more simple touch and less clutter, and Jason can thoroughly enjoy those items he has on display without having to divide his attention among several.

Andrea agrees to allow convenience into the kitchen and the rest of the house as long as not everything need be moved. Convenience here and there will greatly improve the organization and time efficiency of the overall household, but Andrea doesn't have to lose all the comfort of familiarity. They will discuss and unanimously agree on what will be moved.

Both are looking forward to Matthew's input as well. They are eager to see what his organizational system entails and how it also can be incorporated into the household. Once all systems are up and running, the house will be much more effective and efficient, and each person will feel comfortable with his or her contribution. The other parts will grow into a routine and soon they won't be distinguishable from each other; they will simply become one organizational system.

Accomplishing More in Less Time

Now that you know what you want to achieve and have begun your journey, undoubtedly you are eager to begin saving that precious commodity we call time. This chapter is full of shortcuts that will help you to get more done in less time without feeling you are running yourself threadbare. If you are a fan of shortcuts, this chapter is for you. Learn how to pass off those jobs you never wanted to do in the first place. Consider both the pros and cons of multitasking and if it is right for you. Are there rules working against you? Can you beat the odds? Find out how.

The 80/20 Rule

We've all heard of the 80/20 Rule in one variation or another. It is also known as Pareto's Principal and The Vital Few. The rule states that 80 percent of your results will come from 20 percent of your efforts, which also means that 20 percent of your results will come from 80 percent of your efforts. Vilfredo Pareto, an Italian economist, developed this principle when he discovered that 80 percent of the wealth of England belonged to 20 percent of the population. Upon further study of different countries and different time periods, he found that this equation became a pattern applied to all examples put forth.

Since his discovery, several people have applied the rule to nearly all aspects of life and found that it fits quite nicely. For instance:

- 20 percent of your clothes will be worn 80 percent of the time.
- 80 percent of a store's sales comes from 20 percent of its customers.
- 80 percent of automobile accidents will be caused by 20 percent of motorists.
- 20 percent of acreage will produce 80 percent of the crop.
- 20 percent of companies within an industry will conduct 80 percent of the business of that industry.

Though it can be a rather discouraging statement, it is a good guideline to use while examining your management of time. The problem people have with the 80/20 Rule is that for most aspects in our lives, we don't know which is the 20 percent until after the fact. Therefore, it does us very little good to take the time to analyze the rule. But as far as time management is concerned, examining this rule and its effect on your life will help you to spend your time more wisely.

Assign a Value Scale

To make the 80/20 Rule work for you, first assign a scale of value to your different activities. When you consider time well spent, what is it you have accomplished? This value scale will vary from person to person. Some may place highest value on financial security, while others regard health as their top priority. The values themselves will also vary as you go through life. What takes precedence now may not even be an issue later on.

Keep an Activity Log

An easy way to assess how well you use your time is to keep an activity log. For each activity entry, record how long you worked, whether or not the task was completed, and place a number next to it ranking its place on your value scale. At the end of the day, take a look at how many activities are ranked number one and how much time you spent with each. Chances are, in comparison to the rest of the day, very little time was spent on the "valued activities"—those that will produce the most positive results. If this happens to be the case, you have fallen under the 80/20 spell. But that's okay; it is to be expected.

Recognizing the problem is always the first step in correcting it. You might even find that what you value the most didn't even make it to the list. Are you spending time on activities that don't even remotely relate to your goals? If so, you must find a way to incorporate those things that will bring you the best results into your daily schedule. This is key for your happiness, not to mention your sanity.

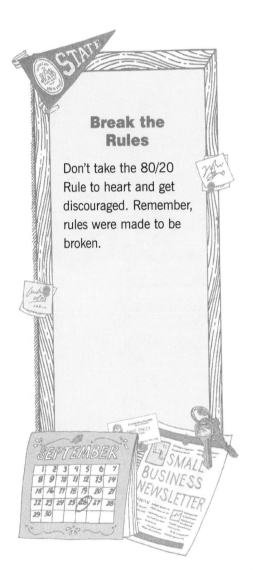

Break the Rules

Don't take the 80/20 Rule to heart and get discouraged. Remember, rules were made to be broken.

Now, take a look at those activities that ranked lowest on your scale. These are the ones we want to concentrate on. All those little chores that get in the way of your life are often should-dos. These can be terribly annoying because you know they are things that need to be done but really have very little impact on your happiness and satisfaction. The should-dos are usually put off until they become urgent, which throws your plan for time management right out the window.

See if you have any alternative means of accomplishing these tasks. Perhaps you can hire someone to mow the lawn while you use that extra time to take your kids for ice cream. Or, if you can't afford to hire help, consider bartering. Because everyone's value scale will be different, it may just work out that you will find someone whose should-dos match up with your valued activities and vice versa. Also, don't forget delegation; we will discuss that in greater detail later in the chapter. It may simply be that you decide you can just forget about the task entirely. Perhaps it wasn't really that important in the first place and certainly isn't now in comparison to the valueds. If you can bring yourself to lower your standards for the should-dos, you can then raise your standards for the valueds.

Once you get rid of some of the should-dos, apply that time toward the valueds. Change the 20 percent to 40 percent. Only good can come from this, so why not make it work? All of a sudden, you will have an improved outlook on life, feel better about yourself and what you are doing, and be motivated to get more accomplished. Your ultimate goal is to spend more time on those activities that bring the most satisfaction. The 80/20 Rule may seem as though it is working against us, but really it helps us to keep our priorities in check. Come back to it once in a while and reevaluate your value system. You may find that the 80/20 Rule has snuck up on you once again.

Multitasking: Pros and Cons

What word comes to mind when you think of time management? Several people believe "multitasking" is the new, trendy word that holds the key to solving all time management problems. Multitasking is the idea that more than one task can be performed at once, thereby saving time. Sounds ideal, right? While there are several advantages to this concept, there are also disadvantages that many people don't take into consideration or sometimes even choose to ignore. But let's first take a look at the advantages.

The Pros

Think about how often you waste time waiting for the doctor, on hold, to pick up the kids, in lines, and in traffic. The list could go on and on. You spend most of those times grumbling to yourself, "I could be doing this or that." There is always something that could be done. For these situations, multitasking would work well. Here are some ways you can use it effectively:

- While waiting in the doctor or dentist's office, finish off that last chapter of the novel you've been trying to schedule in for the last few weeks. You will be glad to have finally found out who murdered Miss Smith and will have successfully kept your mind away from the dreaded drills or shots.
- While watching television, there are numerous activities that can be done. Fold the laundry, exercise, clean, iron, and so forth.
- Multitasking while on the phone can be tricky sometimes. Because you are dealing with a person who expects you to be giving your full attention, you must make it seem so. If you are talking with someone who has a tendency to dominate conversation while saying a whole lot of nothing, then by all means get other things done. However, if it is a friend who needs you to hear her out, put the newspaper aside and give your full attention.

Overlap Activities

Save time by combining activities according to location. For instance, if the Laundromat is next to the grocery store, use the geography to your benefit. Put a load of clothes into the wash; then do your food shopping while you wait.

- While waiting to pick up your kids from soccer practice, balance the checkbook.
- If you have a long commute to work, learn how to speak a foreign language or listen to a book on tape. By stimulating your mind, you will be more alert while driving, as well as more energized once you finally reach your destination. Who knows, you might even be inclined to just smile at the guy who cut you off.
- Open your mail or write personal notes while eating lunch.

The Cons

Because of the technology we have today, multitasking seems forced on us. Between pagers, faxes, voice mail, e-mail, and cell phones, something is always ringing or beeping. Granted, they do make completing tasks faster and easier. However, you must utilize these devices with sense and not get too caught up in the technology race. Cellular phones, for example, are very handy but can also cause problems. Take care when using them while driving, and turn off the ringer when an interruption would be inappropriate. Don't excuse yourself from dinner with your spouse to check your voice mail. Use common sense and don't abuse these devices. They are there to make your life easier, not to control you.

While multitasking works well with jobs that take little concentration, it is recommended you avoid it for jobs that require focus. Because you are working on two or more tasks at once, your attention will have to be divided. Multitasking at the wrong times can actually cause you to lose time. If you don't devote your full attention to an important project, mistakes can and will occur, requiring you to take time to correct your errors. However, if you concentrate solely on what you are trying to accomplish, chances are you will get the job done correctly and quickly the first time.

Some people feel guilty for not multitasking. This guilt spurs a collection of myriad partial tasks. While the number of tasks is doubled, the tasks themselves are quite often completed only

half-sufficiently. So now you are also feeling guilty for not doing as well as you could. The pressure to overachieve has a significant impact on your stress level, which in turn can make you tired and careless. You must keep a realistic outlook. Bear in mind that it isn't how much you do, but how much you do well that marks you as a successful person.

In a world where multitasking gives you the image of success, it is easy to be lured into multitasking too often, even constantly. But be careful when succumbing to its appeal. Your stress level and quality of work are at risk. Save multitasking for those jobs that require little focus and brain activity, and you will reap the greatest benefits. Though the disadvantages of multitasking will weigh heavily, they can be easily overcome by using sound judgment.

Trick of the Trade

A trick all good time managers know is how to make use of their most productive time of day. We can't manipulate time to fit our needs, but we can manipulate ourselves to make the most of time. Some of you may already know whether you are a morning person, a night owl, or a midafternoon ace. But are you using that swell of productivity wisely?

First, figure out when your surge of motivation comes around.

- Coffee, sugar, and stimulants aside, when do you feel the most energized?
- Around what time of the day does your inspiration and motivation hit?
- When is your focus its sharpest?
- Do you ever feel as though absolutely nothing can stop you?

You should also take note of your downtime.

- When are you struggling to complete the simplest task?
- What time of day do you feel lethargic?

- Is there a certain period of time in which you just can't remember the meaning of motivation?
- Do you feel it is necessary to load up on stimulants during any part of the day?

Recognizing these two times of day—surges and downtime—and scheduling activities around them can make a world of difference in your use of time. Take another look at your to-do list. Separate the dreaded activities from the enjoyable ones. If you are having difficulty deciding how to categorize a particular item, question its significance. Will the completion of the task enrich your life or advance your goals? If so, then put it in the enjoyable category.

Once you have sorted through all the activities, take a look at your schedule. Do the dreaded activities coincide with your downtime? Do the enjoyable activities coincide with your upsurge? If so, it's time for a little reorganization.

This may not make a lot of sense at first, but stick with it. It's natural to work on your enjoyable tasks when you are the most motivated, and it is easy to leave the boring tasks for later, when you are sluggish anyway. If time and task match up, then they must go together, right? Wrong.

If you want to make the most of your day, you will match up the boring tasks with your productive period and the gratifying tasks with your unproductive period. Because you are going to be motivated regardless of what you are doing during your productive period, it is best to take advantage of that energy to tackle the tasks you simply don't like. If you allow these tasks to be postponed until a time when you don't feel like doing much of anything, much less a task you hate, chances are it will never get finished. If you hold off on the enjoyable activities (or those that yield the most positive results) until a time when you are normally unproductive, those activities will provide motivation you would not otherwise have. You will get more accomplished throughout the course of the day and achieve a balance of productivity.

Granted, it may be difficult to rearrange your schedule to make this work for every task. But do what you can. Every little bit of time used effectively will benefit you.

Making the Most of Every Moment

By this time, you have figured out how much time you waste in a day and have taken steps to rectify the issue. However, there will undoubtedly be small spans of time you haven't planned for.

Let's say your child is running late getting ready for school. You are dressed and waiting with coffee in hand. You can either stand there and tap your foot impatiently, or you can use the time productively. Whatever you choose is not going to help your child along any faster. But those unaccounted-for moments can allow you to get the little things done and out of the way. However, if you spend the time trying to figure out what to do, the time will be lost and wasted. We aren't going to go overboard here; we're only going to give you a few suggestions to get you thinking.

Give Me Just Five Minutes

Five minutes may not seem like a lot in the grand scheme of things, but those small scraps of time add up rather quickly. Take a look at your to-do list. Is there anything there that won't take a great deal of thought and can be done rather quickly? Consider the following options:

- Water the plants.
- Flip through your magazines and tear out the articles you want to read.
- Affix stamps to the envelopes in your bills-to-be-paid folder.
- Let the dog out for a bathroom break.
- Pull the frozen pork chops out of the freezer to thaw for dinner.
- Sort the mail.
- Unload the dishwasher.
- Hide the remote from your spouse.
- Throw a load of laundry into the washing machine.
- Warm up your car.

While it will probably be rare for you to have even five seconds of free time, much less five minutes, think about how you spend your idle moments. When those times do arise, you have several productive options open to you. Take advantage of them.

Stick with What You Start

In a world where time is always at your heels, it is easy to get caught up in a routine of partial tasks. We fool ourselves into thinking that we are working more and harder if we have several things going on at once, but really we may be slowing ourselves down, as well as risking the quality of our work.

Let's say that you have three partial tasks going on that you float between. You start with task 1, which happens to be the one you like the least, but in following with our advice, you try to tackle this one first. Almost instantly you become bored and think of a hundred other things you could be doing. You convince yourself a change in task would leave you refreshed. So begins task 2. This one is second on your list because it is only slightly more favorable than task 1. Needless to say, you tire of task 2 rather quickly as well. Now your ego plays a part in the decision-making process. Of course, it makes sense to complete the first two tasks and get them out of the way, but you are smart and an efficient worker, so why not take on a third, just to break up the monotony of the first two? Enter task 3.

You enjoy task 3, but knowing that the other two tasks have yet to be completed takes away from the joy you want to experience with task 3. In the back of your mind you are thinking haphazardly of ways the other two can be accomplished. So you run back and forth and back again. Each time you dart from one task to the other, you lose concentration and have to begin anew. The loss of concentration equals the loss of time. It is also likely that because you are darting from one to another, you aren't going to be solely focused on any of the projects at any given time. Which, in turn, means that you

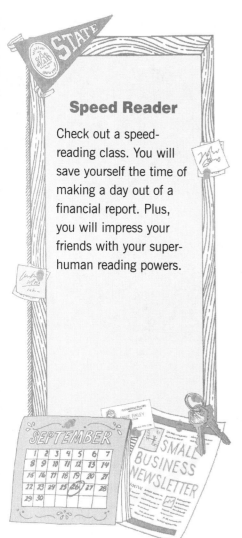

Speed Reader

Check out a speed-reading class. You will save yourself the time of making a day out of a financial report. Plus, you will impress your friends with your super-human reading powers.

aren't accomplishing the quality of work you are capable of, even with the tasks you enjoy.

Sounds like a headache, right? But this is a scene we play out daily. There is always something to be done and never enough time in which to do it, so why not combine everything and at least give it the facade of superhuman accomplishment? There are several reasons/excuses we come up with to justify moving on before a task is completed: "I need a break," "Something more important came up," "I will get burnt out trying to stay focused for too long," "I will have more time to spend working on it tomorrow." Do any of these sound familiar? With a continuous starting and stopping of tasks, will anything ever get done?

It is okay to break up a large task into sections, but define those sections. Don't just tell yourself you will work until you can't work anymore—that rarely becomes the case. Set definite goals to accomplish. Set your mind on accomplishing one goal at a time. Chances are, once you get rolling with the project, as long as it has a definite end in sight, it will be easier to keep it up. If you just can't bear to keep it up, take a short break, not an extended one in which you find something else to work on. Get up and stretch, walk outside for a moment, or just close your eyes for a minute. The break should refresh you without completely breaking your concentration. Once you finish the first project, you will have such a great sense of accomplishment, you will want to jump on the next project. Okay, maybe you won't have that much enthusiasm, but you will feel better about yourself and the work you have done.

Do It Right the First Time!

How many times have you heard your mother say that? Those six little words are words of wisdom. When we're short on time, we often think that getting anything done is actually quite good. Getting a lot done is exceptional. But do we take into consideration how well it was done, or are we just so excited to be finished with it

I'm Not Stupid, I'm Ignorant!

There is a difference between stupidity and ignorance. Don't be afraid to be smart and show your ignorance. Ask questions. You will save yourself time by getting all the information you need up front. People who don't bother to ask questions only make work for themselves later.

Body Language Speaks for Itself

Body language can clue you in to a person's feelings. Consider the following list. Though these equations may not be true in every case, they are common interpretations.

Arms crossed over chest = Defensiveness or anxiety

Swinging arm = Wants to walk away from a situation

Eye blinking = Fast blinking signals stress

Downward gaze = Feeling defeated

Taking notes = Shows interest or involvement

Hand over mouth = Can mean boredom

Arms behind head and leaning back = Looking for power or control

(continued on next page)

that the quality of work doesn't even cross our minds? In today's fast-paced world, a person is judged on how quickly tasks are accomplished. Therefore, the focus lies on the completion, not the quality, of the job. What many people don't realize is that those judgments are immediate and have little effect in the long run.

Saving time is the focus here, but in doing so, you don't want to risk the quality of the work you are doing. Though you may think you simply don't have the time to get the job done well, that is a misconception. Actually, you don't have the time to not get the job done well.

Think back to when you were young and so desperately wanted to go to the neighborhood baseball game. One thing stood in your way: your messy bedroom. Your mother absolutely refused to let you out that door until the room was cleaned. So what did you do? You decided that the baseball game couldn't wait for the time it would take to thoroughly clean the room. You bulldozed clothes into the closet (the clean along with the dirty); shoved magazines, school papers, and candy wrappers under the bed; and pulled your comforter over everything that was lying on the bed, using the pillows to cover the unmistakable lumps. You were then out the door without a second thought to the mess that was waiting unattended.

However, your mother caught on (perhaps due to the smell that seeped out from under your bedroom door) to your trickery. So, think back to how you spent the following weekend. Of course, the room was in an even worse state than before, and because you didn't take the time to clean it correctly the first time, cleaning it the second time around took at least twice the amount of time it would have taken originally. So instead of missing half the ball game last weekend, you have missed a full ball game this weekend.

We are all guilty of scenes similar to this, and not just from our childhood. We have such a demand on our time, it is easy to believe that completing a project regardless of the quality is better than not having completed it at all. We lower our personal standards to raise the quantity of our accomplishments. Though some projects may slide by without notice, others will be stopped and evaluated for quality. When this happens and the work is yours, the standards others have set regarding your work will also lower. This means that you will have to set time aside to work harder and regain your standing. Sometimes the projects themselves will have to be modified or completely reworked. You will have lost the time it took you to pull together the insufficient material in the first place, as well as the time it will take to rebuild the project.

In order to do it right the first time with a reasonable time allowance, you must be prepared. Preparation is key for the smooth execution of most tasks. Never assume you can just "wing it" and pull together an important project without the proper legwork. Shoddy work will most certainly be noticed at some point, and it's not worth risking your reputation.

By taking your mother's advice and doing it right the first time, you will save yourself the time and energy it will take to rework the task. Also, your confidence and overall attitude toward your work will improve, creating a relaxed environment in which you can work effectively and efficiently.

The Importance of Listening

If you have ever had a communications class, you know that listening is important. But did you know that it could save you time as well?

You need to understand that listening is different from hearing. Hearing is the process of perceiving and registering sound through the ear. Listening requires you to actively participate in understanding what is being heard. Quite often people do not make a distinction between the two. Active listening is a skill you can apply to all facets of your life, not just time management. Because it is a skill not mastered by many, it will set you apart from the masses.

There are several ways that active listening can benefit your management of time. For example, active listening will allow you to understand instructions the first time around so you can avoid having to return to a person again and again. It will also decrease the number of errors you make. It will make you more knowledgeable and give you confidence. However, keep in mind that this is a

Body Language Speaks for Itself

(continued from previous page)

Unbuttoning coat = Openness

Buttoning coat = Feels trapped and wants to leave

Standing with hands behind back = Confidence

Clearing throat = Nervousness

Rubbing back of neck = Defensiveness

Hands flat on table = Ready to agree

Stroking chin = Evaluating or thinking

Foot tapping = Impatience

Rubbing the eye = Doubt or disbelief

Rubbing hands = Anticipation

Tilted head = Interest

Pulling/tugging ear = Indecision

skill, and skills require training and discipline; therefore, it will also require time.

Here are some guidelines to active listening:

- **Clear your mind of any prejudices, preconceived notions, and judgments.** You will have time later to form your own opinion.
- **Focus on the person speaking.** Do not allow outside forces to invade your thoughts. Tune out the background noise. Allow nothing to interrupt your concentration.
- **Be silent.** Do not give in to the temptation to dispute or defend. The speaker has the floor and deserves to be heard. Silence doesn't mean just keeping your mouth shut. It also encompasses resisting the urge to prepare a speech in your mind. You cannot give your full attention to the speaker if you are formulating ideas and questions.
- **Be patient.** Do not get frustrated if the speaker is having difficulty expressing him- or herself. Don't tap your foot or drum your fingers on the table, and under no circumstances should you try to finish the other person's sentences.
- **Try to understand what the speaker is feeling as well as saying.** The use of nonverbal communication comes in handy here. It is not always easy to voice emotions, but if you take notice of a slight frown or a wringing of the hands, it can clue you in to other aspects surrounding the speaker's words. Listen for what is not being said.
- **Do not get emotionally involved.** This can be a difficult thing to do at times, but you need to be able to draw rational and objective conclusions.
- **Send signals to inform the speaker that you are listening.** Maintaining eye contact is key. Nodding your head or smiling once in a while shows attention. If you don't

understand a statement, but don't wish to interrupt, you can frown slightly to show confusion. If the speaker knows he has your attention, he will be more confident in relaying his ideas.

- **When the speaker has finished, ask questions.** Don't feel embarrassed about not understanding. This is your opportunity to clarify any and all issues that may be confusing. If you think you understand, but still need a bit more reassurance, reiterate the speaker's remarks. This shows that you listened and how much you were able to grasp. If you leave anything out, the speaker will assist you.

Active listening can build stronger relationships, save you time, and open the door for new opportunities. By practicing active listening, you will no longer have to interrupt your work to double-check on instructions, you won't have to spend time correcting errors that resulted from misunderstanding, and you won't miss out on important information. Allow good listening skills to build you a sound and admirable reputation.

Test Your Listening Skills

Recall a conversation you had last week. Did you hit all major points? What about a conversation you had yesterday? A few hours ago?

Eliminate/Control Distractions

How many times have you used the excuse "I got distracted"? Probably thousands. It's one of the most prevalent scapegoats for missing a deadline, forgetting to pick up your kids, ruining dinner, or just about any blunder you can think of. This is widely accepted because we all have to deal with distractions. Sometimes it even seems as though they rule our lives.

A distraction is anything that pulls your attention away from what you are currently working on. Noise, the lack of noise, emergencies, television, a bird outside the window—these are all distractions. Distractions are inevitable and have the potential to ruin our carefully planned schedules. There are, however, simple steps we can take to cut down on the damage.

Do You Welcome Distraction?

What you first have to realize is that most distractions are a problem only because we allow them to be. In other words, the channel surfing in the other room may very well distract you to the point of insanity; whereas it may have no effect whatsoever on your partner. If you don't enjoy what you are doing, you may subconsciously search for a distraction. In this case, anything that diverts your attention is welcome although you may groan about it. But truly, you are finding a way to place the blame for your own lack of motivation.

If you secretly welcome distractions, it may be that you simply have a lack of focus. This doesn't have to apply to everything you do. Perhaps you find yourself consistently distracted only when you are trying to write a paper or take notes in a meeting. This makes sense if these are activities you dislike. If you find that suddenly the color of the neighbor's grass becomes the most interesting thing you've ever noticed, take a look at what you should be working on. It is very difficult to stay focused on an irritating project, but it can be done.

Control Distractions

You have control over some tangible distractions. For instance, if you are trying to write a paper, turn off the television so your eyes won't wander in that direction. Shut the door and blinds if necessary. Position your computer screen so there isn't a glare beckoning to you. Remove all external distractions that you can. This will help some, but if writing this paper is something you really dread, your very own mind may turn against you.

Daydreaming is a favorite distraction. It doesn't need outside forces; instead it plays on your fantasies and lack of focus. Since you can't very well turn off your mind, you will need to find an alternate way of avoiding daydreams. In this case, you may want to use visual aids. When you go into that "zone," it may seem as though you don't see things in front of you, but your eyes will still register. Within eyeshot, place a memo to yourself listing the reasons why this project is important to you. Or, if positive reinforcement doesn't work, make a list of the penalties you will have to pay if the project isn't completed.

Another suggestion would be to let someone else know you are having trouble focusing. Ask that person to check up on you periodically to see how much you have accomplished. Chances are, you will feel pressure to get more done, and your focus will be a little more steady. But don't allow yourself to be checked on too frequently, because this will serve only as yet another distraction.

What Do Distractions Cost You?

Consider the amount of time distractions cost you. Do you use distractions as your excuse for being late often? If you stay focused on your project it will be over quickly and out of your life. However, if you allow distractions to interfere continuously, it could drag the project out over a course of days. No one wants to wake up in the morning knowing they have to complete a dreaded task that could have been done the day before. That just gives you an even worse attitude toward the task, allowing for even more distractions. Try to focus on a positive aspect of the job, even if it is only getting it completed and out of the way.

Of course, there are distractions you can't avoid. Emergencies such as illness in the family, for example, cannot be anticipated. However, if you are a good time manager, you will have left some time available for the unforeseen.

Keep in mind that distractions aren't always the enemy. If you have a tendency to become distracted quite frequently, this could be a warning sign to take heed of. We live in a very busy age and some people overload more frequently than others. Distracting ourselves may be a natural way of allowing the mind a little downtime. Though it may seem like a contradiction, breaks are an important part of getting things accomplished. So pay attention to your inattention. You just may need to schedule a few more breaks.

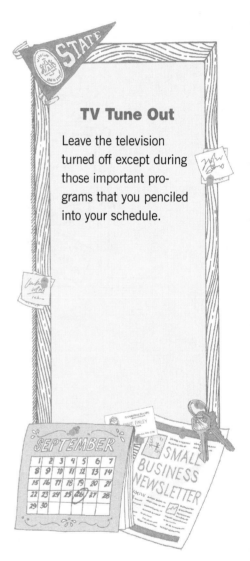

TV Tune Out

Leave the television turned off except during those important programs that you penciled into your schedule.

Interruptions

One class of distraction is interruptions. An interruption is an interference in your schedule caused by an outside force. Most often people are the interruption, and that can sometimes be more difficult to deal with than a distraction. Though some don't mind dissuading people from bothering them, others find it very difficult to discourage someone for fear of hurting their feelings or alienating themselves from social encounters. Regardless, interruptions must be dealt with if you want to strengthen your time management skills.

There are different degrees of interruption. Some you simply have to deal with. For example, a storm just blew a tree branch through your beautiful bay window. That's something that needs to be acted on. But the most common interruptions are ones that can be limited. It just takes a bit of skill and practice.

Got a Minute?

Socialization is necessary for our comfort and happiness, right? But is it necessary at all times? Interruptions from people are a difficult thing to avoid. Yet, if you don't place some time restrictions, your entire day can easily be consumed by nothing more than the ever famous "got a minute?" opening line. Because you are forced to deal with the issue face to face, it is easy to give up your ground. But there are ways to dodge drawn-out interruptions without hurting the other's feelings or being labeled a recluse.

- **Hide.** Yes, this sounds like silly advice, but it works. If you have a project to work on, try to find an area that is out of the traffic zone. People are more inclined to stop and chitchat if they see you. Unless they have something important to say, chances are they will walk right past you as long as you don't catch their eye. Don't draw attention and possibly create a bad name for yourself by crawling under the desk when you hear footsteps approaching. You can subtly conceal yourself by positioning your work area behind a partially closed door. This way you are still open to those who really need your help, but you can escape the wagging tongues of those who have nothing better to do. This idea also works well for people who come by your house to visit. Make use of that peephole. It was installed for a reason. Use your best judgment to decide whether or not you have the time and patience for the interruption.

- **Inform those around you that you have a lot of work to do and you would appreciate it if you could be left alone for a while.** Stress the importance of the task if you feel that will help emphasize your point. Perhaps you could even ask them to take your phone calls or pick up the mail. Chances are, you'll clear the area if you start handing out assignments to all who stop to bother you.

- **Stand up when someone approaches you.** This will make them less inclined to sit and stay a while. Also, maintain professional body language. Don't relax and neither will the interloper.

- **Always keep a bit of busywork close by.** Even if it is a fake fax to be sent to your sister, keep it within reach. If you see a long-winded person approaching, grab the fax and offer to walk him down the hall. Don't let him get comfortable.

- **Look busy.** This shouldn't be too difficult for you to do. Quite often people won't make you part of their rounds if you are visibly busy.

- **Set time limits.** Let the interrupter know right away how much time, if any, you have available. If it looks as though it may turn into an involved conversation, ask if you can schedule a time to sit down and talk. This is a courteous way to plan for the discussion, and it also shows that you feel his concern is important enough to warrant an extended period of time.

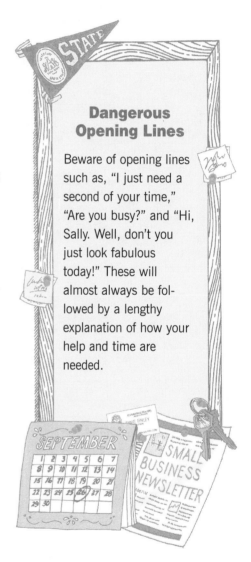

Dangerous Opening Lines

Beware of opening lines such as, "I just need a second of your time," "Are you busy?" and "Hi, Sally. Well, don't you just look fabulous today!" These will almost always be followed by a lengthy explanation of how your help and time are needed.

- **Don't be afraid to shut the door.** An open door is an invitation to many people.
- **If all else fails, place a "Do Not Disturb" or "Beware" sign outside your work area.** If people don't take the hint after that, feel free to unleash the beast.

Seven Sayings to Help You Out

- "I don't have time to talk. I'm really busy right now."
- "Can we catch up on all of this over lunch?"
- "If you don't have anything to do, can you run some of these errands for me?"
- "Now is really not a good time for me."
- "I have a 'Do Not Disturb' sign on my door."
- "Will you excuse me? I need to make an important phone call."
- "I'm sorry, you'll have to schedule an appointment with my secretary."

Are You a Phone Addict?

Bless technology, but do you ever find yourself just wanting to rip the phone right out of the wall? Several of us simply can't deny that ring. What if it is the million-dollar phone call that will change your life forever? You just don't know, so you have to answer it.

Phone calls are an easily accepted distraction because it isn't our fault someone called, phone calls don't last very long, and it may be an emergency. Track your phone usage for a couple of days. Mark down who calls, for what reason, how long the call lasted, and then rate its importance (see the chart on page 85 for an example). You can do this

PHONE USAGE			
Name of Caller	**Reason for Call**	**Time Spent**	**Importance**
Sandy	Mailing address	25 minutes	10
Doug	Scheduling visit	15 minutes	7
Michelle	Department meeting	10 minutes	5
Mom	Just to talk	10 minutes	11
Randy	Sales meeting	20 minutes	8
Doctor Smith	Blood work	5 minutes	3
Solicitation call		30 seconds	12
Sam	Friday night	5 minutes	9
Alicia	Marketing proposal	25 minutes	4
Larry	Status of Martin proposal	20 minutes	1
Tara	Client queries	15 minutes	2
Brian	Stocks	5 minutes	6

for a couple of weeks and become thoroughly shocked, but just a couple of days will do to open your eyes. If you find that your phone calls total more time than you spend actually working, it's definitely time to limit yourself. Here are some suggestions to help you get started on the phone addict's road to recovery:

- **Shut off your ringer and let the voicemail or answering machine pick it up.** If you don't know it's ringing, you won't feel the compulsion to answer. Even if you only do it while you are completing a project, the time saved will amaze you. Not only are you saving the time it takes to carry out the conversation, but also the period of time it takes to get focused again on your project.
- **Use Caller ID.** If you just can't bring yourself to shut off the ringer (or perhaps the phone not ringing would be a major distraction in itself), install an identification feature that will allow you to see who is calling before you decide to answer. This won't lower the number of interruptions, but it will decrease the amount of time spent overall on interruptions. However, this will work only if you refrain from answering every call.

- **Designate a period of time in your day to return and make phone calls**. For optimum payoff, schedule this time to coincide with your least productive time of day. It doesn't take a lot of energy or mindwork to make phone calls, and this could serve as a needed break from the project you are currently tackling. Also, let others know that this is the best time to reach you. If they call in the time slot already allowed for phone calls, then that just cuts back on the number of unexpected interruptions throughout the day.

- **Once you make/answer the call, don't dawdle, get right to the point.** It isn't necessary to find out how each member of the family is doing or what the weather is like in Cleveland. On the other hand, be pleasant. Begin by asking what it is you can do for the person. This will encourage the caller to get right to the point without participating in the usual idle chatter. If at all possible, write down the information you need beforehand so you aren't wasting time trying to remember everything you need to say.

- **Set time limits.** You can easily do this by informing the caller immediately that you have only a few moments to spare. If you do this in a courteous manner, not only will the caller be aware of and try to keep within the time limit, but he will also feel honored that you chose to spend your precious little time speaking with him.

- **By all means, don't humor a salesperson.** Some people feel it is rude to deny a salesperson her right to talk. But think about it: The motive behind the call is to make a sale. If you aren't interested, say so right away. Otherwise, the salesperson will waste your time and hers by reciting the entire speech before you decline the offer. Also, don't tell her to just send you the information in the mail. Not only will this waste time when she verifies your mailing address, but it almost guarantees another phone call within a couple of weeks and more sorting of snail mail.

Schedule for Distractions

There are several types of interruptions, but only you will know which affect you the most. If you don't know, then keep a log of all interruptions that pass you in a day. Group them into categories and begin work on the biggest group first. You may be surprised to find that the technology that you formerly thought to be heaven-sent—such as e-mail, the Internet, and cell phones—is actually costing you more time than it's worth in the long run. Or perhaps you'll find that you spent a total of two hours watching your cats play outside the window. If you can, try to narrow the distractions down into specific activities. This will allow you to better gauge how much time is wasted and how much could be saved with a slight change in your habits.

It is nearly impossible to get through an entire day with no interruptions. It's a good idea to allow time in your schedule for distractions. Expect them; they will occur. But you don't have to let them destroy your plan for managing your time effectively. By allotting time in your schedule for distractions, your other activities won't fall behind. Think of the possibility of your having fewer than anticipated interruptions. That means that you have that extra time to play with.

Don't Be Afraid to Delegate

If you feel as though you need to be everywhere at once in order to get things done, it may be time to stop what you are doing and delegate. For some, this can be a very scary idea. For others, it is a dream come true. Delegation is simply getting the job done by distributing the work. It is a relatively simple idea, but one that needs to be executed correctly if you want to save time and energy. Keep in mind this isn't a power trip. Effective delegation is not barking orders; rather it is inviting someone to accept shared responsibility for the completion of a project.

Those who are serious about time management will learn to delegate. Granted, it will take up some of your valuable time in the beginning, but the time you save in the long run more than makes up for it. There are several advantages to delegating, the most obvious being less work for you. Those whom you delegate to will appreciate the trust you place in them, creating closer relationships. The work itself will become easier, and your stress level will decrease. Sometimes you will even find others who have the specialized skills to tackle a job with more efficiency and accuracy than you would be able to.

Quite often people associate delegation with the workplace. However, if you have friends and family (don't forget the children), this can work in all areas of your life. Because time management isn't necessarily restricted to just one area of your life, neither should be the elements of it.

The Delegation Process

In order to make delegation work for you instead of against you, follow the suggestions listed below. But be sure to keep in mind that this will take time. If you rush through it, you may be costing yourself more in the long run.

- **Make a decision.** Before you start passing out assignments, you must decide what needs to be delegated. Create a prioritized list of jobs that have yet to be completed. Spend a bit of time with each item and consider whether there is someone who has skills suitable to get it accomplished. When you first begin to delegate, it may be a good idea to keep the most important jobs under your control. This will make you feel more comfortable handing out the less important tasks. Also, take into consideration which jobs bring you the greatest gain. Your focus should remain with these, whereas jobs that bear a lower yield are prime candidates for delegation.
- **Choose with care.** Choosing the right person for the job is a major part of the delegation process. Matching a person's skills to the job should be foremost in your mind. However,

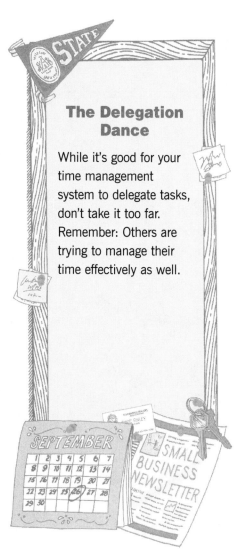

The Delegation Dance

While it's good for your time management system to delegate tasks, don't take it too far. Remember: Others are trying to manage their time effectively as well.

also respect their wishes. Perhaps a person doesn't have the skills to successfully tackle a task but would like to learn them. This person may turn out to do a better job than would a person who already has the skills.

• **Give specific instructions.** Once you have decided who is going to get what job, clarifications need to be made. Explain exactly what needs to be done, why it needs to be done, and when it should be done. Add training if need be, but don't hold an employee's hand. Allowing a person more authority and rein to complete a job will give him the confidence and assurance he needs to prove himself. Also keep in mind that it is more satisfying to work on an entire project than it is to work on just bits and pieces.

• **When the delegation is complete, trust the person to get it done.** Do not stand over her shoulder, watching her every move. The idea behind delegation is to create more time for yourself. You will waste time by worrying and constantly checking up on the project. Plus, you will create tension and nervousness in the person trying to do the work, thus raising the potential for mistakes.

• **Communicate effectively.** It is important to keep the lines of communication open. Let the worker know you are available to answer questions, but encourage him to try out his own ideas first. This will not only show that you support his work, but it will give him confidence in his own judgment as well. You might want to set up prearranged meetings to check on the progress of the project. This would also be a good time to go over any concerns or questions the worker has.

• **Allow for mistakes—they are good learning tools.** If you have done a good job delegating, the little mistakes will be easy to fix.

• **Above all, praise the person for a job well done.**

Delegation Hang-Ups

Even though delegation sounds like an easy fix, some people still would rather take everything on themselves. Here are just a few reasons for this:

- Some people like to think they are superhuman and want to maintain that image. However, these are the same people who find themselves constantly taking on more than they can possibly handle. Yes, they may complete the tasks, but it is unlikely that the tasks are done well. The end result is stress overload, a ton of faulty projects, and one tired and grumpy soul.
- Perhaps you suffer from perfectionism. The very thought of allowing others to possibly screw up your tasks makes you cringe. You like things to be done perfectly and rarely trust anyone else to do that kind of work. However, you are probably the person most in need of delegating skills. If this description seems to fit you, you are most likely at your wit's end trying to get everything done and done well. But sometimes it just isn't possible. Try to learn to divvy up the work. It is better to get a project completed with a few mistakes than not even started at all.
- Another common hang-up is that you just don't have the time to sacrifice. This is a pretty good argument, considering you are already having problems managing your time. But one of the fundamentals of time management is prioritizing and looking ahead to the future. Delegating will undoubtedly take time if you plan on doing it right. But what you have to take into consideration is that it will save you loads of time in the long run. You may not see the results right away, but eventually they will show. If you live in the "now," this will probably serve only to frustrate you. But if you are concerned with your future, delegation is a smart route to take.

Hiring Help

So you've prioritized, planned, scheduled, delegated, balanced your work and play, and are content with your management of time. So what do you do when there are still things to be done? Should you regroup and start all over? Just give up? Of course not. A few changes may be required, but nothing that is going to throw all your hard work and efforts out the window. It may be time to consider hiring help.

Hopefully by this time you have realized that you simply aren't superhuman. You cannot do everything yourself all the time. It is unreasonable to think so. Yes, hiring help will cost you some money, but it will save you the time it would have taken to complete the task yourself. Now, which is more important—a relaxed and happy life or a bit of money? That's basically what it comes down to. If you do your homework and are able to settle for less than perfection, the cost may be just a trifle that is hardly even noticeable.

Deciding What Tasks to Hire Out

There are some basic tasks that are rather easy to let go of. Once you decide to hire out for the completion of these, you will find that quite a bit of time has been suddenly discovered in your life. You will be able to move forward with your goals and devote yourself to the priorities in your life. Here are some suggestions to get you started:

Promoting Responsibility

Hiring neighborhood kids to do odd chores not only saves you the time and trouble, but it raises their self-esteem, encourages them to manage money, gives them a foundation for a good work ethic, and teaches responsibility.

- Yard work can take up quite a bit of time and energy. If you simply want the lawn mowed, it is likely you will be able to find a neighborhood kid willing to do the work for what you would spend at a fast food restaurant. However, if you want to have some serious landscaping done, you might decide to forego eating out entirely for a couple of months and hire a professional.
- If your budget allows, consider hiring someone to fix meals for your family a couple of times a week. Perhaps you

know of someone in the restaurant business who would appreciate a side job. Or maybe you have a grandmotherly figure in your life who enjoys cooking. A bit of pocket change never hurt anyone, so why not seek out her services? After working all day long, it doesn't get much better than to come home to a hot, home-cooked meal ready and waiting for you. You will be able to relax at once and concentrate on your family or other priorities in your life without the burden of having to make your workday that much longer.

- House cleaning is a popular hired-out task. Not too many people enjoy dusting, mopping, and scrubbing toilets. Think about how nice it would be to strike that from your to-do list forever! Maybe forever is exaggerating a bit, but if you don't have to face the housework every week, chances are you will be a much happier person. Prices for house cleaners vary depending on location, size of the house, what chores are to be done, and so forth. But think about how nice it would be to give yourself a break from all those despised chores. There are drawbacks to this wonderful idea, though. In addition to the expense and the risk of damage to your possessions, you need to be able to trust the workers when you are out of the house. Be sure to get reliable references and supervise your housecleaners carefully.

- Washing and detailing your car can be hired out as well. This is another job where the amount you pay customarily relates to the experience and quality you desire. However, keep in mind that quite often a young person who is just beginning to earn his or her own money will be very determined and most likely do excellent and detailed work.

Seeking Workers

Odd jobs are often mundane and boring but are easily hired out. Take a look at your to-do list. Are there items there that could be labeled busywork and aren't that important? Would you feel comfortable hiring someone else to complete the task? If so, then it is time to seek out potential employees.

If you aren't willing to shell out the big bucks for professional services, there are places to look for less experienced workers. The newspaper will sometimes have a "Services Offered" or "Work Wanted" section in the classified ads. Skim the ads and see if any match up with your needs. Libraries, schools, retirement communities, and local shops are excellent places to find postings for hired help. You may also inquire about posting an announcement yourself. Don't forget to check with neighbors and friends; they may be able to offer a recommendation. Perhaps you can spread the word around the neighborhood to see if any of the kids are interested in earning a little extra money.

Once you find a task or two that can be hired out, remove said tasks from your to-do list and breathe a little easier. You have just made room for any other tasks that didn't initially make the cut for your schedule. Or perhaps you would rather just enjoy your newfound leisure time. The choice is yours, but don't waste the time you've made. Wasting this time will equate to wasting your money.

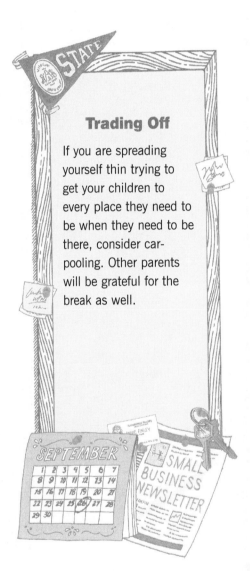

Trading Off

If you are spreading yourself thin trying to get your children to every place they need to be when they need to be there, consider carpooling. Other parents will be grateful for the break as well.

Jason and Andrea Keep on Learnin'

Just when Jason and Andrea think they have it all under control, they come across even more information that is relevant to their use of time. Chapter Four is a free flow of timesaving information. Though not all of it is new, most of it is thought provoking.

Jason

Jason discovers several ways of making the most of his time. Take, for instance, the distractions and interruptions he faces every day at work. Jason considers his work time to be the one aspect that has always been under his control. However, he had not thought of distractions as a time-wasting feature of his daily job. They are simply a part of the routine and structure. In fact, he often uses them as excuses to himself and to others for not accomplishing what he set out to get done. He hadn't considered the idea of his being able to take steps toward controlling, and even sometimes eliminating, these distractions and interruptions.

Eager to put his newfound knowledge to the test, Jason is early for work the next day. He carefully examines the layout of his office. His desk is positioned in the center of the room directly facing the door. The computer screen is facing the window, and the window faces east. The filing cabinet that serves as the department's central filing system is positioned in the back right corner of the office.

This may not seem like a big deal, but to Jason's newly trained eye, he notices several possibilities for distractions and interruptions just from the layout of his office. The position of his desk basically tells anyone who walks by the always-open door to "Come right in, Jason is ready and available to talk to you!" Not to mention the distraction created when someone does walk by, regardless of whether or not they choose to step in. The computer screen is sure to catch a glare from the rising sun in the morning hours. Also, his secretary and others in the department have to walk past him several times a day to retrieve files that are in the department domain. The figure moving past in itself is a distraction, but chances are that person would be tempted to stop and talk with Jason sitting right there and vulnerable.

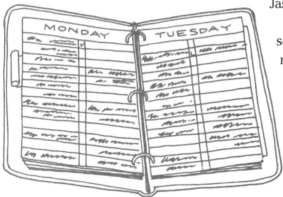

Jason just smiles to himself, removes his schedule from his briefcase, sits down, and starts rescheduling. He schedules time for himself during the morning hours to rearrange his office to fit a layout that will tone down the possibilities for distractions and interruptions. He is enthusiastic about the insight he has gained and is eager to start accomplishing more in less time.

Andrea

Andrea also discovers something very important: Being queen of multitasking is not always a good thing. This knowledge makes quite a dent in her time management system. She thought everything was finally on track and running as smoothly as possible, but she just had to read that fourth chapter.

It is actually a very good thing she did. Even though her time management system requires her to slow down quite a bit, she is still actively participating in multitasking to get things done. Handling two or more activities at once is simply a way of life for her. She has always believed multitasking and time management went hand in hand. She never dreamed there could be cons to this wonderful idea.

Upon self-evaluation, Andrea realizes that even though she is able to get several things done during the day, sometimes twice as much as her coworkers, her quality of work is lower than it should be. She equates success with quantity, not quality.

Andrea looks over her schedule. Every activity has its own time slot, yet she knows she is multitasking. She takes a closer look. There are several items on her to-do list that she doesn't bother to schedule because they are unimportant or unnecessary, but she is still managing to get them done. This is where multitasking finds its way into her otherwise nicely scheduled life.

This wouldn't be so bad if the activities she is overlapping were just busywork. But some of them need and deserve her full attention. For example, during a meeting with her boss to go over an upcoming project, Andrea composes a note to Mrs. Johnson thanking her for participating in the student/parent weekend at Matthew's school. Because she is able to get this note out of the way while talking to her boss, she frees up a time slot on her schedule. But it is likely she misses out on some important information her boss gives her. She will just have to take the time later to get caught up on it. This type of pattern repeats itself several times throughout the course of a day.

Andrea decides that no matter how strong her addiction, she will quit multitasking at the wrong times. Of course, she won't give it up entirely. It does, after all, have its good points. But she resolves to stick tightly to her schedule and let go of those items she deletes from her to-do list.

Using the Internet to Save Time

We live in a fast-paced world, there's no doubt about that. We rush here and there trying to cram all we can into each and every day. Constantly on the lookout for different strategies to save time, we pressure ourselves into trying all of the timesaving devices that cross our paths. However, not all these devices will work in conjunction with everyone's needs. Some will even end up costing more time. But there is one form of technology, when used appropriately, that will allow us to save loads of time and is able to cater to everyone's individual needs: the Internet.

The Internet is a powerful tool these days. People around the world are connected and take advantage of its benefits. Even if you aren't connected, you still have access. Libraries, schools, and some businesses such as some office supply superstores will allow you access, either for free or a small fee. If you don't think you have any use for the Internet, think again. The Internet provides a wealth of information on pretty much any subject you can imagine. If you need to save time, the Internet is a profitable route to take.

This chapter will give you some examples on how the average person can use the Internet to save time. But don't feel restricted by these suggestions. Use the Internet to explore all different ideas you may have. Perhaps you can find creative ways to save time that no one else has ever even considered.

Time-Consuming Traps on the Internet

Before we delve into the numerous opportunities and timesaving capabilities the Internet offers, you must first be warned of its time-consuming capabilities. While the Internet is indeed a form of technology that makes our lives easier, it is also a trap in which a person can easily become disoriented and distracted.

From banners to pop-up windows, there are several distractions thrown in your face with every click of the mouse. Some of these will tempt you to try your hand at winning money, others will attract your interest by offering fantastic deals. While you may think that you are spending very little time checking out these too-good-to-be-true offers, the minutes can very easily turn into hours without your even realizing it.

Even your own hunger for knowledge can be a time-consuming distraction. Because the Internet offers information on such a wide variety of topics, it is easy to let your curiosity get the best of you. Sometimes the amount of information itself is overwhelming. If you are looking for a particular piece of information, you may find yourself spending hours sifting through all the available material.

To avoid wasting time on the Internet, you need to know exactly what you want from it at all times. If you are searching for information, be as specific as possible. If you are checking headline news or stock quotes, don't wander from the page. Whatever your reason for using the Internet to help your management of time, do not stray from it. While the temptation may be great, you simply don't have the time to give in to it.

The Internet is only profitable if you use it wisely. It is easy to get lured in by the vast number of possibilities that it offers. Many people spend hours on unnecessary Web surfing, chatting in rooms, composing and receiving e-mail, and sifting through information. Stay in control of your time and don't let the Internet create needless distraction.

Finding Information with Ease

Because the World Wide Web is just a compilation of information (beware, both fact and fiction), it can be a one-stop resource for your needs. How often have you had to stop what you are doing because you realize you don't have all the information you need? Not only do you have to stop in the middle of something, but then you have to figure out how you are going to find the information you need to continue. This can be a daunting process. There are hundreds of resources out there, but they are often scattered all around. Well, the Internet allows you to access thousands of resources in just one stop. You don't have to leave the comfort of your home or wait for the library to open.

Whether you need to find the phone number of a favorite restaurant or the complete life history of Beethoven, you will be able to find relevant information on the Internet. There are several search engines you can choose from. Because each Web site is not going to register with every search engine out there, it is a good idea to use a few in order to get a good variety of resources. Of course, this depends on how much information you need. If you are just looking for the definition of a word, you may have to use only one particular Web site.

All you have to do is type in the subject you are searching for and click the mouse once. Instantly, thousands of resources will be at your fingertips. You can pick and choose those you think will be most helpful and disregard those that don't look interesting. This is a lot easier than going to the library, for example. Whereas you may have five different books on the subject, you still have to sit down with each and manually search for any specific information you are looking for. This will take a considerable amount of time, not to mention the time spent commuting to and from the library. By using the Internet, you can find specific information quickly and easily.

It is becoming more and more common for people to use the Internet for all their information needs. Students are finding it to be a valuable resource for research papers and to help with homework. Parents are keeping up-to-date with the latest child-rearing tips. Workers are able to keep an eye on the changes in their industry. You can get headline news, weather, stock quotes, statistics, and sports scores all with the simple click of the mouse. How much easier can it get?

Bookmark Feature

If there are certain Web sites you use consistently, you may want to consider using the bookmark feature. This will allow you to store a certain Web address for future reference without having to first conduct a search. Nearly every browser will have a way to do

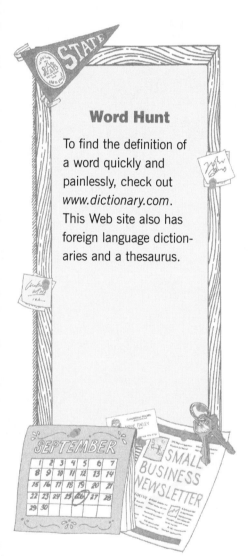

Word Hunt

To find the definition of a word quickly and painlessly, check out *www.dictionary.com*. This Web site also has foreign language dictionaries and a thesaurus.

this. For instance, if you refer to a phone directory of a particular area quite often, mark this site so you can access it with just a couple of clicks of the mouse. This feature is easy to use and will save you quite a bit of time. Depending on the Web site, you may also have the option of signing up for continuous updates sent to your e-mail address. This allows you to keep up with changes without having to revisit the Web site continuously.

Fact vs. Opinion

You must keep in mind that all the information you come across during your search on the World Wide Web may not be entirely factual. Anyone can post information, and a lot of what you will find is based on opinion only. Therefore, if you choose to use the Internet as your main source for information, consider the source. Check to see who posted the information and whether or not it is a reliable reference.

Take advantage of the convenience of the Internet. It is definitely a good resource to have at your fingertips. It will save you time and, in some cases, even money. But, as with everything, it is essential that you use good judgment and common sense. If you fail to do this, you may end up costing yourself time. Relying on false information can create future problems. Depending on what you intend to use the information for, it may not always be your best bet to rely solely on the Internet.

E-mail

E-mail is a widely known form of communication these days. Do you have an e-mail address? If not, you may want to consider getting one, especially if those you wish to keep in contact with have their own e-mail accounts.

Keep in Touch

There are several attributes of e-mail that make it a handy time-saving option. For instance, do you have a rather long-winded friend

that you hesitate to call often because you can't spare the time? By using e-mail to correspond, you will be able to catch up on your own time, and most likely more often. You are in control of when and how long you spend with the correspondence. This saves you from feeling as though you are neglecting your friend, and also from having to cut the conversation short and risk being rude because you have other things you must deal with.

E-mail allows you to keep in touch on a regular basis with family and friends who live far away. Long-distance telephone charges add up quickly. If you have loved ones who live all over the world, your telephone bill has the potential to exceed even your rent or mortgage payment each month. E-mail accounts are often free, and you don't have to worry about peak periods or counting minutes.

Additionally, it is sometimes difficult to find a time when both parties are free to chat. What may be a good time for you during the day to spend on a personal phone call might be the worst possible time of day for the one you want to talk to. By using e-mail, you overcome that obstacle altogether. You both are able to correspond at your own leisure. Regardless of whether it is 2:00 in the morning or 2:00 in the afternoon, e-mail is always available.

Mass Mailings

Perhaps you have news or a message that you would like to pass on to several people. Using the telephone can cost you a lot of time. It is likely that for each person you call and relay the message to, you will run into further conversation not pertaining to the original idea. Feedback itself will cost you time, especially if it isn't necessary. With e-mail you have the option of sending the same message to several people at once without even having to type it over again. With a click of the mouse, you have accomplished a task that might very well have cost you an entire afternoon otherwise.

If you want to be a little more personal than sending out a generic e-mail to everyone, you can simply use the copy and paste features available. Copy the generic information and paste it into the text box, then spruce it up with a personal note. You will have to send this out individually, but it saves you from having to type the same information over and over again.

Address Book

Most e-mail accounts will have an address book feature. This saves you the time of having to search for and type in someone's address. If you just spend a little time typing in everyone's name and address, later you will be able to just click on a person's name and not have to worry about typing out the address or double checking the sometimes odd spellings of screen names.

The Subject Line

E-mail has a feature that all time-conscious people adore—a sub-ject line. Before you even open the e-mail you can know what it is about (that is, if the person sending it to you has filled in the field appropriately). This allows you to pick and choose what you read at any given moment. If you don't have the time to catch up on hometown news, then don't even bother opening the e-mail. It isn't going to go anywhere and you can come back to it when you have more time available.

Contact Businesses

You can also use e-mail to make contact with several busi-nesses. How many hours or days of your life do you think have been spent waiting on hold? If the business has an e-mail address, you won't ever have to worry about that again. Just e-mail your question or comment at your leisure and then check back every once in a while for a response.

Drawbacks

As wonderful as this may seem, there are some drawbacks to e-mail as there are with any technology. As with snail mail, your

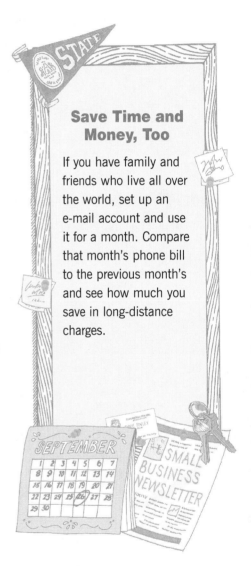

Save Time and Money, Too

If you have family and friends who live all over the world, set up an e-mail account and use it for a month. Compare that month's phone bill to the previous month's and see how much you save in long-distance charges.

address will most likely end up on a mailing list somewhere. This means that you will be receiving junk e-mail just as you receive junk snail mail. Sorting through this can be a pain. However, some e-mail accounts will set up a separate file programmed to sort junk mail from legitimate mail. This works well for the most part, but it isn't 100 percent effective. You can also e-mail a reply requesting that you be removed from their mailing list.

Jokes and chain letters circulate among e-mail accounts rapidly. You will undoubtedly be hit by one, if not both, of these quite often. It is very time-consuming to read and respond to every joke and chain letter you receive. While jokes will brighten your day from time to time, overload will create a huge dent in your time management system. Notify your friends and family that you would rather not be a part of the joke or chain letter circle.

Another drawback to e-mail is the transmission of viruses. These viruses can create a lot of problems, varying in degree of severity, which may cost you a lot of time, money, and lost files and software. You need to try to stay informed of the circulating viruses and buy the most current antivirus software. Most important, do not be tempted to open an attachment from an address you are not familiar with.

Although e-mail is an easy and convenient way to stay in touch, sometimes it isn't always the best way to converse. By typing out messages, you lose the ability to draw meaning from the inflection derived from verbal communication. Also, sometimes it is necessary to allow for immediate rebuttal. Important relationships will require a variety of lines of communication, such as meetings and phone calls.

Try to not get addicted to e-mail, although it is easy to do. Set up specific times of the day to check your e-mail and stick to that schedule. However, do take advantage of the timesaving qualities of e-mail; they will come in quite handy for both your personal and business-related needs.

Personalizing a Search Engine

If you are hip to the idea of using the Internet to save time, consider personalizing a search engine. Search engines such as Yahoo!, Alta Vista, AOL, and Excite all have an option to create a personalized page for free. If you use the Internet to search for particular information on a regular basis, you can't pass up this opportunity.

A personalized page is just that—personalized. You create the page according to your own tastes. The content, the look, and the order of the information are all up to you. You are essentially designing your very own Web page without ever having to think about HTML.

By personalizing a search engine home page, you will be able to access all the information you search for time and time again as soon as you log on. It is the ultimate Internet organizational tool.

Register as a User

You first need to visit your favorite search engine's home page. If a personalization option is available, you will find it there. Just click on the link that will allow you to create your own page and follow the instructions. You will first have to register as a user. This form will require you to fill in your name, e-mail address, password, and usually address information. Sometimes you will be asked for other information, such as your gender, age, or profession. This information will help the engine to offer suggestions on content material.

Customizing Content

Once you are registered, you can begin to customize. The screen will give you the option of changing the content of the page. This is where you decide what is going to be displayed. For instance, if keeping up with sports scores is a priority in your life, you can customize the page to reflect that information. Pretty much anything you want to know on a regular basis can be added here. Stock quotes, headline news, weather information, television listings,

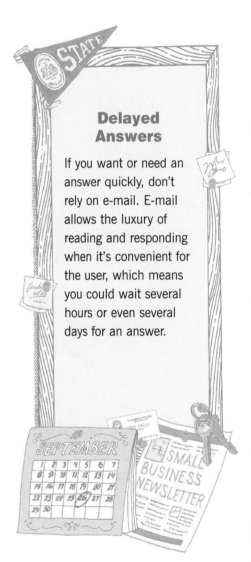

Delayed Answers

If you want or need an answer quickly, don't rely on e-mail. E-mail allows the luxury of reading and responding when it's convenient for the user, which means you could wait several hours or even several days for an answer.

lottery numbers, entertainment updates, or special deals from a particular industry—all these and more can be added to the content of your personalized page.

Customizing Layout

When you have settled on content, you will want to arrange this information in a particular order. Put your prioritization skills to use here. You want to make the visit to your customized page as time efficient as possible, and this is the key. Choose the layout option to design your page. Vital information should be placed at the top and follow down the page in order of importance. For instance, if you check the status of stock quotes most often, place this at the very top of the page. Whenever you log on to your page, this will be the first piece of information you see and will save you the time of scrolling down the page in search of it. If you check the weather in Bali quite often, but not every single time you log on, you may choose to place this information toward the bottom of the page. It is still there, but it won't be in the way of more important issues.

Setting the content and layout will allow you access to all the information you want in a timely manner. With one click of the mouse you will be able to view data that is tailored to your tastes without first having to conduct several searches. For those of you who use the Internet to keep tabs on a particular information category, this is a good time management tactic to take advantage of.

Personal Planner

Are you on the Internet at all hours of the day? Perhaps you stay logged on all the time at work. If so, you may want to consider taking advantage of another feature available to your customized page: the personal planner. Most search engines have this feature available either as a planner or calendar. It works in pretty much the same way as a traditional paper planner, but with a few added bonuses.

Once you have registered with a search engine and personalized a page, it's pretty easy to make use of the planner feature. All you have to do is click on it, and it will take you step-by-step through the process of filling in appointments, recurring activities, and even setting up alerts.

Most will have the same layout as a traditional planner. All you have to do is type in what the activity is and at what time it will occur. Once you enter all this information, an organized daily schedule will appear on your screen detailing what you need to do at what time.

Additional Features

So far, this personal planner is quite similar to a traditional planner. However, there are options available online that paper just can't seem to make happen. For instance, you can set up an alert feature. This will send an alert to your mailbox within a specified time period, notifying you of an activity's approach. It acts almost like an alarm. Therefore, when you are caught up in work and paying little attention to the clock, you needn't worry about missing that important meeting. Your planner will notify you in plenty of time to make it there.

Another handy feature is the ability to mark recurring activities with just a click of the mouse. Think about all that time you spend manually marking the monthly department meeting in your planner. With this planner, you need only set the time and date and mark it as recurring. The activity will pop up automatically on every consecutive occurrence.

Even though these features make keeping an online personal planner a good way to save time, before you set it up consider if it is really worth it. If you aren't on the Internet often, you will have to log on to take a look at what is coming up for the day or to take advantage of the alerts feature. Also, keeping a planner on your customized page is not as portable as keeping a paper planner. Take these things into consideration when deciding whether or not to spend your time setting up an online personal planner.

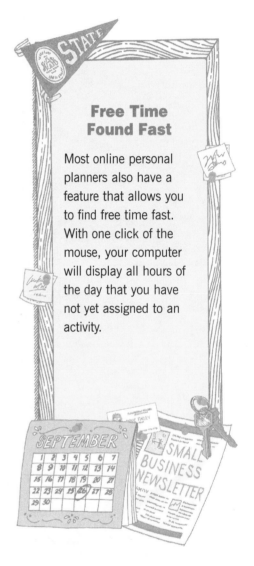

Free Time Found Fast

Most online personal planners also have a feature that allows you to find free time fast. With one click of the mouse, your computer will display all hours of the day that you have not yet assigned to an activity.

If this type of personal planner is tempting to you, but a paper planner is more accessible, reject the temptation to set up both. You should not have two planners going at once. This makes it easy to miss appointments and scheduled activities. You may write down an activity in one planner, but forget to mark it in the other. This can create all kinds of time disasters. If you do happen to keep track of activities in both planners, you waste time filling in the same activities twice. Choose one planner and stick with it.

One-Stop Shopping

How much time do you spend shopping? How much time is spent on the commute to the stores? Trying to find what you need among the endless aisles and racks? What about in the checkout line? A shopping excursion can easily be an all-day job. But it doesn't have to be.

Consider the Internet to be a gigantic mall offering every store you can imagine, but without the hassles of finding a parking space or waiting in lines. Sounds pretty fantastic, doesn't it? Most major businesses, and even quite a few small ones, now offer their services online.

Thousands of stores offer hundreds of thousands of products. What do you need? It is all but guaranteed that you will be able to find it on the Internet.

If you have a certain store in mind and you don't know whether or not it has a Web address, simply do a search. If the business is online, you should be able to use keywords that will take you directly to its home page.

Because online competition is so fierce, you will most likely be offered deals that you would not be able to find in the physical store. But you must remember that even though you may get a discount here, you may still be required to pay shipping and handling charges, so it is likely that you might only break even. However, you will save yourself time, gas money, and the energy it takes to get out and shop.

RESEARCH ON-LINE

If there are certain items you buy on a regular basis, online stores will sometimes set up an automatic delivery schedule for you so you don't have to keep reordering. The order is placed on a certain day of every month—or however you choose to set it up. If you want to cancel, generally all you need to do is send an e-mail.

All in all, online shopping should be a timesaving option to take into consideration. There are many benefits as far as saving time and energy. But don't go crazy. You do need to leave your house once in a while. Don't think that just because you can be sufficiently supplied by the Internet you should never again step into a store. Our purpose is to save time, not to create a hermit.

Travel Made Simple

Planning a vacation? Need a night out on the town? Let the Internet come to your aid. You can save yourself time and hassles by allowing yourself the luxury of not picking up the telephone. Airline, car rental, hotel, and restaurant reservations can be made and confirmed over the Internet just as they are on the phone, but without the holding time.

Planning a Vacation

For those of you who love vacations, but dread planning them, the Internet will become a good friend to you. Because it is chock full of information and possibilities, you will be able to find nearly all you need right at your fingertips. You won't have to go from travel agency to travel agency, haggle over the phone about prices, or go to the bookstore to find information on the place you want to visit. All you need to do is sit down at your computer, have a dream in mind, and type in key words or phrases.

Once you have decided on a destination, it's time for a little research. The Internet can really help you out here. Whether you want to hand over the project to a travel agent or compile everything yourself, you need not leave the computer to do so. From renting a car to finding the perfect sandals, you can do it all on the Internet.

Virtual Shopping

Whether you're looking for airline tickets, books, stocks, computer equipment, hotel reservations, clothing, or gifts, the virtual mall is always open. Internet shopping is easy and convenient, and that is why more and more people choose to shop online rather than head to the local mall. All the big-name stores are represented, as well as some that exist solely on the Web.

Often you will get lower prices by buying on the Internet than you would in actual stores. You can sign up for e-mail lists that notify you of current sales and promotions. On the next few pages you'll find some of the top shopping sites. As you review these, keep in mind that URLs do change frequently.

First of all, you need to know how you are going to get to your destination. Does it make more sense to fly or drive? Even if you are taking a cruise, you need to figure out how to get to the boat.

Flying

If you are planning on flying, there are several sites available to you. Some of the more popular ones are *www.travelocity.com*, *www.priceline.com, www.expedia.com, www.cheaptickets.com, www.lowestfare.com,* and the individual airline companies' sites. You can compare prices, check flight availability, pick your days and times of flight, choose seats, hold a reservation, book a flight, purchase your tickets, have your tickets mailed to you or electronically processed, confirm your reservation, and check flight schedules. You don't have to repeatedly call the airline for information, wait on hold while they find answers to your questions, or go through a series of voice mail menus. Just type in what you want and let the Internet do the rest.

Driving

If you are planning on driving, you can use the Internet to get the information you need. For instance, do you want to rent a car? There are hundreds of businesses online just waiting to serve you. Shop around and find the best deal in your area. You can get price information, choose the type of car you want, and make your reservation right there online.

Once you arrange for your vehicle, you are going to need to know how to get where you are going. Web sites such as *www.mapquest.com* can give you directions to your destination. All you need to do is type in your starting address and the destination address and the site will draw you a map, lay out step-by-step directions, and give you an estimated timetable. These can be printed out and are easy to use. Some of these sites will even offer to locate hotels and restaurants along your route so you can easily make prior reservations.

Online Travel Sites

- Arthur Frommer's Outspoken Encyclopedia of Travel
  www.frommers.com
  From the author of those famous guidebooks comes this informative site. Features include sightseeing guides, customs and hotels for 200 top cities and islands worldwide, helpful articles on budget travel, and travel reservations.

- Expedia
  www.expedia.com
  A comprehensive travel resource, from making airline reservations to a huge travel guide organized by country. Helpful features include airfare comparisons, currency converters, and a low-airfare finder with e-mail notification.

(continued on next page)

Where to Stay?

Once you have your transportation arranged, you are going to need to know where to stay. You can use the Internet to find what hotels are offered in the area you want. You can then visit their Web sites to take a look at the features of each. You can also get information about prices and availability and make your reservations all at the same time.

Do Your Homework

Now that you are satisfied that you will arrive safely and have a roof over your head, you may want to do a little homework on the place you are visiting. If it is a foreign country, you will probably want to check out the native customs so you don't embarrass yourself and your home country. Plus, you will be much more relaxed if you know a bit about your surroundings.

Conduct a search of your destination for timesaving information. If you have a good idea of the area, you will know beforehand what you want to see and where you want to go. You can find out the opening and closing times of points of interest, tour ticket prices, and even bargain deals not available to everyone. You may even want to create a schedule according to the information you find on the Internet. Don't get out of control, though. This is your vacation and you shouldn't turn it into a rigorous drill to accomplish as much as you can within a certain time frame. Once you get there, take it easy and let things come to you.

Other Plans to Make

See how easy it is to plan a vacation with such a collection of information at your fingertips? The same idea can be applied toward planning a night out. Most likely your area or a nearby city will have a home page that features all the happenings around town. Check it out! You may find the perfect restaurant, an interesting production, or a hopping club. Whatever your heart desires, search for it. You will be able to make reservations,

Online Travel Sites

(continued from previous page)

- Fodor's Travel Service
  www.fodors.com
  This personal trip planner can customize trips to over 80 cities worldwide. It also allows you to select hotels and restaurants by price and location. Included are essential information and activities for the guidebooks, articles, and a low-airfare finder.

- Priceline
  www.priceline.com
  Pick the price you want and Priceline will try to match unsold seats and reduced airfares on major airlines for domestic and international flights.

Online Travel Sites

(continued from previous page)

- Travelocity
  www.travelocity.com
  A huge travel guide from SABRE, the airline reservation system. Organized by country, this site features airline reservations, hotel bookings, and a low airfare finder.

order and charge tickets, and get directions—all during one stop at your computer!

If you need to schedule appointments, check and see if the business you need is online. You can set up hair appointments, dental appointments, medical appointments—pretty much any appointment you can think of. You will also be able get directions, business hours, and price lists. Some sites even allow you to download forms you need to fill out prior to your visit.

It is amazing how much time you can save by doing a little planning on the Internet. What may have taken hours of phone use, commuting time, and headaches, can be achieved with one visit to the computer. But because time awareness is our mantra here, be sure you don't get too caught up in the wealth of information available to you. You have a set mission to formulate a plan; don't deviate or you may end up wasting time.

Online Education

Does the idea of gaining more knowledge appeal to you? Would you love to take a class, but your subject of interest isn't offered at any of your local learning institutions? Perhaps traditional classroom schedules conflict with your own. If this is the case, the Internet has come to the rescue.

Yes, the Internet can help you get a degree, brush up on your Chinese, and simply take you back to that classroom setting without the classroom. Online education is a hot new trend that makes it easy for working people, parents, disabled persons, and even people from different countries to participate in a class.

Online classes have all the same attributes as a traditional class, except that the classroom is a Web site. They have qualified instructors, textbooks, assignments, deadlines, class discussions, tests, grades, and college credit. The difference is that you can participate in the class as it fits into your schedule and from the comfort of your own home. This allows you to get the education you want without having to stress out about the affects it will have on your time management system.

Are you interested yet? Even if the idea of going back to school doesn't really appeal to you at this time, read on. You may decide you want to take a class in the future, and the Internet may be the best route to take.

How Do You Sign Up for an Online Class?

First of all, you will need to choose a school that offers online education. If you don't have any schools in mind, take advantage of the Internet. Use search engines to find what you are looking for. Once you find a few sites that grab your interest, study each one. Some sites will offer you a tour or an orientation walk-through that explains in detail how their online classes are set up. Use your decision-making skills to choose the school that will best fit your needs.

Most schools will require you to apply to the program. You can do this by visiting a school's Web site and checking out its Web page on distance learning or online education. Once you decide that the institution offers what you want, read carefully over their admission guidelines. They will have an application you can fill out and submit right online.

Once you are accepted, you can then begin to choose the courses you would like to take. Even though this is an easy process and the Internet makes taking classes convenient for you, don't get carried away here. Remember that this is a real class for real credit. Don't take on more than your schedule will allow, and budget time to complete necessary schoolwork.

How Do Online Classes Function?

Most of the time classes will begin and end alongside the traditional classes, meaning that the class begins on the first day of the term and ends with finals week. Generally, there aren't specific times in which you need to be "in class." You can log on to your class at pretty much any time of day. (Sometimes, however, you will be unable to log on due to system maintenance.)

The Real Thing

Degrees achieved online are exactly the same as those received by "traditional" methods. Your transcripts won't indicate whether a class was taken online or in person.

Virtual Shopping

Auctions
- eBay
  www.ebay.com
  Bid on everything from clothes to cars to real estate.

Books
- Amazon.com
  www.amazon.com
  This online bookstore with over two million titles is searchable by title, author, and topic and offers discounts. The site has reviews and recommendations, plus free e-mail reminders of upcoming releases.

- Barnes & Noble
  www.bn.com
  This chain's online store is searchable by title, author, and topic and offers deep discounts on purchases, many live author chats, reviews and interviews, and recommendations.

You will be given a code or password to log on to the class Web site. This ensures that you have paid your tuition in full and that only those registered for the class have access to the materials offered.

As with conventional classes, online classes often require textbooks. You can order them directly through the school's online bookstore, or you can choose to order them elsewhere online. Chances are, you still will not have to move from your comfortable chair.

A qualified instructor will generally lead the class in all basic forms of learning—lectures, assignments, discussions, and tests. However, lectures will be read, not heard, and discussions are typed, not voiced. All of this is conducted over the Internet. So if you choose to participate in such a class, you need to become good friends with your computer.

Assignments will be given with deadlines attached, so don't think you can stretch the class out over a period of years. Assignments will often need to be downloaded, and you can return them to the instructor via e-mail.

Discussions, often in the form of chat rooms, e-mail, or message boards, will take place regularly. Because of the freedom to participate in class at times convenient to you, you may not always get a response to a question right away. Everyone in the class is on a different schedule, so don't get impatient with the pace of the discussion. Sometimes instructors will set up specific times in which the entire class can sign in to a chat room so everyone can bounce ideas off of each other and get an immediate response.

And, yes, tests will be administered. This is usually the one time you are required to be logged on during specific days or even hours. Because the tests are normally timed, this part of the class requires a bit more structure.

You will then get a grade and, assuming you pass, college credit. This is the same credit you would have received had you sat in the physical classroom on specified days at specified times. And look at all the time you've saved. By taking an online course, you've cut out the time it would have taken to get ready for class (shower, shave, dress), to prepare (find all your books, make sure you have all assignments with you, lug your book bag out to the car), to commute to and from class (not to mention the wear and tear on your car), and to rearrange your schedule to make room for the set class times.

Just these benefits alone should get you excited about going back to school. But before you dive right in there, review your personal goals and your schedule. If school isn't a priority, don't bump another priority out of the way to make room for it.

Using the Internet to Find a Job

Unless you are independently wealthy or so happy in your current job that you are near tears just thinking about it, this section should spark your interest. Nobody likes to go through the frustrating process of finding and securing a job, but it is something we all have to do at one time or another. Amid the storm of resumes, cover letters, hidden opportunities, trips to the post office, and interviews, it is easy to just want to give up. You may spend hours, days, months, sometimes even years searching for the perfect job. Think about all that time, not necessarily wasted but nonetheless spent.

As technology advances, more and more opportunities are open for job hunters. The hunt has become easier to execute, the job easier to secure. This isn't to say it isn't going to be hard work, but the time and energy you put into the hunt will not be so tense. The Internet has become a popular resource for both job seekers and employers. It can help with everything from job postings to preparing you for the interview. What used to take days to achieve now takes only minutes.

Businesses looking to hire employees are now taking full advantage of the Internet. To stay abreast in the employment pool, you need to become savvy at Internet job seeking. You might want to look into job search Web sites and sites where you can post your resume. You can also search sites of specific companies you'd like

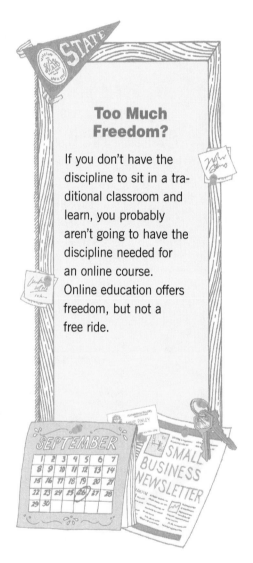

Too Much Freedom?

If you don't have the discipline to sit in a traditional classroom and learn, you probably aren't going to have the discipline needed for an online course. Online education offers freedom, but not a free ride.

to work for—many now have screen space devoted to employment opportunities—and even browse the want ads of online newspapers. All this is available to you in one sitting at the computer. Already, just with the available resources, you have saved yourself a substantial amount of time.

Online Resume

To make the most of your Internet job search, begin by creating an Internet-friendly resume. This doesn't mean that the traditional paper resume is by any means obsolete. You will still run across leads that require you to mail or fax a resume. However, having an Internet-friendly resume on file will allow you to e-mail your resume straight to a prospective employer or post it on an online database. You won't have to print it out again and again. Nor do you need to concern yourself with licking stamps, addressing envelopes, and making numerous trips to the post office. You can send it out as many times as you like without having to do more than move your fingers.

So how do you turn your fancy, eye-catching resume into an online-accessible form? The magic word here is "simplicity." While the basic information should remain the same as your traditional resume, the formatting may require a bit of reworking.

- Put your name and only your name on the very first line. Granted, this is almost always done anyway, but it is important that this is the case for an online resume.
- Do not include any artwork or graphics.
- Set all your text as flush left. Also, keep the individual lines fairly short.
- Don't go overboard with accents. For instance, you shouldn't use the italics, bold, or underline features. If you want to stress something, put it in all caps.
- Keep it simple and plain, no fancy fonts. Use a common font such as Times New Roman.

Save Time Telecommuting

While using the Internet to find a job, consider also the timesaving possibilities of telecommuting.

SAMPLE ELECTRONIC RESUME

Danny Rose
150 West Allen Street
Cambridge, MA 02138
(617) 555-5555
dannyrose@myemail.com

SUMMARY

Accounting manager with eight years' experience in general ledger, accounts payable, and financial reporting. MBA in Management. Proficient in Windows, Lotus 1-2-3, and Excel.

EXPERIENCE

MALCOLM CORPORATION, Newton, MA
Accounting Manager, 1996–present

   Manage a staff of six in general ledger and accounts payable.
   Established guidelines for month-end closing procedures, speeding up closing by five business days.
   Implemented team-oriented cross-training program within accounting group, increasing productivity of key accounting staff.

DAKOTA & SOPHIA COMPANY, Wellesley, MA
Senior Accountant, 1993–1996

   Managed accounts payable, general ledger, transaction processing, and financial reporting.
   Developed management reporting package, including variance reports and cash flow reporting.

Staff Accountant, 1992–1993

   Managed accounts payable including vouchering, cash disbursements, and bank reconciliation. Wrote and issued policies.
   Maintained supporting schedules used during year-end audits.
   Trained new employees.

EDUCATION

MBA in Management, Northeastern University, Boston, MA, 1994
BS in Accounting, Boston College, Boston, MA, 1992

ASSOCIATIONS

National Association of Accountants

Virtual Shopping

Consumer Safety

- Better Business Bureau
  www.bbb.org
  Learn how to recognize common scams, plus find tips on buying safely and descriptions of the bureau's dispute resolution programs.

Entertainment

- Blockbuster Video
  www.blockbuster.com
  Movies for sale or rental, music CDs, CD-ROM games, plus entertainment news.
- Reel.com
  www.reel.com
  Rent or buy movie videos that include thousands of discounted classic, art house, foreign, and rare films.
- Ticketmaster Online
  www.ticketmaster.com
  Buy concert or theater tickets, searchable by keyword, state, or venue.

E-mailing a Resume

If you choose to send your resume to a company via e-mail, keep a couple of things in mind. You will need to get a specific e-mail address for the human resources department or for a contact name. Do not just send your resume to addresses labeled "info" or "webmaster." Also, it is recommended to copy and paste your resume into the body of the e-mail message. Although it looks better to send it as an attachment, most companies these days will automatically delete messages with attachments due to the possibility of catching a virus.

Online Resume Databases

Once you are confident you have a strong online resume, you can check out the online resume databases. You can use these to post your resume on the World Wide Web.

Online resume databases will allow you to reach recruiters and hiring managers worldwide. Hundreds upon thousands of companies will have access to your very own resume. Can you even handle the thought? Try to comprehend how much time, energy, and money would be spent on traditionally mailing or even faxing a paper resume to all the companies that have access to the Internet. And you've accomplished the same thing with a simple click of a mouse.

How to Submit Your Resume

Before you get all excited, you need to decide where you are going to post your resume. Use search engines to pull up any Web sites or newsgroups that pertain to the job you are seeking. There are several Web sites that will not only allow you to post your resume, but will also give you tips on creating a resume, let you search job listings, let you do company research, and even lead you through a mock interview. A few of the most popular sites include *www.monster.com, www.careermosaic.com, www.career-path.com,* and *www.hotjobs.com.*

These sites will most often provide step-by-step instructions on how to submit your resume. Sometimes you will be required

to fill in fields such as name and address, others will allow you to just copy and paste your entire resume into a text box. These sites will also give you additional information pertaining to how long your resume will be posted, what to do if you want it removed, and if there are any fees involved. The fees are often paid by the companies seeking employees, so the job seeker rarely has to pay.

Now that you have your resume all set and ready to go, you can begin the hunt. Even if you have posted your resume for all to see, it is a good idea to conduct your own search. You will waste time just standing by, hoping someone will come to you. Be aggressive. You can't go in for the kill if you haven't begun the hunt!

Jason and Andrea Become Internet Savvy

Since Jason and Andrea have come this far already with their time management systems, they figure they might as well jump on the technology bandwagon. Both have had a little experience with the Internet prior to this chapter, but neither realized that there were so many different ways it could be used. All kinds of information is suddenly at their fingertips. It is almost a power trip of sorts. With just a few key commands and clicks of the mouse, they suddenly have even more control of their use of time.

Jason

Jason isn't so enthusiastic about joining the cyberspace cowboys. It is all just a little too new for him. He prefers the traditional style of research and communicating. Because he realizes there are several different ways the Internet can be used quite regularly in the office, he often delegates that work out to others. He just isn't interested in taking the time to learn something new. The only thing Jason uses the Internet for is to receive e-mail from clients and businesses from time to time.

Your Online Resume

Pros
- A computer is less likely to misplace your resume.
- Your resume can be in a potential employer's hands immediately after a job has been posted.
- You need send only one resume to a company, even though you may be interested in several jobs.
- Submitting resumes online reduces the cost to you.

Cons
- The Internet is less likely to protect your privacy.
- A computer is looking for keywords and your resume could be overlooked.
- Your current employer could come across your resume.

Virtual Shopping

Gifts

- CyberShop
  www.cybershop.com
  Gourmet cookware, foods, electronics, and home furnishings purchased through this site are shipped and gift-wrapped within 24 hours. The directory is easily searchable.

- 1-800-Flowers
  www.1800flowers.com
  This searchable online delivery service offers bouquets, plants, food, and gift baskets.

- Vermont Teddy Bear Company
  www.vtbear.com
  A creative alternative to the traditional gift of flowers. Search for the perfect bear in a variety of categories. Bears are shipped within 24 hours of ordering.

- The Virtual Florist
  www.virtualflorist.com
  An online delivery service for bouquets and gift baskets. This site also offers free electronic cards if your budget is tight.

However, Jason decides that since he is bettering his management of time in every other way, it wouldn't hurt to just take a peek at some of the timesaving options available on the Internet. With a little bit of guidance from his coworkers, Jason finds a wide range of possibilities that appeal to several aspects of his time management system. One feature in particular catches his eye.

Personalizing a search engine is ideal for Jason. He is still a little leery of spending so much time on the Internet. But with his own customized page, he would have to make only one stop. Eager to build, Jason doesn't wait for instructions from his coworkers. He chooses a search engine and just dives in. He finds that it is actually rather easy. The search engine takes him through the process step-by-step and gives clear instructions on how to make his page his own.

Soon Jason has constructed a page that allows him to check stock quotes, sports scores, headline news, and his favorite cartoon all with just one visit to his personalized page. Though this information is important to Jason, he rarely finds the time to retrieve it, much less take the time to peruse it. However, now that it is available in such an easy format, he is fulfilling another important activity, and he needn't spend several minutes, even hours, searching and retrieving. It is readily available in one glance.

With this first venture completed, Jason becomes more inclined to branch out. He decides he will explore all the possibilities. He congratulates himself on keeping up-to-date while saving time in the process.

Andrea

Andrea could easily become an Internet junkie. She is more than ready and willing to begin saving time using the Internet. She simply doesn't have the bond with tradition that her husband does. Anything new and beneficial is right up there on her list with multitasking (and we know how much she loves that). However, she plays it smart. She realizes her hunger for knowledge might get her caught up in hours of surfing, so she makes a list of those items on her to-do list she can take care of on the Internet and sticks only to those.

The idea of shopping online particularly appeals to Andrea. She has several items she needs to purchase, but simply doesn't have the time to spare to drive all over town visiting different stores. Because she knows exactly what she wants, she does a search and compares prices.

For instance, their dog, Barney, refuses to eat anything but one particular brand of dog food. The store that sells it is a nearly 45-minute drive away. Therefore, she often has to block out an hour and a half of her schedule just to buy dog food. The Internet saves her that time. Not only does she find a store that carries it and will deliver, but she also finds a better price than what she has been paying. She sets up a monthly home delivery schedule with the business, and now she doesn't have to worry about being out of Barney's special food anymore.

When she finishes her shopping, she takes a brief look at online classes available. She teaches a class herself every Wednesday, which just heightens her interest in learning more. She already has a good idea of what subjects she would like to study, and she easily finds online classes that appeal to her interests. Suddenly that dream has a chance to become reality. But she knows she doesn't have time right now. So she pencils in a time later in the month to do some serious researching. Classes won't begin until the fall, so she has time to make her decision.

Next, she decides to reward herself and her husband for their Internet timesaving ventures. She first checks her schedule and finds that she can make it work. Finding their favorite restaurant online, she quickly sets up reservations for dinner that evening. She then checks the weather to help her decide on an outfit.

The End Result

Having accomplished quite a bit on their Internet adventures, Jason and Andrea compare stories over the reward dinner set up online. They both come to the conclusion that the Internet is going to become a big part of their time management systems.

Virtual Shopping

Pets
- PETsMART.com
  www.petsmart.com
  Shop for your favorite companion, whether dog, cat, ferret, bird, or reptile. The site offers deals on pet supplies, as well as a wide range of other items and pet tips.

- Petco
  www.petco.com
  All sorts of special gifts, message boards, and pet products are offered on this site touted as "where the pets go online."

Business and Finance

- Ameritrade   *www.ameritrade.com*
  Buy stocks, mutual funds, options, and bonds online. Save money by making trades yourself rather than financing the salary of a broker.
- E*Trade   *www.etrade.com*
  Buy stocks, mutual funds, and options online, as well as track market indexes and favorite stocks.
- Hoover's Online   *www.hoovers.com*
  This site features company profiles, addresses and telephone numbers, key executives, and more. It is searchable by company name, industry, region, and amount of sales. Extra services are available for a fee.

Cars

- Auto-By-Tel   *www.autobytel.com*
  Buy a new or used car, easily searchable by model type, with information on leases, reviews, and other resources.
- Kelley Blue Book   *www.kbb.com*
  Research the retail and wholesale values of new and used cars. You can also get information on financing and insurance.

Catalogs

- CatalogLink   *www.cataloglink.com*
  Browse offerings or order catalogs from many retailers, selling everything from clothing and home and gift items to sports, business, and computer equipment.
- Catalog Mart   *http://catalog.savvy.com*
  Browse or order from over 10,000 catalogs on over 800 subjects, from clothing to business and computer equipment.
- The Gap   *www.gap.com*
  The casual clothing chain's site has a mix-and-match feature to show how different styles, types, and colors go together with varying hair color and skin types. Also included are catalog listings, pictures, and a store locator.
- J. Crew   *www.jcrew.com*
  This site has catalog listings and pictures, plus a store locator.
- Lands' End   *www.landsend.com*
  Features catalog listings for clothing, luggage, bed linens, plus an overstock section with discounts of up to 70 percent off.
- L.L.Bean   *www.llbean.com*
  Browse through catalogs of apparel, sporting goods, travel accessories, and home and garden supplies. This site also includes information on special sales as well as a section on where to go for outdoor activities.
- Spiegel   *www.spiegel.com*
  Offers catalog listings for intimate apparel, electronics, and a deep discount section.

Package Tracking

- Federal Express   *www.fedex.com*
  Track packages sent worldwide by Federal Express. Arrange for pick-ups, fill out and print air bills, order supplies, and find out addresses and hours of the nearest drop-off locations.
- United Parcel Service   *www.ups.com*
  Track packages sent worldwide by UPS. Arrange for pick-ups; calculate rates; order supplies; and find out addresses, hours, and directions to the nearest drop-off locations.
- United States Postal Service   *http://new.usps.com*
  Purchase stamps, make an address change, track a package you sent, or price a package you want to send.

PART TWO

Psychological Setbacks in Time Management

By now you have a firm foundation for the development of your time management system. However, good time management doesn't involve only lists, schedules, and organization skills.

While the basics are important, we still need to dig a little deeper. This part of the book will help you to recognize the causes and effects of psychological and emotional issues involved in the management of time.

This book stresses the importance of creating a system that is tailored to your individual needs. This is due largely to the fact that your psychological makeup is going to differ from every other person's. Your emotions play a major role in your use of time. Though it may be difficult to distinguish their immediate effect now and then, it is evident that your emotions are part of a chain reaction that has the ability to cause glitches and snags in your time management system. For this reason, it is important not only to have a foundation of the basics, but also to incorporate the knowledge and recognition of psychological setbacks in time management.

Part Two is going to help you identify how your emotions affect your use of time by exploring the following particulars:

- Getting and staying motivated
- Defeating sensory overload
- Recognizing self-esteem as an influential factor
- Achieving a healthy stress level
- Making wise decisions
- Rewarding yourself on a regular basis for jobs well done

Unveiling Motivation

E ven if you have the ideal time management system in place and raring to go, it will do you very little good if you aren't motivated. Motivation is what gets you going. It helps you through those seemingly impossible tasks and encourages you to stick with what you start. At times, it can mean the life or death of your time management system.

Motivation takes several factors into consideration. It depends on the type of task that needs to be done, your attitude toward this task, any past experiences you've had with a similar task, your physical health, your stress level, the importance and/or urgency of the task, and your overall mood. All of these factors will influence your level of motivation.

Who Has Control?

It may seem as though you have no control over your motivation. People often believe motivation is derived only from outside forces. While this may be true in some cases, most often personal inspiration, or lack thereof, has the greatest effect.

Either you are motivated or not. It's not in your hands, right? Wrong. You can take action to help yourself find inspiration for the completion of even the most menial of tasks. It will take a little determination on your part, but what doesn't?

Determine the Root of the Problem

Instead of just accepting the lack of motivation and proclaiming yourself lazy, try to figure out why it is you have no motivation. Think about the upcoming task. If you cringe, that's the problem right there. What associations do you make with the task? Is it something that brought you displeasure in the past? Do you expect an unfavorable outcome? Is it a task that was forced on you? Are you too physically tired to put forth the effort? Does your mind conjure up a thousand more enjoyable things you could do instead? Is it something that will take up a big chunk of time? Are you unsure of your ability to complete the task correctly?

Mornings Just Don't Do It for You?

Do you have trouble getting out of bed in the mornings? Place your alarm clock across the room so you have to get up to shut it off.

Time to Take Action

Once you have determined the root of the problem, it is time to take action to dispel those negative responses. One way to do this is to just start. Yes, this advice seems to contradict the entire idea of lack of motivation. How can you start something when you don't have the motivation to do so? By just jumping in there, that's how. Even if you don't know exactly what you are doing, if you just do something, anything that will pertain to the task, the movement itself will serve as a motivator.

Let's say you just can't get motivated to do the dishes. Force yourself to get up off the couch. Don't even think about it, just do it. Once you are standing and realize that it is unlikely you will once again find that perfect cozy position, take a step toward the kitchen. The next step will be even easier to take. Chances are, once you begin a task and see that even the tiniest bit of progress has been made, you will be more willing to continue and go a little further. Taking the step forward and actually involving physical action will get the blood flowing, and motivation won't be far behind.

Rewards

Another trick to get you motivated is to place a reward at the finish line. Rewards will tempt you to get started and follow through. Before you begin the task, set guidelines for yourself. Be specific about what you want to accomplish and within what period of time. Assign a fitting reward to be granted only at completion. By setting your sights on something that will bring you pleasure, it is easy to overcome any obstacle—in this case the task—that stands in your way. Rewards will be explored in further detail later in this chapter.

Physical Setbacks

Sometimes the lack of motivation stems from physical setbacks. If you are tired, for instance, it is unlikely that you will be inspired to do a whole lot. Consider eating a healthy snack. Sometimes getting a bit of food into your system will up your energy level and you won't feel as tired. Perhaps you could even take a power nap. A short nap will help you to dodge that sleepy feeling and give you a fresh outlook. You could even do a few exercises to stretch your muscles and accelerate your heart rate.

A lack of motivation doesn't have to drag you down. Figure out why it is you are so unmotivated and look to conquer the root of the problem. Don't expect to find inspiration in all that you do; some tasks simply have no admirable qualities. However, a small surge of motivation—whether it entails just standing up or thinking of a great idea—will get you started, and once you are started, it is easier to continue.

Excuse Me?

We all make excuses from time to time. For some of us, that's all that comes out of our mouths. For the most part, excuses are harmless in the grand scheme of things, but did you ever stop to consider what effect they have on your time management efforts? Probably not. That's why we are taking care to bring that up as an important aspect in your time awareness.

Try to figure out approximately how many excuses you make in a day. It is difficult to do because it is likely that many of them are habits that were formed way back in your childhood. These tend to be hard to break. But don't concern yourself with quitting them just yet. Right now, just take notice of the time that goes into the execution of an excuse.

Selling Excuses to Others

First of all, time will be spent while you devise a justification that sounds reasonable. But remember, reasonable alone isn't

Healthy, Energizing Snacks

Consider adding the following snacks to your daily diet for that added boost of energy:

- Raw vegetables with or without dip
- Fresh fruit mixed with yogurt, cottage cheese, or peanut butter
- Trail mix
- Whole grain crackers with cheese
- Milkshake made with fruit

always going to cut it. If you are especially concerned whether or not the other person is going to buy your excuse, it will have to be of high quality as well as elaborate. Creative thinking will take some time, especially if you don't have any truth as a basis. Once you have a fantastic idea to save you from any commitments, you must sell this excuse to the other person. This can be tricky because you never know if it is going to be sold as is, or if you are going to have to throw in some additional features to sweeten the deal. Look out for others' bargaining skills. You might find that others have excuses to your excuses. Then what? More creative thinking. More time.

For those of you who have a conscience, it is quite possible that a little guilt will weasel its way in. If you've ever felt guilty before, you know it isn't an easy thing to get rid of. For as long as it makes its home in your subconscious, you will be unable to devote your full attention to anything else you try to accomplish, which causes you to lose even more time.

Selling Excuses to Yourself

Up to this point, we've only discussed making excuses to other people. But what happens when you make excuses to yourself? This is when the issue of wasted time really comes into play. Let's say you have a big project coming up. Now this isn't really something you are all too interested in, but it is going to take quite a bit of time to complete. So you go through all the proper time management functions—planning, scheduling, delegating, and so forth—and then you have nothing left to do but get to it.

You know that little devil that sits on your shoulder? Well, this is one of his favorite visitation periods. All of a sudden, excuses galore pop up in your head telling you reasons why it would be better to postpone beginning the project or possibly just disregarding it altogether. So you have a hundred excuses, now you have to weed out the ones that are just ridiculous and don't even border on reason. Then the decision-making process comes into play. You will want to take a look at those that are left and state

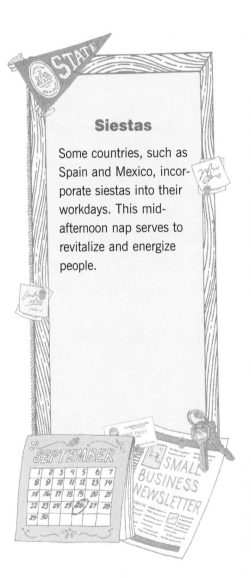

Siestas

Some countries, such as Spain and Mexico, incorporate siestas into their workdays. This mid-afternoon nap serves to revitalize and energize people.

the pros and cons of each. Select the best answer. Try to produce an argument that will convince even you of its undeniable truth; then begin the project anyway. You know you have to do it, but making excuses seems an appropriate venue. What have you accomplished? A whole lot of nothing. What have you spent? A whole lot of time.

ACCEPTABLE VS. DOWNRIGHT UGLY	
Acceptable	**Inexcusable**
"I have a doctor's appointment."	"I'll do it tomorrow."
"I really have too much going on to handle a new project."	"Maybe I'll get to it after the movies."
"I'd love to, but I don't have time. Perhaps you could call Jenny."	"I don't want to."
"Thanks for thinking of me, but I'm really not available for those dates."	"I don't feel like it."
"I have to prioritize, and this one is low on the list. I'll have to finish my other projects first."	"It can wait."
"I don't feel qualified to lead this project."	"Someone else can do it."
"Thanks, but I'm really not interested."	"I forgot."

Excuses Waste Time

Do you see how making excuses can tie up your time for no reason at all? Next time you catch yourself making an excuse, try to calculate just how much time it is costing you. Sometimes you just can't get around making excuses, but quite often you don't have any need for them. As far as others are concerned, if you want to refuse a request, just do so. Don't spend a lot of time trying to come up with a justification as to why you can't do the favor. You will just waste not only your time but the other person's time as well. As for yourself, try to break the habit. You know what you need to do and whether or not you are going to do it. Don't spend time looking for ways out, especially when you know you aren't even going to take them.

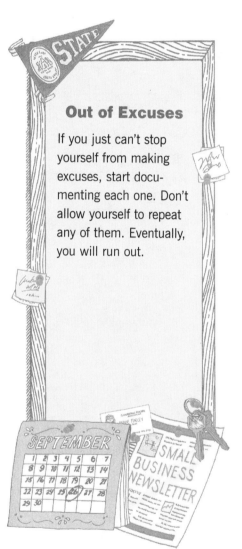

Out of Excuses

If you just can't stop yourself from making excuses, start documenting each one. Don't allow yourself to repeat any of them. Eventually, you will run out.

Parkinson's Law

Parkinson's Law states that work expands to fill the time allotted for the work. In other words, if you give yourself an hour to clean up the yard, it will take you an hour. If you give yourself four hours to clean up the yard, you will do the same work in four hours. You need to understand this concept and see if it is evident in your current use of time. Perhaps recognition of this rule is all you need to solve your time management problems. Chances are it is not, but we'll leave it as a possibility. The following are a few effects this theory can have on your time management efforts.

- This principle could damage your schedule. For instance, according to Parkinson, if you block out too much time for an activity, you will use all that time to complete the aforementioned activity. However, if you had scheduled a smaller block of time, you would still have completed the activity.
- Parkinson's Law can cause you to give greater importance to activities that really have little value. For instance, if you allow a great amount of time to wash your car, you will use all that time to do so. Even though you could easily run it through a car wash and take just a few minutes, all of a sudden, with so much time, grand ideas begin to pop up in your head. Not only do you wash, but you also decide to wax, vacuum, and pull out the old toothbrush to manually clean every single ridge in your tires. All the detailing is unnecessary, especially when placed alongside other important activities you could have accomplished within that same time allotment.
- It can also trigger your tendency to procrastinate. If you realize that the same amount of work can be done in half the time, you may put off beginning a project until you are right upon its deadline.

By taking into consideration Parkinson's Law, you can make use of your time a little more sensibly. Take a look at how much time

Words of Wisdom

"You will never find time for anything. If you want time, you must make it."
—Charles Buxton, author of *The Ideas of the Day on Policy*

you currently allow yourself to complete a project. Is it reasonable? Is there a way to make better use of that time?

Taking Breaks

For some of you, this section is what you've been waiting for when you started reading this book. For others, the thought of taking breaks just sends your stress level to the roof. Regardless of how busy you are, breaks are important.

If you feel like breaks are a waste of time or that you have too many things competing for your time as it is, pay careful attention to this section. You may find that your quality of work and health are at risk. Just to give you an idea of how a lack of breaks can cause you harm, let's go over a couple of examples.

Interrupting Momentum

Let's say you are finally working diligently on the novel you promised yourself so long ago that you would get to. The momentum is strong and your typing fingers have a mind of their own. You are completely focused and the work you are doing is of excellent quality. You are pleased that you have managed to find the time to sit down and write. However, it isn't a lot of time, so you must push yourself to get done all that you can while you are on a roll. A break is out of the question. What, and interrupt the momentum? Never. So you plow through. But eventually your mind tires and you get stuck. The infamous writer's block has hit you square in the head. You simply cannot continue. However, you don't give up. You still have a bit of time left to work with. So you sit and think and stare and use all your powers of concentration. All to no avail. You are in a rut filled with quicksand. There's no way out. You run out of time and have to put it aside. You now have a tremendous headache and are feeling like a failure. That disappointment (and headache) sticks with you throughout the course of your day. Your other activities are affected, and you dread having to return to the novel in fear of never leaving the rut.

This could easily happen to anyone regardless of the kind of work being done. In fact, it's probably happened to you several times already. You place blame on your lack of creativity, the amount of stress you are under, or the lack of time. But in reality, a break would have made the difference. You may think it is absurd to stop yourself when you have the momentum going strong, but if you don't, that momentum will be short-lived. By taking a break in the middle of progress, you have something to come back to. You already have ideas of what you want to accomplish next, so on returning from the break, you are ready to resume. You won't have to waste time trying to come up with something to do next. It is already laid out before you. Your drive will not exhaust itself and you will keep a clear head throughout the project.

Physical Effects

Now, let's take a look at how a lack of breaks affects your health. Let's say you are sitting at your desk working on a computer all day long. You have all the protective equipment—the antiglare screen, the appropriate wrist rest, and so forth—so you feel safe. Knowing you have a deadline to meet, the idea of a break just isn't an option. Perhaps you even decide to work through lunch. Your back begins to ache slightly, but not enough to cause alarm. So you wiggle a bit in your chair and continue on. Soon your wrists are straining, but that's okay because your fingers are still going strong. Your eyes are crying out for relief so you blink a couple of times and you're okay. Still you push. Eventually, you finish your project, meeting the deadline, and now you can relax. You feel good about what you have accomplished and laugh at the ridiculousness of ever needing to take a break. Until you get up. You stand up from your chair and everything is blurry. You squint to try to focus on something. But you don't have time to worry about that now, your body seems to be falling apart. Your legs are buckling beneath you. You are feeling a bit light-headed and your lower back is throbbing. Now you won't be able to enjoy your well-deserved rest because you are in too much pain.

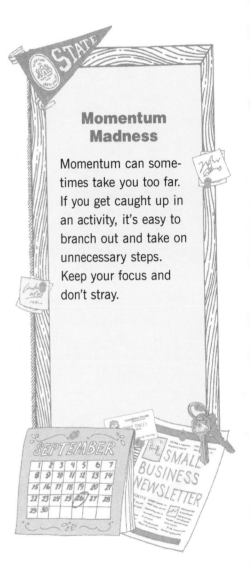

Momentum Madness

Momentum can sometimes take you too far. If you get caught up in an activity, it's easy to branch out and take on unnecessary steps. Keep your focus and don't stray.

Yes, you may have protective gear at your workstation, but these devices can go only so far to protect you. You have to take it upon yourself to schedule breaks. A consistent routine like the one above can easily lead to serious long-term effects. You may believe that you can shake off the discomfort at the end of the day, and that may very well work for a while. But refusing breaks altogether will slowly deteriorate your health.

Types of Breaks

Breaks don't always have to be a set 10 minutes long, nor do they require you to leave your work area. Breaks are simply changes; and change is good. There are several different kinds of breaks you can take. For instance, you can do small exercises to relieve tension and prevent headaches and any other aches you may be apt to encounter. Do shoulder rolls, massage your wrists, shrug your shoulders, stand up and stretch, sit down and stretch, roll your head, breathe deeply, and so forth. All of these can be done in less than a minute and have a significant positive impact on your work and health.

You may choose to take longer breaks than this, which is fine. But don't allow the breaks to be so long that you lose touch with what you are working on and/or spend just as much time breaking as you do working. While breaks are important, it is also important to keep your priorities in check. Small frequent breaks with a couple of extended breaks thrown in are recommended. The main goal is to keep you fresh, in both body and mind.

Put Off Procrastination

"Procrastination" is thought by many to be a dirty word. But really a procrastinator is a highly skilled person. Think about it: procrastination requires the ability to create convincing excuses, convincing enough to persuade not only others but yourself as well. If you are a procrastinator, give yourself a pat on the back for being such a creative person, then kick yourself for using your creativity to feed a bad habit.

Procrastination is simply the postponement of an activity that could—and most of the time should—be done sooner rather than later. Doesn't really sound that bad, does it? Just do what needs to be done and that's the end of that problem, right? Sure, if you live in never-never land. In the real world, however, procrastination can be your worst enemy in getting things done.

Don't get down on yourself about it, though. Everyone procrastinates. For some it is simply an occasional annoying lag in their lives that makes them human. For others it becomes a life-altering addiction. However, most of us fall somewhere in between, applying it only to certain aspects of our lives. Regardless of your degree of dawdling, the results are ultimately the same—an increase in stress, a decrease in self-esteem, a job hastily finished (or sometimes not finished at all), guilty feelings, and, of course, the loss of valuable time.

But it is a habit, and habits can be broken. Let's first take a look at the possible causes of the problem and then try to find solutions.

When You Just Don't Want to Do It

Probably the most common reason we put things off is because we simply don't like the work that needs to be done. This cause seems to nail even the most diligent of workers at one time or another. Everyone wants to be happy, so why voluntarily succumb to an activity that will undoubtedly torment you? Sounds like a rational argument, right? But you must take into consideration the big picture. Sure, you aren't going to enjoy the activity while it lasts, but then it will be over, gone from your list. Think about what great pleasure you will receive from taking that bright red marker and crossing out the formidable feat on your to-do list. To prolong the completion of a dreaded activity will actually bring you even greater discomfort in the long run than it would to just get it over with.

Progress Report

Document a progress report on a weekly or monthly basis to help keep you motivated.

Let's say you absolutely detest doing laundry. You know it needs to be done, but you can survive for a few more days. So you put it off, even though you have a perfect time slot just waiting to be filled. Instead, you use that time to make a couple of calls, lounge on the couch, or just revel in the fact that you aren't doing the laundry. Now that time slot is filled with unproductive activity and the laundry still needs to be done. You go on with your daily, more pleasurable activities, convincing yourself you are a happier person to have not completed the task. Unless you have the ability to selectively erase your memory, the knowledge of that little bit of undone work will gnaw at the back of your mind, putting a damper on more pleasant times. Not to mention the fact that the laundry pile is going to grow and create more work, forcing you to grant even more time to a chore you hate. But if you tackle the laundry when it needs to be done, not only will it be gone from your mind until the next bout, but also less of your time will be spent agonizing over it.

Fear

Fear plays a big role in procrastination. Though this cause may be a little more difficult to diagnose, it can be the strongest element at play. You may not like the idea of admitting to fears, but if you are honest with yourself, you may find out that a certain fear is all that has been holding you back.

Fear of Failure

Ask yourself these questions:

- Do I ever hesitate to answer a question even though I am almost positive that I know the correct answer?
- Do I ever pass up an opportunity to take on a new task even though it would likely reap great rewards?
- Is "I can't do that" a common phrase escaping my lips?
- Do I find myself placing a disclaimer on a project before it is completed?

- Do I often find myself relinquishing a position of responsibility or command, preferring instead to remain in the background?

If you answered yes to any of the above questions, it is probable that you suffer from the common fear of failure. Each of us has struggled with this; fear is a normal human reaction. Many people advertently or inadvertently use the fear of failure to postpone or deny activities or actions that could very well better their lives, given the chance. The fear overrides the possibilities.

For instance, place yourself in a marital situation. It's safe to say that no marriage is perfect; it's a given that every couple will have some problems to work through. It is how you handle these problems that determines the success of the union. Perhaps you are concerned with a bad habit your spouse has, and you would like to be able to face the problem head on. But the divorce statistics run through your head and you talk yourself into thinking that maybe the habit isn't really that bad, and it will probably go away on its own. You decide to tackle it later when you feel more secure in the relationship. Time goes by and you have become quite frustrated with your partner's habit. So frustrated, in fact, that you can barely speak at all, much less confront the issue. Due to your fear of failure, you have put off handling the issue and now it has escalated to the point of damaging an otherwise healthy relationship. Allowing your fears to override your interests will cause you to miss great opportunities; will hollow out your self-esteem; and, in some instances, will even cause you to lose control over the situation you fear.

Contrary to popular belief, failure is not bad. Our failures teach us even more than our successes do. Children are the best example here. Failure has very little negative impact on their lives. How often do you see a child give up after the first try? They don't allow a sense of failure to stand in the way of what they want to accomplish. Instead, they use it as a learning tool.

Fear of Success

If the fear of failure doesn't quite describe you, but you still have a little hesitancy in dismissing the fear factor altogether, ask yourself these questions:

- Do I ever feel as though I just can't live up to what others expect of me?
- Have I set relatively low expectations for myself?
- Do I ever pass up an opportunity to get ahead because I feel I don't deserve it?
- Do I avoid or dismiss praise?
- With the assignment of a new task, do I ever feel a sense of panic even though I know I can accomplish it effectively?

If you answered yes to any of the above questions, then it is possible you have not a fear of failure, but a fear of success. Believe it or not, this is actually quite common. Everyone agrees that success is a high priority in his or her life, but what happens when you reach that ideal peak? Will you be able to maintain that peak or will you have nowhere to go but down? Once your talents are recognized, they also become expected. Can you take that pressure, or will it be too much to handle?

Though there are several causes of a fear of success, most often low self-esteem is the primary issue to be dealt with. Fearing success doesn't necessarily mean you do not want to succeed, but rather that you are unsure of your ability to maintain that standard of success. If you rationalize it, however, you will see that the effort and skill it took to reach that peak is under your control and definitely something you were quite capable of handling. You have already gotten past the difficult stages. Although maintaining that level of success will undoubtedly take work, the challenge is one you can comfortably face. You have proven yourself to everyone else already; now accept that fact for yourself.

A Procrastination Secret

Sometimes, though rarely, procrastination of a task will force you to question its importance.

Getting Past Procrastination

Everyone welcomes procrastination at one time or another, whether it be because they fear something, dislike the work to be done, aren't sure exactly what needs to be done, can't get motivated to begin, have several things come up unexpectedly, or any of a variety of other justifications. This is a practice you need to curb if you are serious about managing your time wisely. The following are some suggestions on how to get past procrastination:

- **Realize what has been holding you back.** When you discover the reason behind your procrastination, you will have the issue to face in front of you. Make a list of specific activities and chores you have been putting off and analyze the list to assign a cause to each item. You may find that a single cause repeats itself in several items on your list. Group these together. Tackle the reason, then tackle the task.

- **Accept responsibility or not.** Decide whether an activity needs to be done and whether it is you who needs to do it. Once you determine that you will take on the chore, accept the responsibility for the completion of the task and its rewards, as well as the consequences if the task is not completed. If you aren't comfortable taking the responsibility, use your delegation skills (delegation is explored in greater detail in Chapter 4) to appoint someone else to the task. By making this one decision, the task is now on its way to completion.

- **Create a to-do list, but keep it short.** By determining what your priorities are, you can create a shorter list, thereby not overwhelming yourself. Another good idea is to place the job you dislike the most, first. You will look forward to moving down the list and therefore will get more accomplished. You may also want to write down the benefits of completion next to the task. This can be good for a little added motivation.

- **Don't allow yourself to indulge in self-defeating attitudes.** Getting down on yourself serves only to waste time and disable you.
- **As soon as a creative excuse cries out for attention, challenge it with rationalization.**
- **Reward yourself.** This is a pleasurable and important step. Defeating procrastination is a difficult thing to do. Don't hesitate to give yourself a pat on the back or whatever reward you feel necessary for accomplishing the feat. Not only will it boost your self-esteem, but it will motivate you to complete future tasks.

The Pains of Perfectionism

We all know that procrastination is a huge time waster, but many people don't realize that perfectionism can be just as bad. In fact, perfectionism can even be a catalyst for procrastination. For example, a perfectionist needs to clean out the junk drawer. But because he hasn't found the perfect organizer to fit nicely within the drawer, he won't even begin to work on the problem. Or perhaps he just doesn't have the time to sit down and go through each scrap of paper to determine its worth, and if he can't do the job well, then it just won't be done at all.

Perfectionism sounds nice and admirable, but it actually hinders your ability to produce results. Some of us would love to be labeled a perfectionist. After all, doesn't perfectionism go hand in hand with success, and isn't that what we all desire? In the mind of a perfectionist, yes, success is achieved only through perfection. But realistically, perfection does not exist, and, therefore, the perfectionist never attains success.

Okay, now that all your hopes and dreams have just been destroyed, let's take a look at this more closely. Perfectionism labels anything short of perfect as unacceptable. This means that accomplishing a task to the best of your abilities just doesn't cut it. Your best will never be good enough. You will constantly strive, somewhat compulsively, toward unrealistic goals that will always evade your grasp. Doesn't sound like much fun, does it?

Perfectionists view all mistakes as failures. Quite often they take an "all or nothing" approach toward things. This will hamper their productivity, and it is their accomplishments and productivity that they use to gauge their self-worth. A self-defeating cycle is created. First, unrealistic goals are set. Inevitably these impossible goals cannot be met, creating a sense of failure. That failure brings about low self-esteem and an even greater compulsion to get it perfect the next time. Thus, the cycle begins again.

Putting Perfectionism in Its Place

The ideas behind perfectionism aren't all bad. Striving to get something accomplished perfectly is an admirable goal, as long as you equate perfect with your best efforts and realize that perfection in itself does not exist. Because perfectionists set extremely high standards of achievement, their goals are set at a challenging level. This can actually be beneficial to those who use the motivation in a healthy manner.

Again, being grounded in reality is a must here. It is okay to challenge yourself, but to place unnecessary stress on yourself will do you nothing but harm. Perfectionists also usually like to get a jump-start on a project and put all of their energy into its progress. However, on the flip side of that, a project might never even be started if there isn't the probability it will be done flawlessly. The intentions are good, but they must accompany a realistic outlook.

Here are some suggestions on how to put perfectionism in its place:

Practice Imperfection

Your imperfections are what make you human. Recognize them, respect them, and join the social club we call the human race.

- **First of all, you must learn to forgive yourself for mistakes.** You are human after all. Mistakes are tools we use to learn. Pay attention to them, but don't dwell on them. Learn from them and move on. Also, don't regard mistakes as failures. This will lead only to heightened stress levels and low self-esteem.

- **When completing a task, don't pick it apart all over again searching for flaws.** Reward yourself for a job well done, even if you think it still could be better. Let it go.
- **Ask yourself, "What is the worst that could happen if this project is not completed perfectly?"** And be honest with your answer. You will find that you may place too high of an importance on nearly everything you do.
- **Take risks.** Jump on those projects you would normally not give a second look. Don't let your disposition toward perfection stand in the way of taking on activities that you know won't turn out faultless. It's just these types of activities that will actually be good for you. Recognize what you do accomplish instead of what you don't.
- **Do not allow yourself to feel as though you are in constant competition with those around you.** This is a huge step for a perfectionist, but it can be done. Once you realize that you are your own person and that others aren't better than you, they are just different, your outlook on life will change for the better. Your stress level will lower, your level of self-esteem will rise, and you will find yourself accomplishing tasks you never thought possible.

The Two Ps

Both procrastination and perfectionism have the potential to dominate your life—but only if you let them. By recognizing the causes and effects, you can take control. Of course, changing habits like these isn't going to be easy, and you will undoubtedly slip back into the old routine every now and then. But remember to take it easy on yourself. You are allowed, even encouraged, to make mistakes.

Reap the Rewards!

No, I'm not teasing you. Rewarding yourself is an important aspect of time management. Without a reward here and there, who is going to be motivated to get anything done? For some tasks, the achievement and completion are reward enough. You need tasks like these to give you an overall feeling of satisfaction. But the focus here is on those bothersome tasks that you don't really care for or simply flat-out despise. These are the tasks that require incentives.

Take a look at your to-do list. Take note of those tasks that don't directly relate to your list of priorities. You probably have a lot of those humdrum daily necessities that always seem to find you no matter how far you run or how well you hide. Well, get ready to change your attitude; you will like these tasks by the end of this section. Okay, so maybe you won't necessarily like the task itself, but at least you won't be dreading its turn on the list.

This book will give you a few basic examples to get you started. However, the reward system is entirely up to you. Get as creative or fattening as you want. As long as you stick to a few simple guidelines, you will stay in control and have fun at the same time.

Reward Guidelines

Okay, first the guidelines. "Rules" sounds like such a harsh word, and this is supposed to be fun. But if you think calling them rules will help you stick to them better, then go with that word.

1. The reward cannot exceed the activity in terms of proportion. For example, if the dreaded task happens to be watering the plants, you cannot reward yourself with a trip to Hawaii. That is simply unacceptable and will knock the entire scale of rewards off balance.
2. The activity cannot exceed the reward in terms of proportion. For example, if the dreaded task is spring-cleaning the entire house from top to bottom (garage included), you cannot reward yourself with one single lick of a chocolate ice cream cone. That is unreasonable and does not serve as an appropriate incentive.

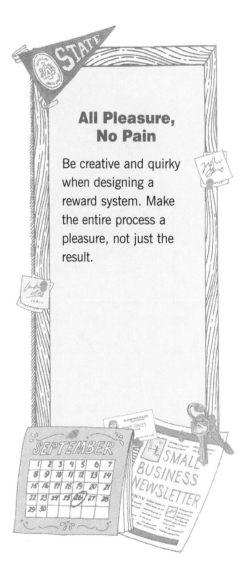

All Pleasure, No Pain

Be creative and quirky when designing a reward system. Make the entire process a pleasure, not just the result.

3. A reward cannot conflict with a to-do. In other words, you cannot reward yourself by procrastinating or eliminating an item on your to-do list.

4. A reward cannot conflict with any goals or priorities you have set. For instance, it is forbidden to reward yourself with a strawberry cheesecake if one of your goals is to lose weight.

5. A reward must be carried out within a reasonable time frame following the completion of the activity. This rule guards against those sneaks who get the bright idea to accumulate rewards. You cannot stockpile rewards because they will lose their individual meaning if grouped with others. A reward does not work as a reward if it does not reflect upon the task completed.

Reward System

So now that we have the guidelines out of the way, let's get to the fun part. As stated before, the reward system is to be created by you alone. Only you will know the impact of a particular reward. Therefore, get those creative juices flowing. But remember, you must always abide by the guidelines!

The following are a few suggestions to help give you an idea of how to balance the reward with the activity. Feel free to use them to get you started:

*   *Activity:* Cleaning up the yard, including any necessary mowing, trimming, watering, and planting.
    Reward: Treat yourself to a movie in the cinema across town.
*   *Activity:* Sitting through a two-hour-long seminar about a still-undeciphered topic.
    Reward: Taking your phone of the hook and displaying a "Do Not Disturb" sign for the rest of the day.
*   *Activity:* Painting the house.
    Reward: A day at the spa.

- *Activity:* Sorting and folding laundry.
  Reward: The most fattening single-serving dessert you can find.
- *Activity:* Tackling that pile of papers that has been ceaselessly growing for the last week.
  Reward: Take a leisurely stroll to admire the changing of the seasons.

Jason and Andrea Get Motivated

Jason and Andrea both have a good time management system in place. They take pride in the hard work and determination that brought this system into their lives. However, they can't seem to do more than just look at what they've written down on paper. Even though their motivation and drive have brought them to this point, it suddenly seems as if those things aren't enough to get them to implement the system.

Jason

Jason battles motivation in his personal and home life. This seems quite unreasonable to him, considering the fact that the main reason behind his wanting to incorporate a time management system in the first place was to spend more time with his family and himself. Even though his system allows plenty of time for these things, he is still at a standstill.

After reading this chapter, Jason discovers that he has a problem with procrastination. However, his procrastination doesn't stem from not wanting to do the job or not knowing how, but rather from his wanting to do the job perfectly. His fear of failure is so extreme, he can't force himself to begin to make use of his time management system at home and in his personal life. This is most likely one of the main reasons he is used to bringing his work home with him on a regular basis. He is procrastinating his life outside work.

Because it is so important to him that he has a stable and healthy relationship with his family, the idea of failing in his attempts stops him from undertaking the effort. That idea of perfection, which he originally reasoned would motivate him, actually discourages him.

Jason is able to pinpoint the reason behind his procrastination. This is the first step in conquering his lack of motivation. Just having the fear named and out in the open is encouraging. He then knows what it is he is battling. Beforehand, he could only get down on himself for not seeming to care about time with his family.

But because fear is not a tangible item easily struck down, Jason has to work hard on his self-esteem and inner strengths to overcome this. His line of offense is to first accept the fact that mistakes will be made and that perfection isn't a possibility. If he can learn from and use those mistakes to better himself, he will be making the most of his time at home and in his personal life. When he comes up against that brick wall, he will recognize that fear, accept responsibility for it, tackle it, and gain the motivation he needs to complete the task.

Jason has high hopes for his time management system. Now that he knows what has been holding him back, he has no excuse to keep him from moving forward with it. He understands that he is not in competition with anyone and that his life is much too important for him to bow to fear. He is excited about the prospects, and that in itself serves as a form of motivation.

Andrea

Andrea needs motivation to help her get going in the opposite direction. She needs the motivation to slow down, not speed up. Whereas Jason's time management system is set up to incorporate more time and energy into his home life and personal life, Andrea's system was created to help her focus on only those tasks that meet her priorities and goals.

Andrea's time is spent on a wide variety of activities. She never has a problem getting motivated to begin or finish a task. She doesn't have time for that. One task immediately follows another, and she doesn't stop to think about what she is doing. As discovered earlier,

her focus has always been on the completion of several tasks, not on how well they are completed or how important they may or may not be. Although she has shifted her focus to concentrate on using her time wisely, she still finds it is difficult to maintain the motivation to slow down.

After reading this chapter, Andrea discovered that she is a master at making excuses and that this skill hinders her motivation. Her excuses often justify (in her mind anyway) breaking away from her schedule and placing too many items on her to-do list. She uses statements such as "It will only take me a second" and "It is easier to just do it myself" to pardon her unwillingness to stick to her system. She lacks the motivation it takes to buckle down and break her habits.

Now that she has discovered her own trickery, she is better able to fight it. But because making excuses is in itself a bad habit, she is going to have to work hard to take notice each time she conjures up one. It has almost become second nature to her. However, she is determined to make her time management system work. This determination will spur some motivation, and keeping a constant watch on her priorities can unearth even more. She is prepared to stop herself each time she finds she is making an excuse, and immediately look over her list of priorities. This will go a long way toward helping her stay true to her system and find the motivation she needs to do so.

The End Result

Both Jason and Andrea have discovered ways to help them stick to their time management systems. Even though motivation will allow each to go in a separate direction, its outcome will be the same. Jason will stand up to and conquer his fear of failure, allowing him to make the best use of his time at home and in his personal life. Andrea will break her habit of making excuses to pardon her deviation from her system, allowing her to use her time wisely and focus on the important things in her life. It is a rocky road ahead of them, but their determination serves as a motivator to get them on the right track.

Do You Suffer Sensory Overload?

ometimes it seems as though no matter how hard you worked on your time management system, or how much effort you put forth into abiding by it, your senses just become overwhelmed with the amount of work you have sitting in front of you. Perhaps you suffer sensory overload just trying to figure out how to apply that time management system you worked so hard to create. Does any of this sound familiar?

Slay the Giant!

A huge stumbling block you may be facing is the size of the projects you take on. The size, regardless of importance, can be intimidating. If intimidation is allowed to take hold, there is no stopping the number of obstacles that will suddenly materialize.

Not Enough Momentum

Procrastination is one obstacle that stems from the intimidation of a big task. If you see a giant looming in the distance, what are the chances you are going to run up ahead to get a closer look? Not very good. Most people take the same approach with giant tasks, lingering behind as long as possible, putting off that necessary confrontation. Even though they know in the back of their minds that the task is just going to be that much harder to complete if they wait until the last minute, that fear of tackling it paralyzes their courage and reasoning abilities.

Whatever else you choose to do will be tainted by this oppressive fear. You will be unable to give your full concentration to any one project. Erasing your subconscious just isn't possible, or the problem would be solved. Unfortunately, the only solution here is to face your fears. Well, brainwashing might work, but that's a little risky and not recommended.

Too Much Momentum

On the other hand, you may jump right into the project and work nonstop, which can be yet another obstacle. Perhaps you

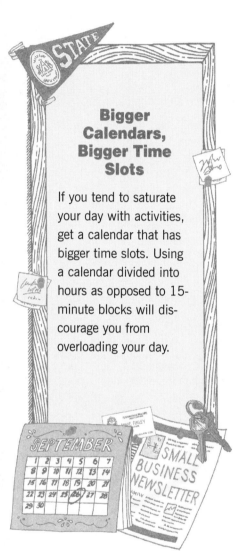

Bigger Calendars, Bigger Time Slots

If you tend to saturate your day with activities, get a calendar that has bigger time slots. Using a calendar divided into hours as opposed to 15-minute blocks will discourage you from overloading your day.

consider anything big to be important. Your judgment can become jaded by the size of the project. The project may have no connection whatsoever to your priorities, yet you promote the project to a position higher even than your top priority. This can create chaos in your schedule. If you place such importance on a project, then it will ultimately consume most of your time. Other things get pushed aside, and the urgencies begin to build up. Your schedule will be in disarray for a long time thereafter.

Lack of Strategy

Another drawback when you dive in and begin work right away, is that you don't take the time to design a plan. Without a plan, a big project will just swallow you whole. You need to organize a schedule and abide by it. Have a strategy in mind, lay out the steps, and then take action. If you fail to do this, chances are you will end up doing more work than necessary, thereby wasting even more time.

The Plan of Attack

So what is the appropriate action when faced with a giant task? Break it down. It's unreasonable to think that you can and should conquer a huge task in one sitting, but neither should you refuse to face it. Be confident that you have the skill and ability to effectively deal with and satisfactorily complete a big project. Have faith in yourself and stand up to your fears.

First, you have to know the deadline. It may already have been set by a higher authority, or you may have to set it yourself. If the latter is the case, take your time in analyzing how much work is going to be required to complete the task correctly. Be realistic in the time span you give yourself. If it isn't that important and doesn't reflect on any of your priorities, then by all means give yourself as much time as you can. Perhaps you may even decide that you will spend only 10 minutes a day on it. That's fine. Remember, you must always have your priorities in mind when scheduling. If the deadline is already set for you, it may be a little trickier to balance

your priorities. However, it can be done. Work with it, and remember you must not sacrifice the important stuff.

Once you know the time boundaries you have to complete the project, you then need to create a plan of action. Define what needs to be done. Create a clear picture of the completed project in your mind. Contemplate any possible problems or obstacles that may occur, and prepare a counterattack. Next, treat the project as you would a goal. Break it down into steps. Don't worry about the size of the steps right now, just divide them into the basics. Then you will want to figure out what actions need to be taken to complete each of the steps. Once you have a rundown of the activities involved, start scheduling. Most people will prefer to start to schedule at the beginning, moving forward. However, you may also consider starting at the end and moving backward. Sometimes this tactic works better for bigger projects. Find the midpoint in your time allotment. Determine where you want to be at that time and set it as a goal. If at that point you find that you aren't as far as (or possibly, that you are further than) you anticipated, you will be able to rework the schedule accordingly.

By breaking big tasks into smaller sections, your fear begins to weaken. It won't seem so overwhelming if you shift focus from the size of the task itself to the size of the individual steps. Granted, you are essentially fooling yourself, but the end result is the same. If the steps and their time allotments are set on a realistic scale, you will have tangible evidence that you can, in fact, get the work done. Your confidence will build, and the determination to complete the task will set in.

Make a Trade

By now you should possess excellent scheduling skills, even if they aren't broken in quite yet. However, even with all your skill, sometimes you will reach a point where you simply have too many tasks left to schedule and no time available. But before you begin slashing personal time and breaks, take a moment and think.

What are some of the other options you have available to you? If you have done your job well and balanced your personal, work, and home life, and have refrained from scheduling anything that was not important or urgent, you may think that all your options are exhausted. But they're not. Where there's a will, there's a way. Ever hear that before?

An Exercise

Look closely at your schedule. Then look closely at your leftover tasks. Now take out a colored pen. Mark all the urgencies that show up on your schedule that cannot be delegated out. Those have to stay.

Next, delegate, hire out, and flat-out strike those items that you can. No, this doesn't mean you can cut out a night's sleep—don't forget your priorities and health. But any of those items that you don't have to do yourself or that don't necessarily have to be done today are up for the axe. You may have to be a little more lax than usual here. If you refrain from delegating work because you just don't think the job can be done as well by someone else, you obviously aren't that concerned about your time. Sometimes you just have to let go. Your schedule isn't always going to be jammed, so if you need to, consider this a one-time deal.

Now compare what you have left on your schedule to the leftover tasks. How do they rank in importance on each list? If there are more important tasks on your leftover list than on your schedule, get ready to make a trade. Match up those highly ranked items on the leftover list with the low-ranked items on your schedule. Are you going to be able to make a swap—one task and its time slot for the other? If the particular tasks don't share the same allowances, move on down the list. You may even have to double up activities to make up for a single one.

Ask yourself what it is going to cost you to make the trade. Then ask yourself what it is going to cost you to refuse the trade. Since they are all important (if you have any unimportant items still listed, please strike them now), consider how much time you have left before they become urgent. This and their rank of importance are going to be the two main determining factors of who makes the cut for today. Make use of those decision-making skills. They come in handy all over the place, don't they?

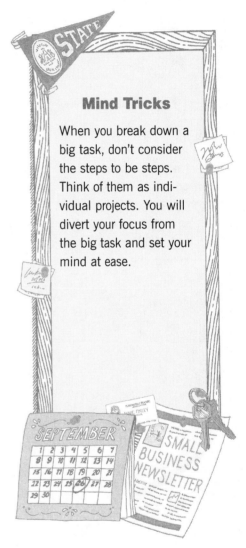

Mind Tricks

When you break down a big task, don't consider the steps to be steps. Think of them as individual projects. You will divert your focus from the big task and set your mind at ease.

Once you decide on a trade, make it, and immediately reschedule the ousted item. Just because it didn't make the cut doesn't mean it isn't important. Remember that your schedule is not set in stone. That is why you should use pencil to mark activities. Don't think that just because your schedule did not work out as planned you have failed as a good time manager. On the contrary, you put your time management skills to good use and were able to make your schedule work. That right there shows that you have the abilities and skills necessary for excellent time management. Perhaps it's time for a reward.

Emotions

Another big enemy—or sometimes ally—of your time management system is your very own emotions. Yes, your emotions can be the life or death of your management of time on any given day. If you don't believe this to be true, answer the following questions: What did you do the last time you were sad? Did you mope around the house? Obsess over it all day long? Call in sick to work? Go shopping to cheer yourself up? Unless you stuck to your schedule and were able to give your full attention to the projects you worked on, your emotions probably affected your time management system.

Gauge Your Reaction

Because emotions have such an impact on everything you do, it is necessary to take them into consideration when setting up a time management system. This isn't to say that you are always going to be able to gauge your emotions days in advance. Who knows why on some days we wake up in a horrible mood and on others can't seem to wipe the smile off our face? But if you can estimate what your feelings will be regarding a particular activity and what your reaction to those feelings will be, you will be able to get even further ahead in using your time effectively and efficiently.

For example, let's say you have a big project coming up that is going to take a few weeks to complete. The head honcho himself

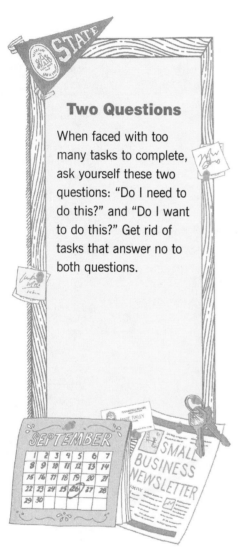

Two Questions

When faced with too many tasks to complete, ask yourself these two questions: "Do I need to do this?" and "Do I want to do this?" Get rid of tasks that answer no to both questions.

gave this project to you. It could very well mean a promotion for you if completed satisfactorily. So, you set your goals, break down the big task into smaller tasks, and create a very evenly balanced schedule. You now feel pretty confident that all will be done well and on time. Time passes and you are doing well with your progress and everything is right on schedule.

However, in the last week, you realize what this project could mean for you. Not that you didn't in the first place, but now that the pressure is on to get it completed, you suddenly begin to panic. You don't deal well with pressure, you never have, and you begin to think that you aren't going to be able to finish what is left to do. The fear takes hold of your activities. You freeze up and procrastinate. You get some work done but cannot handle the amount that is left. You miss the deadline and the promotion as well.

In this instance, you should have been able to gauge your emotional reaction to a pressing deadline. You have had experiences with deadlines in the past, and know that you do not handle the pressure very well. Add to this the pressure of a possible promotion, and you are sure to succumb. Considering all this information you had right in front of you, you should have been able to come up with a better plan for time management. So what could you have done?

Analyze Your Reaction

Let's take a look at the information. You are good at scheduling and sticking to your schedule. That is a strong suit for you. So you would want to use that to your advantage. Your schedule needs to reflect not only the work that must be done, but also the effect your emotions will have on that work. So, in this case, your confident period is in the beginning when the project is new and there is still quite a bit of time left to work on it. You feel self-assured and have an overall positive feeling toward it.

However, as the project wears on, you become less and less confident. You pick up feelings of fear and anxiety. You dread working on the project even though you know you must. Your schedule should take these feelings into consideration. The first few

Making Good Use of Emotions

When you are so angry that you are ready to hit the next person who looks cross-eyed at you, use that energy to tackle a big task. Take your anger out on a project and release that tension while using your time effectively.

weeks of your schedule should hold the bulk of the project. When you are confident, you are at your best. You can handle that amount of work and will get it done well. Then that leaves just a few tasks for the last couple of weeks, when you are at your weakest and unlikely to get a whole lot done. An evenly balanced schedule is not always the best route to take. Sometimes you have to account beforehand for outside factors that can throw off that balance.

Emotional Control

Emotions also take a toll on your time management when you give them control. We can't always control how we feel, but we do have some control over the reactions we have to those emotions. Say, for instance, you are easily angered. Just any little thing will get under your skin. Now, you can either obsess about all that makes you angry and blow up at everyone who crosses your path, or you can accept the fact that you are angry and curb your reaction to it. For instance, perhaps you could exercise daily to help relieve some of those pent-up feelings.

There are tons of books written on handling your emotions, but what it comes down to is strength of will. This isn't to say you should bury all your feelings deep inside you—that is just asking for trouble. But you can use reason and willpower to overcome the control your emotions may have over your actions.

Pounce on the Paper Problem

We all have a certain fondness for paper. How can we not? Magazines, books, loose-leaf paper, mail, sticky notes, file folders, business cards, and anything else made of or containing paper can bring us good news, surprises, wealth, notoriety, knowledge, and opportunities galore. Paper makes us look busy and smart. It helps us live our daily lives. So why make a fuss about it? Nearly every time management guide will address the paper problem in one way or another. It all comes down to one reason: Paper can be the death of time management.

Taking Stock

The above is not an exaggeration. Paper not only clutters your desk, it also takes over your ability to prioritize. Let's look more closely at this.

First, take stock of all the paper items that surround you where you sit. Now, let's pretend you are a detective and have the capability to dust for prints. Just how many sets of your fingerprints do you think would be found on each paper item? Granted, there will be some items that are used consistently, but focus on those that you really have little use for. Even though you may not use them regularly, there will most likely still be several sets of prints found on each.

Why would you bother handling something over and over if it is of little use to you? Because it is there and in the way, and because it is paper and paper is important. Besides, you don't want all those trees to have died in vain, now do you? Paper is a problem that just keeps coming back for more. Once you have it, it is hard to get rid of. Each time you handle a certain piece of paper more than once, it becomes a strain on your time management.

One Touch Only

Most paper products that you come across during the course of a day need to be handled only once. Let's take a memo for instance. Say you receive a memo informing you of a company meeting in a week. Most people will look at the memo and put it aside until later. There's a good chance that that one little piece of paper will be swallowed whole by the stack of vagrant papers on your desk, never to be seen again. This can create all kinds of snags in your time management.

Because you didn't write down the day and time of the meeting, you are unsure if it is this week, next week, in Conference Room C, in the lounge, shortly after lunch, or a morning meeting. You vaguely remember seeing the information written down somewhere, so you automatically reach for the stack of vagrants. Yes, it is in there, but finding it is a different story. You handle the same papers you've handled a thousand times before to no avail.

Destructive Control

Don't bury your emotions. This form of control is unhealthy and unwise.

Time Spent

Okay, so you've already spent time trying to wrack your brain for the lost information, trying to remember where you saw the information and where you placed it, taking a chance on sorting through the never-ending stack of papers, and failing to find it. Oh, but wait, we aren't done. You still haven't gotten the information you need. So you resolve to ask a coworker. You hate doing this, so you take even more time to get it done. Finally, you have the information you need. Take a look at how much time you have spent. Pretty bad for an otherwise good time manager, don't you think?

How could you have used your time more efficiently? When you first received the memo, you should have immediately entered the appointment in your planner and thrown the memo away. You would have had the information where and when you needed it.

You should try to apply the "handle paper only once" rule as often as you can. Granted, you are going to have to hang on to some documents, but for the most part, you should be able to get the information you need and be done with it. Think about all the time you will save if this becomes a regular part of your routine. No more intimidating stacks of vagrant papers, no more having to suck it up and ask for help, no more wasted time. You'll be surprised to find what an impact paper has on your management of time.

Making Wise Decisions

Decisions are simply a part of life. Whether you realize it or not, you are constantly making decisions on how to spend your time. They may be subtle and take very little thought, but they are decisions just the same. To take control of your time, you must control your decisions and how they are made. Wise and rational decisions lead to effective and efficient time management.

There are going to be some decisions that are more important than others. Some are going to be easy to make, while others will call for extended thought on your part. But keep in mind it is the

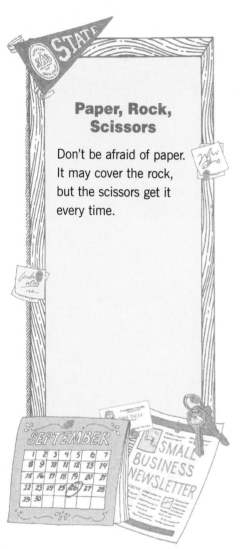

Paper, Rock, Scissors

Don't be afraid of paper. It may cover the rock, but the scissors get it every time.

quantitative sum of all these decisions that will determine the out-come of your life. Therefore, it is important that you do the best you can with each.

Factors and Influences of Decision Making

There are several factors that play a role in your decision making at any given time. Facts and consequences are the hard-core truths you simply cannot run from. So, of course, those must be taken into consideration. If you try to overlook these, you will ultimately make poor decisions. Your emotions and how you feel toward a certain decision also weigh heavily. Your attitude, mood, preconceived notions, psychological issues, and knowledge all play a role as well. So you can see that making a wise decision while taking all these factors into consideration is no little task. However, don't let it overwhelm you. Once you get the system down and understand your tendencies, the decision-making process will become second nature and an instinctive reaction.

Before we get into the steps of decision making, you need to evaluate yourself and the current influences on your process of making decisions.

- You know that facts and consequences are involved, but do you give them the attention they deserve?
- Do you thoroughly evaluate the facts and consequences and allow their weight to be distributed properly when making a decision?
- Do you take the time to research all the facts and deter-mine the likeliness of each consequence?
- Do you gather a few facts, just enough to get you by, and hope for a positive consequence?
- Is there a lot of guesswork involved in your decisions, or are you secure in the knowledge you have?
- Do you take a systematic approach? Or is there just a jumble of ideas and possibilities?

Try to get a general idea of how you normally handle making decisions. Of course, some decisions deserve more consideration than others, and your approach may vary at times, but if there are any habits you have, these need to be identified now.

There are also several psychological factors that play a part in your decision-making process. What is your overall disposition toward decisions? Quite often we allow our emotions to answer that question for us. If we're in a bad mood, the inclination to make hasty decisions, or no decision at all (consciously anyway), is compelling. If your self-esteem is at a low point, you may be reluctant to decide for fear you cannot make the right decision. Or in this case, you may even make wrong decisions in a sub-conscious, self-defeating effort. If you are too involved in yourself, you may make bad decisions because they deliver instant gratification, even though they may hurt you in the long run. Making decisions sometimes becomes a terrifying experience for those who suffer from depression, anxiety, low self-esteem, mania, dependency, or sorrow.

Recognizing the psychological factors involved, regardless of what they may be, may help you to overcome the barriers of poor decision-making techniques. This isn't to say you have to rid yourself of all psychological obstacles before you are able to make a wise decision. Rather, just recognizing the obstacles and minding their effects will have a tremendous bearing on your method.

If at all possible, you should try to separate your emotions from the decision itself. If you can maintain an objective point of view, your decision will be made in the best interests of all. However, this is quite difficult to do at times, and you may want to bring in an uninvolved third party to help. As long as you keep a base in reality and let the facts, rather than your feelings, sway the direction of the decision, you will have done the best you could and that is all anyone can ask for.

Now you are ready to try your hand at taking control of your decisions, thereby taking control of your time management, thereby taking control of your life. Think you can handle it?

The Five Steps of the Decision-Making Process

1. **First, you must recognize that a decision needs to be made.** This is pretty much a given, but you wouldn't believe how often people don't even make it this far. Choices arise before you constantly, and whether you face them or not is up to you. Start making a conscious effort to identify every decision you have an opportunity to make. You can't make a decision if you don't know it exists.

2. **Identify and assess the various choices.** This is a very important step, one that many people don't take nearly enough time with. In order to make the best decision possible, you must weigh all the alternatives. For major decisions, you may want to use a sheet of paper and list the pros and cons of each possible decision. Your goals must be considered at this stage. Will the choice benefit you in the long run? Does it help you to achieve your goals? Is it important? Gather all the information you can. Depending on the decision, researching could take you less than a minute or a full month. But knowledge is key, so the effort is worth it.

3. **Select a solution.** Because you are going to commit to it, make sure it is the best choice. Try to remain rational and not allow too many psychological factors to come into play. If you have your pros and cons set before you, this shouldn't be too hard. However, not every decision is going to require such an extensive effort. So you need to have a clear picture of your goals and priorities at all times, and from there determine how they will relate to the decision you will make.

4. **Execute the decision.** Whatever solution you have chosen, it's time to act on it. You must let the other alternatives go. Once you decide, don't waste time considering what might have been. It won't do you any good.

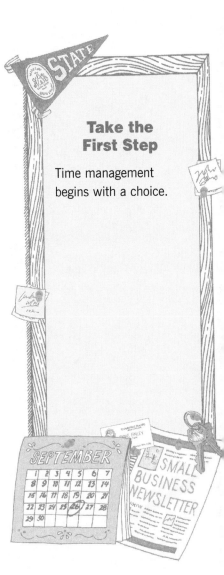

Take the First Step

Time management begins with a choice.

Even if you make a bad decision, you can only learn from it, you can't go back and implement one of the other choices. So it's best to just let go and not torment yourself with it. If you have taken your time and weighed the different choices carefully, this step should be no problem for you. However, if you find that you are constantly obsessing over decisions made, it may mean that you are not taking enough time with step 3.

5. **Follow up on the choice made.** Evaluate the results of your decision. Sometimes the results are evident immediately following the act; other times, you will have to wait a while before an evaluation can be made. However, don't be indifferent toward the outcome. For a decision well made, reward yourself. If you make a bad decision, learn from it. Why was the decision a poor one? Perhaps you need to work on strengthening a particular area of the decision-making process. Don't abandon the process simply because you make a mistake. Mistakes are tools we use to gain knowledge.

Wise Decisions Equal a Wise Use of Time

The decision-making process will take some time to master. But once you make it a habit, you will find that it saves you loads of time. Consider the following situation. Let's say someone has asked you to run for the school board committee. Without thinking, you say yes because you like to please and it sounds like something you should do. Now, because of that decision, your life is consumed by campaigns and elections for the next few months, which forces you to place most of your goals and priorities on the back burner. You don't really care to be on the school board; in fact, you would rather not because it will just take up more of your time in the future. But you made a choice without working through the decision-making process. Therefore, you wasted your valuable time.

THE FIVE STEPS IN ACTION

Identify the Problem:	• A formal proposal is due Friday and it has not been started
Assess Choices:	• Work overtime • Take work home • Postpone deadline • Put all other work on hold and work solely on the proposal • Delegate some of the tasks to fellow employees • Blow off the project and miss the deadline altogether • Call in sick on Friday
Identify a Solution:	• Work overtime AND delegate some of the tasks to coworkers
Execute Your Decision:	• Come in an hour early on Monday and Wednesday • Stay late Tuesday and Thursday • Come in early Friday morning for finishing touches • Pass on some of the research to others who have some spare time • Have proposal well done and completed for Friday's meeting
Follow Up:	• The proposal is completed • In the future, schedule things better so it isn't a last minute scramble • Take everyone who helped out to lunch • Be willing to help others in a similar situation

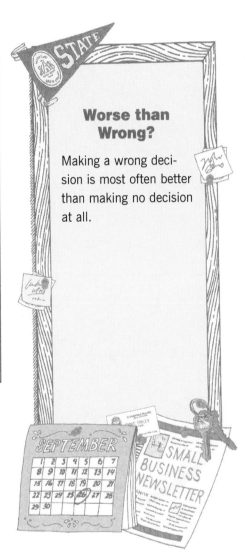

Worse than Wrong?

Making a wrong decision is most often better than making no decision at all.

Now, if you had carefully proceeded step-by-step through the decision-making process, you would have reached the conclusion that running for the school board committee simply did not favor your best interests. You would have been able to put the campaign and election time to better use. But no, you felt the process was something only scientists need to go through and you paid the price.

Not only will it save you time, but by carefully examining each decision to be made, chances are you will make the right choice more often than not. That should leave you with a good feeling. You will have more confidence in yourself and, therefore, achieve more.

In the case of those decisions that don't bring you the best results, you will have the insight you need to get it right the next time.

Fear

We are all afraid of something and there's nothing wrong with that. It's when we allow our fears to have a significant impact on the way we spend our lives that something needs to be done. You've all heard the phrase "face your fears," and this is especially true when it comes to making decisions. Inner fears can hold you back, force you into making bad decisions or no decision at all, and ultimately cause greater problems than you initially feared.

Making Mistakes

One of the main reasons people postpone—or even avoid altogether—making decisions is because they are afraid of making a mistake. This fear can lead to severe time-consuming consequences. Mistakes are a natural part of life. Without them we could never learn how to do things the right way. But because we were all raised with the negative implications surrounding mistakes, we inherently believe they are bad.

Mistakes are made when a decision has gone wrong. But that doesn't mean you should give up on making decisions. Use that fear for the greater good. Turn it around so it works for you, not against you. You are terrified of making the wrong decision, yet you still have to make that decision, so what are you going to do? Don't let your fear allow you to procrastinate or, worse yet, to not make the decision at all. Instead, let it force you into taking extreme care with the decision-making process.

Fear-Driven Wise Decisions

This process is tried and true. It was created to help you be objective and think clearly. Let your fear drive you to spend quality time with this process. The more careful you are with making the decision, the more likely it is to turn out right. Even if it doesn't,

Decision Deadline

Set deadlines for making important decisions so you aren't tempted to procrastinate.

you have more knowledge to use later on down the road. Consider mistakes as learning tools. The more you make, the smarter you get (that is, if you choose to learn from them).

Jason and Andrea Unload Their Overload

Just like everyone else, Jason and Andrea sometimes suffer from sensory overload. Even though they have worked hard to incorporate an effective and efficient time management system into their lives, it is not foolproof. Nothing ever is. There are always going to be times when you simply take on too much. This is why it is important to learn ways to battle sensory overload. If you let these rare instances get out of hand, they could easily throw your time management system way off track.

Jason

Following Jason through his trek with time management, we've discovered that a favorite area of emphasis is separating his work life from his home life. He struggles to designate specific times to each of these areas and works hard to break habits formed over several years.

Even with all his work, he still encounters times when he feels it is necessary to bring his work home with him. Let's not be too hard on him. After all, with years of 60-hour workweeks, it is difficult to accomplish all he is used to accomplishing within a 40-hour workweek. His time management system helps him to make the most of his work time, but even so, he is sometimes overwhelmed.

Jason used to revel in big tasks. He quite often equated importance with size. Therefore, all big tasks he undertook were high on his list of priorities. This was ideal, considering he felt he needed to bring work home with him constantly to get these important tasks completed. Since he was afraid of home time, this provided him with an excuse to hide behind his work. Now, however, his time management system won't allow for this.

Let's take a recent example. Jason has been assigned a task that is large in size and will take a lot of time and energy to complete. He suddenly becomes afraid of work time because he knows he can't complete the project at home with his new schedule. The tables have turned. What once was a savior is now his enemy. He is just sure this big task is going to be the death of his time management system. Enter sensory overload.

But instead of panicking, Jason looks at the situation objectively and hopefully. He realizes that it makes sense to break the big task down into smaller parts. If he considers each of these parts to be their own individual tasks independent from the assignment, he doesn't feel so overwhelmed. This calming feeling alone is going to go a long way toward saving his system.

If he can schedule each of the small parts to fit effectively within his work time, he will be able to get it all accomplished without having to take his work home with him. But the trick here is to shift his focus from the big to the small. He is going to have to maintain that new outlook if he wants to defeat sensory overload. His list of priorities and careful scheduling will help him do this.

Andrea

Andrea's schedule has always been overwhelmed with several little items to take care of. In the past, she used multitasking to handle the load. Now, however, since she has incorporated a time management system, she realizes that multitasking is not always the best answer. She has cut down on the number of small tasks by assigning a value system and learning to say no. However, she cannot backtrack and apply those skills to the past. Therefore, she has commitments coming up that were made a long time ago during her "yes days." She is now afraid that those commitments are going to have a slaying effect on her management of time. Sensory overload kicks in.

Andrea is not one to balk at a challenge. She knows these engagements have the potential to harm her carefully structured schedule, but she is going to try to make the best of the situation. One activity in particular is going to need a lot of work. She was asked several months ago to oversee a local charity auction. This event is important to the community, and as Andrea is a leader in the community, it may reflect badly on her to back out of the position. So she buckles down for battle.

She recognizes that this activity is going to take a lot of time out of her schedule. She will need to create committees, check their progress, answer questions, and conduct several meetings. She looks at her schedule for the weeks ahead. Although she does have some time to play with, it isn't nearly enough to fit all these activities comfortably. Something is going to have to give. Time to make a trade.

By carefully considering the importance and urgency of activities on her schedule, Andrea is able to postpone and even cut a few while still sticking to her time management system. But even so, this isn't enough to make room for the auction duties. Recognizing that she simply doesn't place a greater importance on this auction than on the activities she has scheduled, Andrea is going to have to suck it up and make a hard decision.

The decision-making process comes in quite handy here. She weighs the pros and cons for each option she has. Finally, she reaches the conclusion that she simply cannot fill the position she agreed to. This was a very difficult decision to make, but since she carefully considered all alternatives, she knows she must stick to it.

Andrea relinquishes her position to another individual who is more than willing to take on the role. But because the auction is important to her, she offers her services to one of the committees. Although she is not leading the project, she is still contributing and she doesn't feel guilty about deserting it altogether. She is able to maintain her time management system by making careful and wise decisions regarding her scheduled activities.

The End Result

Jason and Andrea realize that these are not going to be the only instances in which they will suffer sensory overload, but by using the skills they have learned, they will be able to overcome the obstacles and maintain their time management systems.

**Struggling
with
Self-Esteem**

Your attitudes and self-esteem have a significant impact on how you use your time. They can be used as an excuse to hinder your time management efforts. A negative attitude will put a damper on any hope of doing a job well. You may be trying to maintain an image and therefore work yourself to the brink of death. You may think very highly of yourself and yearn to be a perfectionist. There are several different ways your self-esteem will affect your use of time, which is why it is important to devote an entire chapter to it in this book. But before we can dive into these issues, we need to first define self-esteem.

What Is Self-Esteem?

Self-esteem is the value you place on yourself. Self-esteem encompasses your identity, independence, intimacy, trust, intelligence, competence, talents, confidence, and pride. Now, it is the level you have reached with each of these items that determines whether your self-esteem is good or poor.

- **Your identity is who you are—your physical, mental, and emotional qualities and characteristics.** What sets you apart from your friends and family? If you think you are the same as everyone else, think again and dig deeper. Keep in mind that identity equates individuality.
- **Independence is how comfortable you feel with being in control of your life—decisions, actions, thoughts, and feelings.** These are all within your power, but do you take control or do you divvy up control among the different factors in your life?
- **Intimacy involves the connections we make with others.** There are different levels of intimacy and the degree to which you are at ease with these connections can limit your relations. Are you comfortable with intimacy or do you shy away from it?
- **Trust is our belief in others.** For some people, this must be earned after extensive testing; for others, it is given away

Refuse Conformity

Your self-esteem reflects the pride you take in your individuality.

freely. Your ability to trust others may stem from life experiences or your own securities and insecurities. Do you feel you make good judgment calls? Do you trust yourself to trust others?

- **Intelligence is not just knowledge and/or smarts.** It also includes sense and reason. Everyone has intelligence, though some choose to display it more often than others. You can always gain more knowledge, but do you take advantage of that? Do you shelter your intelligence, or do you employ it on a regular basis?

- **Competence is your ability to effectively respond.** Everyone has a set of skills and abilities that can be used to acknowledge a feat. However, little can be accomplished until you exercise these skills to the best of your ability. Can others rely on you to effectively complete a task? Can you rely on yourself?

- **Talents are those gifts that you were born with.** Everyone has a talent, though many do not take the time to discover and exploit it. Can you name your talents? Or are you convinced you have none?

- **Confidence is your belief in yourself and your abilities.** Without confidence in yourself, you will never be able to make the most of your skills and talents. You will miss out on opportunities and experiences. Do you have the confidence you need to be the best you can be?

- **Pride is your acknowledgment of your identity.** How much pride you take in yourself directly relates to your level of confidence and competence. Do you acknowledge it when you do a job well? Or do you just brush it aside and move on?

Take some time and think about those questions. If you are still unaware of your level of self-esteem, take the following test and see how you rate.

SELF-ESTEEM TEST	
When taking the following self-esteem test, please rate yourself according to the following scale: 3—Often 2—Sometimes 1—Rarely	
I have a tendency to apologize excessively.	
I have difficulty maintaining eye contact with those whom I speak and listen to.	
I am comfortable only in a routine.	
I am afraid to voice my opinion in the presence of a large group of people.	
I feel anxious quite often, especially in unfamiliar situations.	
I am uncomfortable with taking on a leadership position.	
I consider myself to be a striving perfectionist, but most of what I accomplish is far from perfect.	
I often wish I were someone else.	
I feel as though I am in constant competition with my peers.	
Criticism greatly upsets me.	
I aim to please others constantly.	
I worry a lot.	
I often harbor feelings of hopelessness.	
I am unhappy with my physical appearance.	
The future scares me.	
I often feel as though nothing is in my control.	
I tend to exaggerate stories of success and/or boast often.	
I look to others for approval and rely on their support.	
I trust only a very select few, or no one at all.	
I constantly feel as though I have let down those people who care about me.	
I am often afraid of rejection.	
Total	

21–35

Low means good! Although everyone struggles with his or her own personal self-esteem issues, you have a pretty good handle on your own self-worth. Look at the areas where you answered with a 2 or 3 and remember to give yourself a little more credit and encouragement.

36–50

Low self-esteem could be the root of many of your problems. You aren't giving yourself nearly enough credit. At the end of the chapter, we're going to give you a few helpful tips toward improving your self-esteem. Pay extra close attention. These tips may give you the opportunity to turn your life around.

51 and higher

Warning! Low self-esteem can be extremely detrimental to your emotional and psychological well-being. If you've scored in this range, you may want to consider seeing your physician or seeking professional help. It is important to get to the root of the problem immediately, and perhaps a professional can help you focus on the positive things in your life rather than the negative.

Now let's take a look at the different types of self-esteem and see how each affects your time management efforts.

The Mirror Test

Look in a mirror. What is the first thing you notice? Do you have a positive or negative reaction to this observance?

Low Self-Esteem

Low self-esteem is something we've all heard of and perhaps have even used to describe ourselves. But do you know the effects low self-esteem can have on your overall well-being? Low self-esteem can lead to a dependency on others, depression, an overall sense of doom, failure, missed opportunities, and self-defeating acts. Doesn't sound like much fun, does it? This isn't to say that everyone will reach this degree of downtrodden spirits, but it is possible if you don't work to improve your self-esteem. Even the most confident of people will at one time or another suffer bouts of low self-esteem. We can't escape it in this pressure-filled and demanding world. However, those confident people will take note of the negative impact of low self-esteem and work to change it. Will you?

Low self-esteem is especially dangerous in that it continuously compounds itself. One negative thought will feed off of another, which will feed off of another, and so forth. It is not treatable like an illness. You can't get an antibiotic for low self-esteem. However, there are steps you can take to improve it on your own. But that's the catch—it must be done on your own. Self-esteem, as stated before, is the value you place on yourself, and no one else can make it better for you.

Low Self-Esteem Affects Time Management

So how does low self-esteem affect your time management efforts? There are several obstacles it may create. The following paragraphs explore the possibilities. Though it is unlikely that a person with low self-esteem will suffer each of these scenarios, even one or two will have a tremendous impact on time management.

Low self-esteem can make you doubt yourself and your abilities. For instance, once you begin to manage your time well, that doubt will swell. It may be hard for you to believe and accept that you are doing a good job, and therefore, your efforts will take a plunge. You essentially destroy your own plans yourself. Negative thinking can and will make mistakes happen.

You may be afraid to try new things. Let's say you view your current routine as a comfort zone even though you realize changes need to be made. However, the thought of change paralyzes you, and you may not even be able to begin strengthening your time management skills. Because time management requires you to determine what parts of your current routine aren't working well, you shy away from it, not wanting to be faced with the fact that you must give up your comfort zone.

Low self-esteem can make you feel as though the pace of life is too overwhelming. If this happens, you may feel like you cannot keep up. It becomes a hopeless case and anything you try will ultimately be overrun by those things you cannot change. A panic mode can set in and damage your ability to think rationally and realistically.

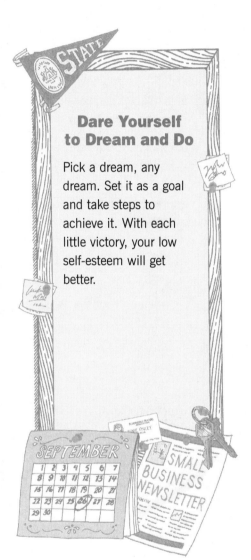

Dare Yourself to Dream and Do

Pick a dream, any dream. Set it as a goal and take steps to achieve it. With each little victory, your low self-esteem will get better.

Low self-esteem may cause you to lack assertiveness. This could cause you to take on too many tasks because you cannot bring yourself to refuse the request of another. You may be afraid to delegate tasks for fear you may upset someone. You allow interruptions to occur constantly. You may allow—or perhaps even depend on—others to make decisions for you.

It is likely you will set unrealistic goals for yourself. Because you are down on yourself, you will feel the need to overachieve. The goals you set have the potential to be far too demanding and out of reach. When you fail to meet these goals, your self-esteem will just drop even lower and your goals will be set even higher. It becomes a vicious circle of frustration and failure.

Often, low self-esteem causes you to worry about how others perceive you. Perhaps image becomes everything to you and a chain reaction occurs. You will overload your schedule so you seem more important and successful. Busywork takes the place of priorities. Your scheduling efforts become useless.

Lists can serve as reminders of how incompetent you are. Even if you mark off all but one item, it is that one item that will weigh heavily in your mind. You will likely disregard all the things you have achieved in favor of brooding over that one thing you failed to get done.

Perhaps procrastination will become a ruling force in your life. Let's say, because you do not have confidence in yourself, you are afraid to begin a new project. You will put it off for as long as you can. Then suddenly it becomes an urgent matter. But because you still feel as though you cannot do it well, the matter will either be dropped altogether, regardless of importance, or you will do a poor job of handling it.

Perfectionism may be what drives you. Because you feel as though what you do isn't good enough, perfectionism is your goal. You waste time trying to do a job, not well, but perfectly. When it doesn't turn out perfectly, you get down on yourself even more.

You may compare yourself to others. If you see that someone else has his act together and manages time very well, you may try to adopt his system. While this may work for a while, if it is not

tailored to your needs specifically, it will ultimately fail. This will cause you to rate yourself even lower in comparison.

Low self-esteem can be very damaging to you, physically, emotionally, and psychologically. Though for our purposes we show how it will affect your time management efforts, bear in mind that it will also affect several other aspects of your life. Time management will help set you on track for a happy and healthy life, but having good self-esteem will take you even further.

High Self-Esteem

There is also such a thing as high self-esteem. While this may sound as though it is ideal, it really can be just as bad as low self-esteem. Just like high blood pressure and low blood pressure are equally dangerous to your health, high and low self-esteem are equally dangerous to your time management efforts. What we are trying for is the middle ground—basic good self-esteem. So what is high self-esteem if it isn't good?

High self-esteem is when you think too highly of yourself. I'm sure you can all think of someone who fits this description. Of course it isn't you, so let's just take this time to learn how we can help our poor overly egotistical friends. If you think high self-esteem will produce good time management skills, think again. It can hinder you just as much as low self-esteem.

High Self-Esteem Affects Time Management

High self-esteem will lead to the idea that you are better than everyone else. Because of this your priorities are going to be all out of whack. As we all know, time management does not work for the benefit of our lives if our priorities are not in place. Having high self-esteem will not allow you to focus on those things that are important in your life. Your focus will be self-centered, which isn't always a bad thing, but when it is consistently so, it does not allow room for anything else.

If you have too much self-esteem, you refuse to delegate work to others. Therefore, your schedule is always overloaded with activities that aren't necessarily your responsibility and could be completed just as well by someone else. But what you don't realize is that by jamming your schedule, you will undoubtedly take away from the quality of some of the projects that need to be completed. It isn't that you can't do a good job, it's that you simply don't have the time to do a good job.

Your relationships with others will suffer. From time to time, regardless of what you may think, you are going to need help. If someone is turned off by your attitude, he is likely to shy away from helping you. This can create a big dent in your time management. Perhaps you don't know how to do something, but Joe next door is an expert. First of all, it is going to be a very difficult step to realize you don't know everything. Second, walking next door to ask for help is next to impossible. Third, if you do finally ask for help, Joe may help you but not do a thorough job of it because he has difficulty responding to your haughtiness. Because of your high self-esteem, you waste time coming to the conclusion and acceptance of the fact that you simply don't know how to do something. You waste time debating whether or not to ask someone for help. You waste time learning only a half lesson (that is, if you do ask for help). Or you waste time trying to learn it on your own (if you don't ask for help). However, if you have good relationships with people, asking for help will not be a big deal at all.

You may try to maintain an image of perfection. As we already know, perfectionism hinders your efficient management of time. While others may view perfectionism as an ideal, you will see it as a must. It will be a standard by which you live your life. So, in actuality, your aim for perfectionism is even more damaging than low self-esteem.

If you do have high self-esteem, this section isn't meant to cause you upset. Nor does it mean to sound condescending. Don't suddenly switch gears and take a dive toward low self-esteem. Like everyone else, you will undoubtedly have periods of both high and low self-esteem. Simply realize that the value you place on yourself

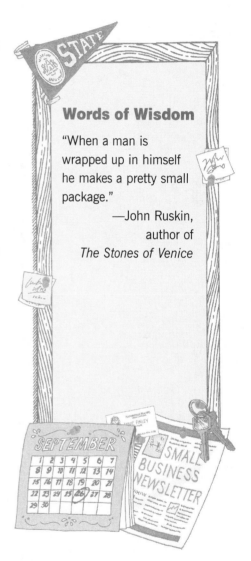

Words of Wisdom

"When a man is wrapped up in himself he makes a pretty small package."

—John Ruskin, author of *The Stones of Venice*

has significant effects on your habits, your relationships, and most importantly your management of time.

Low and high self-esteem are enemies of time management. As you can see, there are several ways they can hinder your time management efforts. All is not lost, though. Work on improving your self-esteem with a goal of good self-esteem. You can do this right alongside strengthening your time management skills. Soon you will not only have your life in order, but you will also feel good about yourself.

Good Self-Esteem

Good self-esteem is the ultimate goal here. However, keep in mind that it is almost impossible to maintain good self-esteem 24 hours a day, seven days a week. Face it, outside forces influence our lives, and with that, our moods and behaviors. But this is completely normal. If we don't have bouts of low and high self-esteem, we would never know what good self-esteem is.

What you want to do is to create a balance that will allow you to live your life to the fullest while still taking into regard those outside forces that may serve to pull you down once in a while. You can't hide from life and Utopia doesn't exist, so you just have to do the best you can with what you've been granted. Good self-esteem will help you do just that.

Improving Self-Esteem

You aren't stuck with the current value you place on yourself. If you feel as though you are worthless, you can alter that for the better. If you feel as though no one can touch your superiority to the human race, that can be altered as well. What you need is a base in reality. Even though it is very difficult to do, try to take an objective view of yourself. This may seem as though it is impossible, considering the fact that you can't separate from your body. But if you are grounded in reality, things aren't going to be as bad as they seem.

What separates us from animals is that we have the ability to reason and rationalize. Now use these skills to their full potential!

Because everyone's self-value is going to be different, not all of the following suggestions are going to pertain to you. But it won't hurt to try them out. You might just have a little fun along the way.

- **Learn to forgive yourself.** This may be a very difficult thing for some of you to do. We tend to hold grudges against ourselves quite often, even though the forgiving of others isn't a big deal. These grudges will swell into a knot of bitterness. You may hold onto them for years and years, never allowing yourself to be truly happy. However, if it had been someone else who did wrong, the deed would have most likely been forgiven and forgotten within a matter of moments. Why be so much tougher on yourself?

- **Surround yourself with stable, happy people.** The moods and attitudes of those around you will have an impact on your own. If you have a tendency to associate with downtrodden and despairing people, you will eventually feel the same yourself. However, the enthusiasm and stability of others will rub off on you as well. Try to form a support group with these people. Seek out those who will listen to you if you need to talk and who will encourage and stand behind you. Sadness begets misery. Happiness begets bliss. Other people's moods will beget your own. What type of people do you surround yourself with?

- **Trust yourself.** You are intelligent and capable of making wise decisions. If you don't trust yourself, you won't trust others. Granted, you don't always want to trust others, as sometimes that can lead to overwhelming disappointment or dangerous ground. Use your judgment and trust your judgment to be favorable. Trust is a building block of healthy relationships. Therefore, it all creates a circle. Trusting yourself leads to trusting others, which leads to healthy and stable relationships, which lead to fewer worries, which leads to more happiness. Sounds like a pretty good plan, huh?

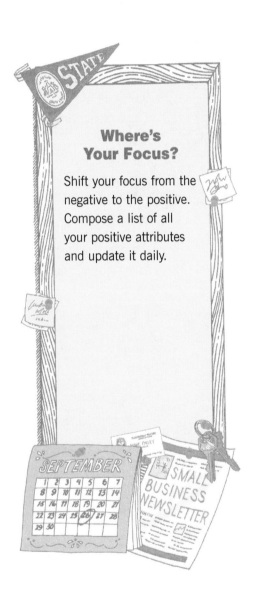

- **Set realistic goals.** This is very important. By setting realistic goals, you open yourself to the probability of success. Schedule time to accomplish these goals. They shouldn't be so far out of reach that you spend most of your time trying just to see them. They also shouldn't be so easily executed that you really feel as though you haven't accomplished anything. Make them just challenging enough to entice you, while keeping them at a level that can be reached. With each accomplishment you will begin to feel better about yourself and your abilities.

- **Reward yourself.** Let every good deed you do be known (even if only to yourself). You should never just shrug your shoulders at an accomplishment. Acknowledge it. You achieved something through your own efforts. It wasn't luck or chance that got you to this point. It was you—and you deserve some praise. See the section on rewards for some helpful suggestions to get you started.

- **Learn the decision-making process and incorporate it into your everyday life.** Making wise decisions will boost your self-esteem considerably. Once you are comfortable with the decisions you make—and you will be if you follow the process—you will begin to make more and more on your own. No longer will outside influences get to you. You will have the knowledge, intelligence, and sense you need to take control of your own life and be at ease with doing so.

- **Take care of yourself.** Eat healthy, sleep well, and get exercise. The way you feel physically will affect the way you feel mentally. If you are well rested, you are more likely to be ready to get up and face the world. If you have been depriving yourself of sleep, any chore is going to seem like torture. You simply won't have the motivation you would normally have. Exercise will invigorate you. Also it will tone your body, which leads to a better physical appearance and, therefore, better self-esteem. Eating well will give you the energy you need to make it through the day and anything you must face. Not to mention the fact that you are less likely to fall ill if you eat healthy.

- **Consider your mistakes tools for learning.** Those suffering from low-self esteem are devastated by their mistakes. However, we can't learn without making mistakes. Everyone does, even those with high self-esteem and good self-esteem. You must learn from your mistakes and let them go. Do not hold on and obsess over them. That is a waste of time and energy.

- **Take some risks.** No one likes to leave his or her comfort zone. But, really now, how are you going to experience the full potential of life if you don't take risks now and then? Don't be afraid to do it. Try new things. Opportunities are constantly turning up—reach out and grab hold of one. You may just find something you've always dreamed of. You will be pleased with yourself for even taking the initiative to try. Think of how good you will feel if you succeed.

- **Focus on your positive attributes.** For some this may be appearance, for others it may be skills, and for still others it may be values. Perhaps you have a combination of all of these. Whatever it may be, give it attention. Everyone does at least one thing very well. Have you found your niche? If not, go out and find it! If you have, then concentrate on it. The more you work with it and give it recognition, the higher the value of your self-worth.

- **Don't rely on the opinion of others.** This is a big one. In today's society it is easy to view ourselves as we think others view us. But really now, what do those others matter? Do they live side by side with you and experience your experiences? No. They have their own lives to lead, and if they are focusing on you, then it is their priorities that are screwed up, not yours. Don't create an image you think will pass well in society; you are neglecting yourself. Focus on your own priorities, goals, dreams, and values. Let your image reflect who you

are and be proud of it. There are very few things more sacred than individuality.

- **Learn to laugh at yourself.** Don't take the world too seriously. There's no reason to become mortally embarrassed every time you trip up. If you take everything to heart, you will be down on yourself all the time. Laugh at mistakes or disappointments you encounter and then let them go. If you keep rehashing an embarrassing or uncomfortable situation, you will discourage yourself further. Laughter will lighten your mood and that of those around you.

- **Above all, you must accept yourself.** This means accepting everything about you—your appearance, your beliefs, your strengths, your weaknesses, your values, your talents, your faults, your standards, and so forth. Because there are so many attributes that make up a person, it is reasonable to be displeased with some of them. However, if you cannot change these, do not focus on them. Accept them for what they are and move on. Focus instead on your positive attributes. Acceptance is the key to good self-esteem. You cannot allow others to accept you until you've accepted yourself.

Okay, so now that you know how you can work to build self-esteem, are you going to do it? If you really want to tackle time management, you will. It will take a bit of effort to reach good self-esteem, but that will be just one more thing you can pride yourself on once you reach it.

Positive Self-Talk

Do you ever pay attention to what you tell yourself, either aloud or inside your head? Well start. It could be that you have problems with low self-esteem, and consequently time management, because you speak negatively to yourself. Some people don't even realize they are doing it. But it is important to take notice of this. Regardless of what you may think, the influence you have on yourself is stronger than the influence others will have on you. For example, if you tell yourself time and time again that you are worthless, you will believe it to be so even though others may tell you otherwise. This is why it is important to pay attention to the ideas you give yourself.

Negative Statements

Are the words "I can't" a staple in your vocabulary? What are some other negative statements you make about yourself? Be honest. We all do it, but it is how often and to what degree that make the impact. These statements will eventually bring you down. They will excuse you from trying anything new and, therefore, from failing. They become a sort of disclaimer you make to yourself and the rest of the world. Because they offer you a way out, they become easier and easier to accept.

Don't allow yourself to get into this pattern. It's true that sometimes you will sincerely feel as though you can't do something, but try it anyway. Unless it endangers your life, it's likely the experience will only benefit you. But how do you reach the point of confidence you need to try something new? Positive self-talk will work wonders for your self-esteem and confidence.

Negate the Negative

Every time you catch yourself making a negative statement, say the opposite. For instance, if you tell yourself you cannot make a speech in front of a group of people, flip that statement around. Tell yourself you can make a speech in front of a group of people. Say it out loud. Say it several times. Make yourself believe it. Don't allow that negativity to creep back in there. Do this every single time you begin to make a negative statement about yourself. Soon, you will believe in yourself and your abilities and not be so quick to turn down new opportunities.

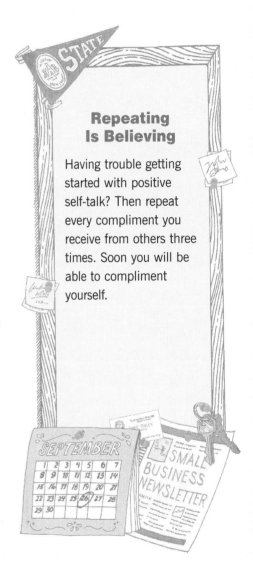

Repeating Is Believing

Having trouble getting started with positive self-talk? Then repeat every compliment you receive from others three times. Soon you will be able to compliment yourself.

Random Positive Statements

If your self-esteem is pretty low and you find it difficult to convince yourself of positive statements in contrast to negative ones, begin to make those positive statements at random. Don't wait until a chance arises to think either positively or negatively; get a jump on the gun. Start out your day with a positive statement. Look at yourself in the mirror and tell yourself something nice. If it is hard for you to sincerely compliment yourself, think about what positive things others have said about you or what you would like others to compliment you on. Set a goal to say a certain number of positive statements throughout the day, every day.

Voice the Positive

Say it out loud. There is a certain believability that comes with a voiced statement. It is easy to think things to yourself, but once they are given a voice, they suddenly have a more concrete meaning. If you feel silly saying such things out loud, do it anyway; you actually have added a bonus. If you are uncomfortable with voiced self-statements, it is likely that you will feel uncomfortable arguing with yourself out loud. This means that the positive statement you voice isn't going to have a negative voiced statement following it up. Sure, you may think negatively in your head, but the voiced statement will carry more weight.

Practice these positive statements, even if you don't truly believe them at first. Eventually they will work in the same manner as the negative statements, but in a healthy and encouraging way. They will become easy to believe and give you the confidence you need. Don't underestimate the influence you have on yourself.

Handling Criticism

Handling criticism in a healthy and constructive way can be a difficult thing to do at times. Often, we take criticism on a very personal level, thinking that any suggestions offered are a direct shot at our inability to perform well for whatever reason. We begin to feel bad about ourselves and believe that our efforts are a waste of time. For this reason, it is important to your time management efforts, as well as your self-esteem, to learn to take and even welcome criticism as best you can.

What Is Criticism?

Criticism is the open evaluation and analysis of your work, ideas, feelings, appearance, and pretty much anything that you are involved with. There are different types of criticism. It can come in the form of concern when someone is worried that you are participating in an unhealthy or unfavorable act. On the flip side, it can come in the form of anger and confrontation. There is also constructive criticism, which focuses on helping you to improve.

Criticism finds fault. But this doesn't have to be bad. It is only as bad as you make it. You are in control of your response to criticism and the effect criticism has on your outlook. Don't forget that. As soon as you forget that, your ability to reason, your self-esteem, and your time management fall to the wayside.

How to Handle Criticism

Handling criticism is something that is not taught in schools, and quite often not even by parents. Because it is the psychological issues criticism evokes that become the problem, it is difficult to enlighten others except on a case-by-case basis. However, there are some general guidelines that will help you to face criticism effectively.

- **Stand and face the criticism; do not run away from it.** Running away will only make the criticism appear larger than it is. Pay attention to what the speaker is saying, and don't get defensive. As soon as you become guarded, you no longer concentrate on what is being said. You become lost in the idea that the other person is out to hurt you.

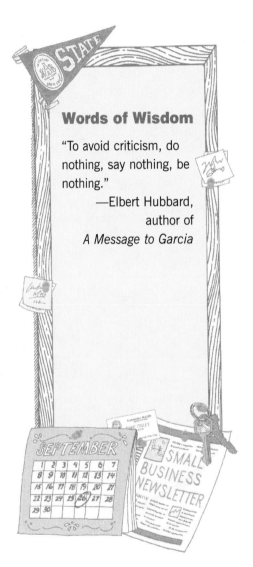

Words of Wisdom

"To avoid criticism, do nothing, say nothing, be nothing."

—Elbert Hubbard, author of *A Message to Garcia*

- **Apply the skills you learned in the active listening section.** Even if the speaker is flat out wrong in his criticism of you, you still may be able to learn something, and it isn't wise to pass up an opportunity for knowledge. Often, you can find life lessons in criticism.

- **Try to be objective.** If at all possible, separate your emotions from the situation. Yes, this is a very difficult thing to do considering criticism has the ability to make you feel exceptionally vulnerable. However, you need to be able to keep your reason. Adjust your attitude and consider the criticism to be of a concerned nature, regardless of whether or not it really is. This will help you to be more accepting of what is being said.

- **Draw your own conclusions.** Do this based on the facts and accuracy of the criticism. Are the criticisms being made deserved? Can you determine a reason behind the criticism?

- **Learn from constructive criticism.** Perhaps the person giving criticism can also offer suggestions on how to improve. Don't be afraid to ask for help. Obviously, if the person realizes that something was done wrong, he or she has an idea of what would be the right thing to do. Acknowledge your mistake and think of it as an opportunity to better your life.

- **If the criticism is undeserved, dismiss it.** Don't allow the thoughts and feelings of someone else to affect your behavior, especially if they are unjustified. You can argue, but often it will get you nowhere and the other person is likely to throw even more criticism your way. You have done your part by being an active listener and allowing the speaker his say. Aside from that, you have no other obligation in the situation. His words need not loom over you, nor should they hold bearing on future actions.

Criticism Can Save Time

Handling criticism is a difficult thing to do and will take some effort and restraint on your part. However, if you allow criticism to be a teacher, it can do wonders for your life. There are simply things that we overlook and others pick up on. You should learn to use the observations of others to your benefit. If you welcome criticism—deserved criticism—you will find that others will be more willing to approach and help you with an adjustment that needs to be made. This will save you the time it would take to make this conclusion on your own and figure out a way to amend it. Whereas if you handle criticism poorly, you may go through life wasting a lot of time stumbling upon mistakes that could have been brought to your attention earlier.

Jason and Andrea Take Time for Reflection

In their busy lives, Jason and Andrea have never stopped to really think about their levels of self-esteem. Yes, they both have their moments when they feel down and out, but these usually pass rather quickly, so they move on without giving them a second thought. Initially, they both believe they have good self-esteem; they aren't suffering from depression, after all. But as they progress throughout the chapter, they begin to wonder whether their self-esteem is really as good as they originally thought.

Jason

Jason enjoys his comfort zone. He considers himself to be, and takes pride in the idea that he is, a traditionalist. His work life is quite structured and rather routine. He knows exactly what he is doing; if anything new should arise, he pawns it off on his coworkers. In his line of thinking, he knows what works well for him, so why bother learning something new? We did see Jason venture into cyberspace in Chapter 5, but even so, he was quite hesitant to do so.

Even though Jason places an overall high value on his self-worth, there are particular areas in which his level of self-esteem drops. Now this is quite normal and happens to everyone. But because Jason is determined to leave out nothing when it comes to making the best use of his time, he is willing to do a little self-reflection and analysis.

What he discovered is that he has low self-esteem when it comes to trying new things. He has a deep-set fear of the unknown. He is afraid that if he were to try something new, he would fail and other people would think less of him. He has always considered his refusal to leave his comfort zone actually beneficial to his self-esteem. If he doesn't try anything new, he won't fail. Therefore, he retains his high value.

However, his traditionalist ways stem from low self-esteem, not reason. He covers up the fact that he has doubts in himself and his abilities by excusing his actions on the basis of the old adage "If it ain't broke, don't fix it." His way of doing things, though somewhat stuck in the Stone Age, seems to be working well for him, so why would he ever want to bother with learning something new?

Learning something new will benefit his management of time in several ways. First of all, it will exercise his mind. If he is used to a set pattern of things, chances are, he has not had the opportunity to really put his mind to the test in some time. This in itself will create low self-esteem. The longer you go without exercising your mind, the less confidence you have in your ability to do so. Jason can discover many different techniques and technologies designed to save time, if he will just take that step forward. But this is a battle that he must confront on his own. No amount of reasoning or persuasion will get Jason to leave his comfort zone if he is not ready to believe that he can.

Jason decides that in order to combat his low self-esteem, he needs to venture out into the unknown. He is not going to let his fear get the best of him, nor stand in the way of his time management system. But because Jason is a reasonable man, he knows that fear is going to hold him back somewhat, regardless of his determination at the moment. So he chooses to take small steps out of the boundaries of his comfort zone. He will begin to try new and different things on a small scale to build his self-esteem bit by bit.

Andrea

Andrea likes to be liked. This has been a motivating force with her for years. She simply cannot stand the idea of not pleasing someone. But is this really a self-esteem issue? It seems as though this is a normal inclination that everyone possesses. It depends on what degree you take it to. Yes, being liked by lots of people brings about a good feeling, and it is natural to want to feel good. But striving to be liked by the masses and jeopardizing your own system of beliefs and values in the light of others' is where your self-esteem comes into play.

As Andrea is well aware, she has a tendency to take on too many tasks. She has allowed herself to create a habit of saying yes automatically to pretty much any request for her time. This has left her with no choice but to multi-task and put the important things in her life on the back burner. Andrea has come a long way in man-aging her time throughout the course of this book, and she realizes where she needs to keep tight con-trol. Even with all of this reasoning backing her, she still finds herself accepting requests—even when they aren't that important. So why does she do it?

Andrea has an area of low self-esteem that makes her want to—and sometimes even need to—please others. She feels that if she were to deny their requests for her time, she would no longer be held in their favor. This is an issue that many people face but seldom recognize. Andrea never acknowledged the idea herself. She always thought her helping others actually raised her level of self-esteem. She never dreamed it was spawned from low self-esteem.

Now this isn't the case every single time. Andrea is a good person and derives pleasure from doing good things. But in those instances in which she takes on a task that is unlikely to bring her

any satisfaction or that doesn't match up with her priorities and importants, Andrea is allowing her low self-esteem to get in the way of her management of time.

Now that Andrea has discovered this obstacle, she has decided to take steps to improve her self-esteem. First of all, she will try to abstain from determining her own self-worth based on the opinion of others. This is going to be a difficult task, but as we know, Andrea likes challenges. She is going to use her list of priorities as the deciding factor when determining whether to accept or deny a request. Because she is a reasonable person, she will stop to remind herself that to deny a request is not going to damage the relationship she has with a true friend. If it does, then that person does not care about Andrea's life's demands and therefore is not worth her time anyway.

The End Result

Both Jason and Andrea have found ways that their levels of self-esteem affect their use of time. Just this acknowledgment in itself will begin the process of reaching good self-esteem. Had they not taken this time for reflection, all their efforts to manage time efficiently and effectively may have fallen by the wayside in light of their inner struggles.

Is Your Stress Level Skyrocketing?

You have to deal with stress. Period. You can't escape it, so you might as well make the best of it. You may realize that your use of time has a tremendous impact on your stress level, but did you know that your stress level has a tremendous impact on your use of time?

This chapter is going to take you through the causes and effects of stress, not only as they impact your time management, but also as they impact your physical and mental health. Every aspect of your life will affect another, so to live the best life you can, it is important that everything work in conjunction and harmony. Your time management system will be the innocent bystander that gets plowed over by a rampaging stress level. So, to protect the innocent, you need to take control of your stress level—and this chapter is going to teach you how.

Stressless—Is That Even a Word?

Try as you might, you cannot escape stress. Stress is your body's reaction to demands placed on it. There are several different types of stress—some bad, some good, some annoying, some fatal. It is how you deal with stress that can mean the difference between the good and bad. If you are having difficulty managing your time, you undoubtedly have a problem with stress. The two just seem to go hand in hand. Since this book is helping you manage your time, it should also help you manage your stress level.

Each one of us has felt stressed out at one time or another, but what we have to realize is that stress is there constantly. It doesn't go away, and it doesn't just show up haphazardly. It is when our stress level gets out of control that we begin to feel its effects and therefore come to the conclusion that we are stressed. As soon as you realize that you are actually stressed all the time, you will be able to differentiate between the types and effects of stress.

Effective Stress Management

The causes of stress vary, depending on the lifestyle you live. The keys to effective stress management are:

1. **Identifying the source.** What is it that causes stress on your body? Does it have a positive or negative effect?
2. **Taking inventory.** Do the stress producers outweigh the stress reducers?
3. **Adjusting to achieve balance.** You aren't powerless against the effects of stress. Create a balance between the stress producers and the stress reducers.
4. **Maintaining methods of healthy living.** Learn how to reduce the negative stress on your body and lead a healthy and relaxed life.

Before you dive headfirst into this process, stop and think about what a significant impact stress has on your life. You may think it is just an annoyance that gets you down once in a while, but in reality, it can have severe effects that you may not be aware of. If you had thought about skipping out on this chapter, read the following effects and think again.

Potential Physical Effects of Stress

- Rapid heart rate
- Muscle tension
- An increase in blood pressure
- A change in sleeping patterns
- Dizziness
- Nausea
- Fatigue
- Back pain
- Rapid breathing
- Headaches
- Clammy skin
- Rashes

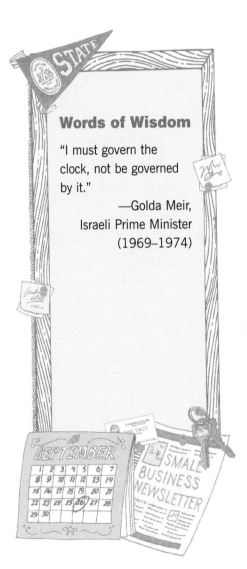

Words of Wisdom

"I must govern the clock, not be governed by it."

—Golda Meir,
Israeli Prime Minister
(1969–1974)

Potentially Serious Health Problems Linked to High Levels of Stress

- Heart disease
- High blood pressure
- Stroke
- Weight problems
- Diabetes
- Sexual dysfunction
- Digestive problems
- Ulcers

Potential Psychological/Emotional Effects of Stress

- Nightmares
- Low self-esteem
- Lack of concentration
- An increase in nervousness
- Irritability
- Anxiety disorder
- Forgetfulness
- An increase in the use of drugs and alcohol
- Depression
- Anger

Hopefully, the above lists have made you aware of the seriousness of stress. Good time management will help you to reduce your stress level somewhat, but there are also other actions to take. The following sections will take you step-by-step through getting your stress level under control.

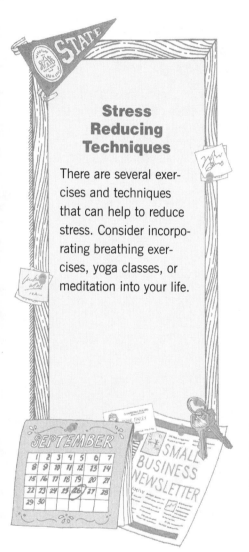

Stress Reducing Techniques

There are several exercises and techniques that can help to reduce stress. Consider incorporating breathing exercises, yoga classes, or meditation into your life.

STRESS TEST

When taking the following stress test, please take into consideration the last two to four weeks and rate yourself according to the following scale:

3—Often
2—Sometimes
1—Rarely

I have trouble sleeping.	
I feel like I'm not in control and life is passing me by.	
I worry a lot.	
I drink caffeine/smoke cigarettes/consume drugs or alcohol on a daily basis.	
I have difficulty making decisions.	
I get headaches on a regular basis.	
I'm never motivated.	
I have poor exercise habits.	
I suffer from low self-esteem.	
I sometimes feel as though my life has no purpose.	
I don't ever have time to relax.	
I often feel stressed at work or at home.	
I sometimes wish I could drop everything, run away, and hide from the world.	
I am disorganized and spend a lot of time searching for things.	
I have difficulty accepting criticism.	
I often view things with a negative attitude.	
I suffer from periods of depression.	
I am easily irritable and argumentative with other people.	
I have poor dietary habits.	
I often suffer from digestive problems.	
I have difficulty concentrating.	
Total	

21–35

Congratulations! You scored on the low end of the scale. This means that you are probably handling your stress very well. Although you may get stressed out from time to time, you are definitely taking action to counteract stress producers with stress reducers. Keep up the good work!

36–50

If you scored here, you definitely need to work on your stress reduction techniques. Pay extra close attention to the next few sections. We'll give you some pointers on how to counteract stress. Also, keep an eye out for the stress reducers. You need to incorporate some of these into your daily routine.

51 and higher

STOP! You need to reevaluate your lifestyle immediately! If you've scored in this section, you may want to consider seeing your physician. High stress levels can have a severe impact on your health. Try to diagnose what is causing your stress, and plan an immediate course of action.

Identifying the Source

Before you can begin to level out your stress, you must take stock of stress-producing activities. Take a look at the activity log you kept at the beginning of the book. Consider your feelings and reactions to each of the activities that took place. At any point did you feel nervous, panicked, anxious, eager, rushed, or confused? Did you have any physical ailments that accompanied these actions? What was your reaction to the completion of the activity? Take note of those that heightened your stress level. Write them down and try to determine the length of time they caused you to feel stressed. If the stress outlives the activity, it may be time to look again at your priorities and debate whether or not the particular activity has any true bearing on your life.

If you are having difficulty remembering your reaction to these activities, start recording your responses to them in a diary or journal. Reflect on your feelings and attitudes toward everything you do. It doesn't necessarily have to be a physical action you take; it could be a thought or feeling that stimulates you. This is a time for self-awareness and should be taken seriously. Granted, it will take some time and effort on your part, but the results are well worth it. Your health and performance may be at risk.

As stated before, stress isn't always negative. Don't overlook those activities that bring you pleasure and a sense of accomplishment. These are also stress producers. However, this type of stress yields positive consequences. If at all possible, identify every source of stress, good and bad.

Because it is impossible to eliminate all stress, pick out those activities that caused the greatest change in your stress level, focusing on those that are recurring. We will work to reduce the negative effects of these stress producers, thereby smoothing out your overall stress level.

Taking Inventory

You now have a good idea of what causes your stress, but do you know what relieves your stress? Take a look again at your activity log. Are there any actions you took to remedy the effects of stressful situations? How did you handle them? How did you react upon completion of those tasks? In order for your stress level to even out, you need to create a balance between the stress producers and the stress reducers.

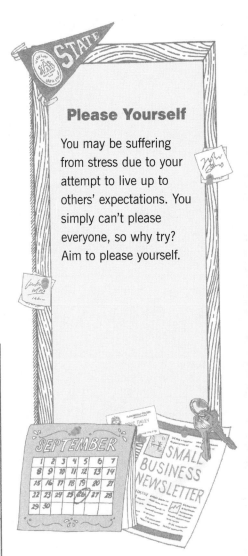

Please Yourself

You may be suffering from stress due to your attempt to live up to others' expectations. You simply can't please everyone, so why try? Aim to please yourself.

Time Began	Activity	Time Ended	Stress Producer	Stress Reducer
5:45 a.m.	Alarm clock goes off—15 minutes of snooze time	6:00 a.m.		X
6:00 a.m.	Dress, start coffee, stretch	6:20 a.m.		X
6:20 a.m.	Jogging	7:05 a.m.		X
7:05 a.m.	Shower	7:20 a.m.		X
7:20 a.m.	Dress, hair, makeup, etc.	8:00 a.m.	X	
8:00 a.m.	Coffee, breakfast, morning paper	8:30 a.m.		X
8:30 a.m.	Commute to work	9:00 a.m.	X	
9:00 a.m.	* Greet fellow employees * Answer voice mail and e-mail * Check planner for daily schedule	9:30 a.m.	X	
9:30 a.m.	Organize desk, final preparation for meeting	9:40 a.m.		X
9:40 a.m.	Personal phone call	9:50 a.m.		X

(continued)

Time Began	Activity	Time Ended	Stress Producer	Stress Reducer
9:50 a.m.	Use restroom, refill coffee, head to conference room	10:00 a.m.		X
10:00 a.m.	Meeting with VP and marketing	11:30 a.m.	X	
11:30 a.m.	Down time—talk with fellow employees, refresh in restroom, relax	12:00 p.m.		X
12:00 p.m.	Walk to deli	12:10 p.m.		X
12:10 p.m.	Lunch and gossip with coworkers	12:50 p.m		X
12:50 p.m.	Walk back to work	1:00 p.m.		X
1:00 p.m.	Paperwork/research	1:50 p.m.	X	
1:50 p.m.	Chat with coworker	2:05 p.m.		X
2:05 p.m.	Paperwork/research	2:45 p.m.	X	
2:45 p.m.	Outline proposal	3:00 p.m.	X	
3:00 p.m.	Write proposal	3:05 p.m.	X	
3:05 p.m.	Personal phone call	3:15 p.m.		X
3:15 p.m.	Coffee, restroom break, chat with coworkers	3:35 p.m		X
3:35 p.m.	Write proposal	4:40 p.m.	X	
4:40 p.m.	Break	4:50 p.m.	X	
4:50 p.m.	Clean desk, organize things for tomorrow	5:05 p.m.	X	
5:05 p.m.	Commute	5:30 p.m.	X	
5:30 p.m.	Post office	5:45 p.m.	X	
5:45 p.m.	Driving	6:00 p.m.	X	
6:00 p.m.	Grocery shopping	6:35 p.m.	X	
6:35 p.m.	Drive home	6:50 p.m.	X	
6:50 p.m.	Unwind, relax with drink	7:10 p.m.		X
7:10 p.m.	Prepare/eat/clean up dinner	8:00 p.m.	X	
8:00 p.m.	Phone calls to friends	8:30 p.m.		X
8:30 p.m.	Drive to Laundromat	8:40 p.m.	X	
8:40 p.m.	Laundry, read magazine	9:40 p.m.	X	
9:40 p.m.	Drive home	9:50 p.m.	X	
9:50 p.m.	Drop laundry—collapse on couch in front of TV	11:00 p.m.		X
11:00 p.m.	Wash up, go to bed			X
Total			**20**	**19**

If you still don't have a good idea of how to relieve stress, picture yourself completely relaxed. What is it you see? Are you lying down? Reading a book? Refusing to stifle that yawn? Whatever works to ease your body and mind is a stress reducer. Participating in enjoyable activities is also a way to reduce the negative effects of stress. Do you reward yourself with a fun activity following a stressful activity?

If you are like most people, your stress producers will heavily outweigh the stress reducers. Although there are little things that can be done to lower your stress level, such as stretching or taking a deep breath, more often than not with the completion of one activity, a new activity instantly begins. This only compounds stress, which can cause it to reach dangerous levels. If you don't allow yourself a break, tension will rule your life on a day-to-day basis.

Adjusting to Achieve Balance

Okay, we've established that stress just isn't going to go away, so what can we do about it? How do we achieve the balance that is so important for our physical and mental well-being?

Your handy priority list comes into play once again here. Maintaining a focus on what is important will allow you to focus less on the trivial things of life that have a tendency to grate on your nerves. If you realize that the task you are working on isn't of great importance, you will be less intense toward its completion. Try to put everything you do into perspective. If it doesn't take up a lot of space in the big picture, it doesn't warrant considerable stress.

If you are able, eliminate as many stress producers as possible. For instance, if driving in morning traffic sets your teeth on edge, consider public transportation. Or, if that isn't an option, inquire if anyone would be interested in carpooling. Perhaps you could even take a different, less popular route to escape the crowds.

Make stress reducers a part of your schedule. Take breaks often, even if they are only two minutes long. Those two minutes will do you a world of good in the long run. If a warm bath relaxes you, make it a part of your routine. Stretch frequently if you are going to be working diligently for an extended period of time. Don't give the stress time to make it to your muscles.

While you can't control every aspect of your life, there are several ways you can get around the amount of stress placed on you. Be creative. Do something out of the ordinary, if need be. The important thing is to make the proper adjustments, whether in attitude or action, to balance the producers with the reducers. Whichever you allow to gain ground will determine your state of stress.

Maintaining Methods of Healthy Living

There are several ways you can curb the negative effects of stress. If you can't eliminate the stress, don't feel powerless. You can still live a healthy and happy life. The following are some suggestions to help you deal with stress affirmatively:

- **Eat healthy.** This isn't to say a nice chunk of chocolate once in a while is going to ruin all your efforts for stress management. But keep in mind that a healthy life is a happy life.
- **Get enough sleep.** With a good night's sleep you will wake refreshed and ready to take on the world. Stress will have a harder time worming its way into your day if you are well rested.
- **Exercise.** It is good for you not only physically but emotionally as well. With the exertion of exercise you are able to get out pent-up frustrations and tension. Plus, if you are physically fit, you will feel better about your appearance, which in turn raises your self-esteem level.
- **Don't take life too seriously.** Have fun and laugh. Laughter is the best medicine, after all.
- **Treat yourself to a massage and/or bubble bath.**

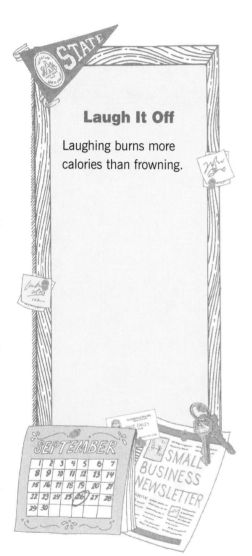

Laugh It Off

Laughing burns more calories than frowning.

- **Don't bottle your emotions.** If you keep drowning your emotions, never allowing them to surface, the pressure will become so great you will eventually explode.
- **Don't worry about things that are beyond your control.** Let go. Unnecessary worry only creates unnecessary anxiety. You are also likely to adopt an overall feeling of helplessness, which may spill over into your other activities.
- **Use escapism (healthy escapism) in moderation.** Don't go overboard and run away from your problems, but it helps to take a step back once in a while to try to get an objective view of the situation. Take a drive in the country or a walk in the park to get away from the situation temporarily and clear your head before trying to tackle it once more.
- **Maintain a positive attitude.** Don't expect the worst or you may very well make it happen.
- **Reward yourself.**

A Tasty Reward

Keep in mind that "stressed" spelled backward is "desserts"!

Setting Up a Routine

While some people will be bored to tears at just the thought of a routine, others live their lives by one. There are pros and cons to the use of routines. Just like habits, there are the good and the bad. Routines can greatly benefit your management of time, but they can also hinder it. So where do you draw the line? When is a routine in your best interests and when will it drag you down?

We will get to the pros and cons in just a moment, but first let's examine your life and see what routines you already have set up, if any. For instance, you may wake up at the same time every day, put on a pot of coffee, shower, eat, brush your teeth, and so forth. A routine doesn't have to be every day, though. It may occur once a week or once a month. If you do the same activities in the same order on a regular basis, you have yourself a routine. Now, do you want the good news or the bad news first? Let's go with the good news.

Pros

There are several advantages to using a routine. A routine becomes a habit, and habits require very little prior thought. Let's take the above example for instance. Your morning routine does not require you to stop and think about what you are going to do once you wake up or after you shower or after you eat. The following actions are already assigned; you simply go through the motions. So you save yourself the time not only of thinking, but also of making a decision.

Routines are easy to schedule. If an activity is completed on a regular basis, you will have a pretty good idea of how long it is going to take you. Even though your estimates of time are often up in the air, your routine should be quite a reliable guess. You know how much time to allow yourself to get ready for work in the morning because it is something you do every day. Because of this, you set your alarm clock for a specified time and know at what time you should be walking out the door. Already your day has begun on a successful note—and all due to a routine.

Others can schedule around you more easily if they are aware of your routines. Often it is very difficult to make two schedules mesh. However, if you have a routine that will not falter, the other person can easily find areas in his or her own schedule that can complement yours. It is kind of like shooting: It is much easier to hit a still target than a moving one.

Routines will give you a sense of safety and comfort. If you don't have to wonder what is going to happen minute by minute, your stress level will not be nearly as high. Even though the rest of your schedule and surroundings may be chaotic and disorganized, you will find peace in the comfort zone of your routine. In contrast to the never-ending uncertainties of life, with a routine you will know what is going to happen and when.

Routines possess quite a few qualities that can make your life simpler. Think about how you can incorporate a routine into your time management system.

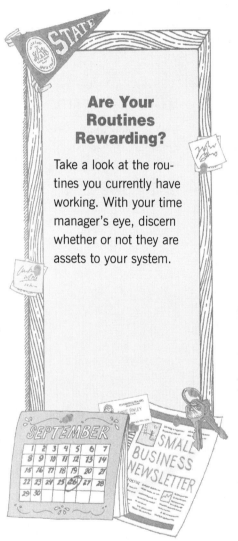

Are Your Routines Rewarding?

Take a look at the routines you currently have working. With your time manager's eye, discern whether or not they are assets to your system.

Cons

As with pretty much anything, there will be an upside and a downside with routines. Now that you know all the benefits, you should be warned of the dangers.

First of all, routines can overload your schedule. You should not schedule one routine right after another to fill your whole day. If you schedule for routines, make sure they are dispersed throughout the day. It is unrealistic to think that you can live your life according to one big schedule. It just doesn't work that way. Unexpected events are sure to occur, leaving you unprepared and defenseless. However, if you are aware of the unforeseen possibilities, you will at least be mentally, if not physically, prepared. Remember that good time management will have a firm base in reality.

Believe it or not, routines can actually affect your self-esteem, and not always in a positive way. It was mentioned above how routines will serve as a comfort zone. This is good to have in your hectic life, but not at all times. You cannot hide out in your comfort zone. If you get used to doing this, you will eventually create a box around yourself that separates you from the world. You will become more and more dependent on the comfort zone, believing yourself to be incapable of dealing with any other interaction. Your self-esteem will plummet, as will your management of time and overall quality of life.

Routines can sometimes be unhealthy and boring, but if used wisely will have a tremendous positive impact on your time management system. The key is to know when enough is enough. Don't let yourself get stuck in a rut. You need that excitement that chaos brings every once in a while.

Good Routines

If you aren't sure where to draw that line, consider some of the following ideas for tasks that work well within a routine:

- Taking your medicine or vitamins at the same time every day
- Walking your dog during specified times throughout the day

- Making one (and only one) trip to the post office every week
- An end-of-the-month review of your priorities and goals
- Exercising

Bad Routines

Now let's take a look at some activities that don't work well within a routine:

- Going clothes shopping every day
- Making negative statements about yourself
- Falling in love every day
- Losing your car keys
- Being late

Suit Yourself

Now that you have an idea of what you should and shouldn't do with a routine, take a look at your schedule. Where can you incorporate a routine that will benefit your life? Do you have any routines that are hindering your quality of life and maybe even your management of time?

Learn to Say No

A big stumbling block for nearly all time managers is the inability to say no. "Yes" is such a positive and pleasant word, and because we like to think of ourselves as nice and helpful, our use of that word seems appropriate. However, that one little word can become the enemy when it comes to managing your time.

Reasons You Say Yes

There are several reasons why you may feel the urge to say yes too often. Perhaps it's a supervisor or parent asking you to do something, and, out of fear or respect, you are uncomfortable denying his or her request. Perhaps you consider yourself to be

an upbeat and positive person, and having such a negative word as "no" in your vocabulary could shatter that image. Maybe you worry someone will not like you if you refuse them. Perhaps the thought of running out of things to do terrifies you, so you actually jump on the opportunity to accept a request. Perhaps you feel as though you don't have a good enough excuse to justify using the word "no." Or it may simply be that you do not know how to say no.

Consequences of Saying Yes

These reasons don't seem so bad, but take a look at some of the repercussions. If you are a habitual yes-man/woman, it is likely you are placing the priorities of others in front of your own. You will rush through your own work to complete the work of others. Perhaps you may even disregard your own work. You will take on more projects than you can handle and resort to ignoring those things that are important to you just to get the work finished. Your level of stress will reach unbelievable heights. You will not eat and exercise regularly, causing your health to deteriorate. Your loved ones will feel neglected.

This is a lot to sacrifice for the benefit of someone else, and, chances are, you don't have any true obligation to anyone else. In the long run, recognizing that you can learn to say no and still be the good guy socially will free up your time considerably.

How to Say No

First, you have to convince yourself that the word "no" does not always have a negative effect. Yes, the word itself is a negative, but no, that doesn't mean it will have negative connotations each time you use it.

Let go of the idea that people will dislike you for saying no. In fact, your ability to say no and defend your own priorities should invite, if not demand, respect.

Quite often people have difficulty saying no because they can't come up with a good enough reason to excuse themselves. You

don't need an excuse. You don't need to get defensive and explain yourself (unless of course it is your boss or spouse bearing down on you with those frowning eyebrows). As long as you decline graciously, there should be no reason for any further conversation. Making excuses only prolongs the conversation. It also allows the other person an opening to offer suggestions as to how to get around your excuse. Say no and move on.

If you are in the habit of accepting proposals automatically and just can't seem to help yourself, slow down. When faced with an offer, force yourself to wait. Take a breath and think before opening your mouth. This will allow you the time to consider the effect your decision will have on your life. Also, as an added bonus, you give the impression that you consider the other person's proposition to be significant and worthy of thought.

If you simply can't get it out of your head that saying no is not discourteous, don't give up. Bear in mind, it is discourteous to accept a task you are unable to finish or one that you do finish, but poorly. Perhaps you could soften the refusal by recommending someone else for the job or an easy way to accomplish it. By offering suggestions, you will show your interest and indicate that you regret being unavailable for the chore. You may even decide to play a small role in its completion, as long as it does not interfere with your own schedule. However, don't succumb to guilt and don't lose your focus.

Above all, if you mean no, say no. Don't try to delay the issue with a maybe. Don't nod your head and look so put-off by the idea that the other person regrets approaching you. Don't stammer over excuses before deciding one way or the other. Do not allow your priorities to leave your mind. Learning to say no may mean saying yes to your life.

The Luxury of Leisure

Ask anyone in pursuit of time management skills why she feels she needs them, and the phrase "leisure time" will pop up in her

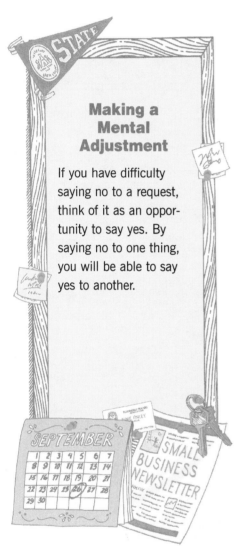

Making a Mental Adjustment

If you have difficulty saying no to a request, think of it as an opportunity to say yes. By saying no to one thing, you will be able to say yes to another.

answer somewhere. Leisure time, like money, indicates success. It is something we all outwardly strive for—even if it's not really something we want—but what happens once we get it? Would we know what to do with it? Some of us may do nothing but revel in the fact that we actually have leisure time. Then, once it's over, it will have done us very little good, and so we strive for it again. Others will run away from it. The thought of not having anything to do is terrifying, so any potential leisure time is filled with nonsensical tasks.

Leisure Hang-Ups

So how do we get past our leisure hang-ups? The trick is to rid your mind of any and all guilt you may feel toward having leisure time. Relax. You deserve free time—free from the constant demands of life, free from the little surprises that aren't always welcome, free from your own driving motivation to be superhuman. Free. Do you even know what that means? If not, it's time for a little reflection.

You know what your goals and aspirations are. You even know what your priorities are. But what do you enjoy? Have ever sat down and thought about this question? Or have you been so busy accomplishing what is expected of you, that you have just forgotten? Forget the phrase "leisure time," and instead change it to "me time."

Put aside all thoughts of work, your spouse, your kids, your obligations, your needs, and your worries. Can you do that? Well, try. Now kick back, relax, and let your mind swarm with things you think may be fun. Yes, fun. Pretend that money is not an issue, neither is location.

How Will You Handle Leisure?

You have the luxury of leisure in the palm of your hand. What are you going to do with it? Perhaps you have always wanted to learn to tango. How about going skinny-dipping in the Mediterranean Sea? Fly-fishing? Visiting the pyramids of Egypt? Smelling the flowers in your neighbor's backyard? Playing baseball? Wrestling a grizzly bear? No matter how far out your ideas of fun

are, they are yours. Hopefully, just thinking of all the possibilities has put a smile on your face. Now what would you do if you were actually able to carry out some of them?

This is what leisure time is for. It is the time to bring enjoyment to your life. Note that the word "time" is involved. We know how valuable time is, and leisure time is no different. Start with the most realistic of all your possibilities and truly consider it. Perhaps you can take tango lessons the first and third Thursdays of every month while your daughter is at Girl Scouts. Don't laugh at the idea; try to make it work! You will thank yourself later.

Jason and Andrea Battle Stress

Jason and Andrea both understand the repercussions stress can have on their health and overall quality of life. However, they didn't realize that it also has a serious effect on their efforts to manage time. This chapter was a wake-up call for both of them. They each handle stress differently and, therefore, aren't always aware of the stress the other is under, which in turn can create even more stress. Creating a healthy and happy life is their ultimate goal. Battling negative stress will help them to achieve this.

Jason

Stress for Jason has always manifested itself in the form of headaches and most often occurs in his personal life and home life. This isn't to say that either one of these areas is unpleasant, it's just that he feels the most tension here. Work, though challenging and deadline oriented, rarely gives him headaches. He therefore assumes that he is under no stress in the office.

However, what Jason has learned is that he is never without stress. A major factor that contributes to how he handles the stress is his management of time. Therefore, he will obviously feel

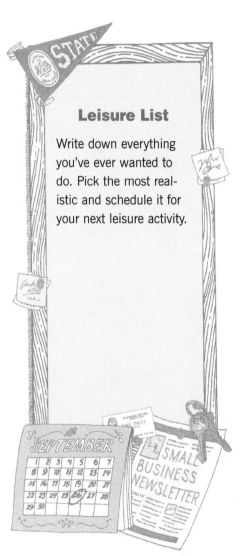

Leisure List

Write down everything you've ever wanted to do. Pick the most realistic and schedule it for your next leisure activity.

the effects of stress more so at home and in his personal life because these are the areas in which his management of time is the weakest.

Jason takes the stress test and finds that he actually has a rather high stress level. He is surprised by this outcome, considering his headaches aren't all that frequent. But headaches aren't the only side effect of stress, as he originally thought. He also suffers from a lack of concentration, forgetfulness, irritability, impatience, and muscle tension. Hoping to escape these side effects, Jason takes steps to reduce his stress level, not only at home and in his personal life, but at work as well.

First, he decides that he has no choice but to end his work day when he leaves the office. He cannot continue taking work home with him on a regular basis. Although this idea has already been addressed in his time management system, the stress factor adds to its importance. Also, he realizes that this practice has been creating stress for his family as well.

Next, he is going to concentrate on taking life a little less seriously. His diligence and drive carry over into every other part of his life, creating stress all over the place. He resolves to smile and laugh more and to find the humor in simple everyday life.

Finally, he is going to seek the help of his wife and son to make decisions. Not all decisions of course, since he still needs a bit of independence. But as it stands now, he shies away from asking for help. Sometimes decisions, especially if they affect the entire family, need consultation. This will strike a sour note with his ego, but he knows it is the smart thing to do.

These three steps aren't going to get Jason to a perfectly balanced stress level, but they will help considerably. Now that he realizes what stress is, he can work to handle it well on a day-to-day basis.

Andrea

Andrea knows she is under constant stress but has always thought it helps her to get things done. She considers stress to be a motivator and actually gives most of the credit for her accomplishments to stress. Most of the stress she encounters is actually self-inflicted. She has set high standards for herself in terms of a high quantity of tasks. While high standards are often a good thing, when they are set as high as Andrea's they become somewhat unrealistic and therefore quite stressful.

She doesn't even bother to take the stress test, since the outcome would only create more stress. However, she does take a look at the stress producers versus the stress reducers in her life. Her daily schedule itself is a big stress producer. Activities are pretty much scheduled back to back, and she knows some of them will be multitasked with something else. Each one of the activities creates an anxious feeling inside her. Because of her old habits, she feels she should rush herself at every turn. She also incorporates stimulants such as caffeine and sugar on an almost nonstop basis throughout the day.

Stress reducers are few and far between. Because she realizes the importance of breaks after coming this far in the book, she does manage to schedule two into each day. However, the breaks are too long, for Andrea anyway. It is quite likely she would start out with the best intentions of taking a break and then end up bored and taking on an activity to pass the time. She has scheduled neither exercise nor enough sleep.

Andrea realizes that her management of time is going to have the greatest effect on balancing out her stress level. She also decides on three major steps to take toward a balanced stress level.

First, she will take out the eraser and fix her schedule. She is going to break the big breaks up into smaller, more frequent, ones and stick to them. By scattering them throughout the day, she will have a chance to stop and take stock of what she is doing and its importance. This will go a long way toward breaking up her stay-on-the-run attitude. So, the breaks will reduce her stress not only physically but mentally as well.

Next, she is going to incorporate an exercise routine into her schedule. Even if she can buy only 15 minutes a day, she is going to write it down and make it happen. She figures if she can work this into the middle of her day, the exercise will have the greatest effect on lowering her stress. Right around early afternoon is when her body begins to ache and tense up. Stretching will help ease this muscular tension.

Finally, she is determined to create more time for herself. She already cherishes those brief moments she can find to be alone with her thoughts. But since these happen very rarely and seem to end before they begin, she never really focused on them. Now that she is in control of how she spends her time, she plans on making the most of this necessary luxury.

The End Result

Both Jason and Andrea have calculated steps to take to reduce their stress levels. They first had to recognize the sources of their stress, and then decide what changes to make. However, in doing so, they have also taken steps toward their ultimate goal of managing time. Now, whether this little fact played a role in their decision to reduce stress is irrelevant. The fact remains, they will better their stress level, thereby bettering their management of time and vice versa.

Jason and Andrea have successfully completed the first nine chapters. They have welcomed time management into their lives. Now they are able to concentrate on and find time for what is important to them and work on creating the ideal happy and stable family. Since they have managed to get their own lives under control, they are eager to share their newfound knowledge

and experience with their son. After all, he was the catalyst that forced them to acknowledge their need for time management in the first place.

Matthew will benefit in several different ways from his parents' control of time. As a teenager, he is at an opportune time in his life to learn the skills needed for time management. He will learn firsthand the effects a successful time management system can have on the overall quality of life. And he will never have to walk home in the rain again.

PART THREE

Applying the Basics to Your Life

If you have made it this far, you have already set your plan in motion. Take a minute to congratulate yourself. You have come a long way toward fulfilling your time management dreams. You've successfully completed the hard part.

This part of the book will give you suggestions on how to apply those basics to your life. It will cover your home life, your work life, and your personal life. But you needn't stop there. If there are other important aspects of your life, let your time management system take a foothold in those as well.

Because everyone's life is different, it is important to remember that your time management system will differ from someone else's. Not every suggestion offered is going to complement your system. However, don't dismiss entirely those suggestions that don't seem to apply to you. You may find that, with a bit of alteration, a suggestion may be a perfect match. Also, consider branching out from those suggestions offered. They are designed as general ideas that could fit easily into the average person's life. But you are a unique individual; therefore, some will work out and others will need adjustment.

The rest of the book explores:

- Organizing your house
- Relocating with ease
- Making the most of your commute to work
- How to delegate effectively in the workplace
- Organizing for convenience

- The importance of effective communication
- Using your vacation time wisely
- Utilizing your time management skills to lead a healthier life
- Finding time to further your education
- Creating and using personal time

While these suggestions will help you make the most of your time management skills, the most important section of each chapter is where we discuss how to maintain a constant time management system for each aspect of your life. This idea is essential to incorporate. Without maintenance, all your hard work thus far will have been for naught. A time management system can work only if it is being put to use.

Time management encompasses three main tactics: devise a strategy, apply it to your life, and maintain management. So far, you have done two out of three. You are now ready for the final stretch. Get ready, get set, and go manage your time!

Your House on Your Time

You go to work, you go to parties, you even take weeks at a time away on vacation, but you always come back to your home. Because your home is the central point for all your activities, it is imperative that you apply your time management system here. The condition and organization of your home can directly affect the condition and organization of your life outside. By getting your home life in order, you will start and end each day on a peaceful note.

Practicing What You've Learned

Time management for the home means keeping the house clean, feeding the children regularly, and occasionally relaxing in front of the fireplace, right? Well, sort of. Those things are certainly part of it, but there's also a lot more involved. And everything you've learned in the previous chapters of this book can apply to it.

Step One

What is your attitude toward the time spent at home? Really think about this. Are you comfortable, peaceful, and time unaware in your house? Or do you dread going home because there is never enough time to get things done there? Is your time valuable at home? Can you define the relationship you have with time?

Answer all of these questions. Compare your home life to your work life if it makes it a little easier to pin down. Also keep in mind that your home life does not include your personal life. In other words, your home life is made up of primarily activities that are accomplished at home. For example, while laundry may be a very personal matter, it is going to fall under the classification of home life instead of personal life.

Once you know what your attitude is, you are going to be able to either work with it or around it, whichever is the safest. This knowledge is your foundation.

Step Two

Track your use of time. Keep a time log of all of your activities and time spent on these activities. Record everything! This is extremely important. We don't want any guesswork as to where your time is going. That would be cheating. So, if you really spend 45 minutes savoring that chocolate sundae, then don't mark it as 5 minutes. This is for your own use, no one else's. You may want to keep a log for a few days, maybe even a week. It is hard to get the full effect of time spent from just one day. Since some days are hellish and others are a breeze; it pays to get an average.

Step Three

Determine what your priorities are. Don't allow anyone else to set your priorities. Your priorities are what matter to you and you alone. Sure, they may incorporate your family and friends, but the value is placed by only you.

Remember that we are just focusing on the home right now. Don't let work or your social life come into play here; they have their own time set aside for later.

Use the master list you created at the beginning of the book. Remember, you should have it within reach at all times. Scan over it and pull out those items that apply to your home. If you think of any more, add them now. Then rank each one in order of importance.

Step Four

Now you need to shift your focus. Don't concentrate on the completion of tasks. Of course, you need to be aware of them, but don't allow yourself to focus just on getting them done. You need to focus on your priorities and what is important in your life. Everything else is the small stuff. Are the tasks you complete currently in line with your priorities? You should concentrate on the quality and not the quantity of tasks.

Step Five

Set goals. It's not as bad as it sounds. You should have a set of goals made already. Again, pull out the work you did at the beginning of the book. Did you create a division for your home life? If so, use these goals to get you started. If not, you should take the time to go through this process right now. See Chapter 2 for instructions.

Once you have both short- and long-term goals set, consider the steps it will take to reach these goals within the given time allotment. Are they realistic? Will you be able to fit them into your schedule? Don't take on too much. Your goals shouldn't all have to be completed at the same time. Remember to be as specific as possible.

Step Six

Create a to-do list. Start off daily. What are the things you need to accomplish at home today? Include the steps toward your goals, urgencies, important items, and even throw in a few wants. Yes, you may end up with a rather large list, but don't worry about that now. Once you have several items, use your prioritization skills to rank them in order of precedence. Remember, this list is not set in stone. It can and will be changed as you go along. Right now you just want to record the possibilities.

Next to each item, give an estimated time for completion. Be realistic. It is important to get as close as possible to the actual time it will take you to complete the task. However, you may also want to tack on just a little extra time. It is better to overestimate than underestimate.

Step Seven

Create your schedule. Your to-do list should be used as the foundation for creating your schedule. This is where you are going to incorporate all that needs to be done into your life. You will give time to tasks based on importance and urgency. Look over your to-do list, starting at the beginning. Because you have already ranked the items, it should be easy for you to decide which ones make the cut.

Remember that these items apply only to your home. It would create a pretty nasty mess of your schedule if you plan to do your laundry while you are in a meeting at work. What are the times of day you are available to work at home? Disregard the time slots that are designated for work or your personal life. You may find that leaves little time for the home, but this is reality and that is all you have to work with.

Don't overload yourself, and allow a little cushioning. You want to get things done, but you also need to add a little downtime. Don't forget the importance of breaks! All this should be added to your schedule.

Step Eight

Organize. Your home is Grand Central Station for the rest of your life. That's why it is important to be as organized as you can be at home. If things run smoothly at home, chances are things will run smoothly on the outside. Let's face it, you are yourself at home. You may put on a bit of a facade at work, but your home is where you are who you really are.

Step Nine

Reward yourself! This is extremely important. You have turned your home into a relaxed and ordered paradise. You deserve a reward. It has been a lot of hard work, and you have passed with flying colors. If you maintain your basic time management skills and apply them regularly to your home, you do not have to do the grit work again.

Cleaning the House

Even if you have decided to hire someone to clean your house, chances are you will still need to do it yourself from time to time. But it doesn't always have to be the headache you anticipate. If you get a time-efficient pattern down pat, upkeep will require very little of your time.

Okay, in case you haven't done this for a while, let's go over the basics of house cleaning. We have dusting, scrubbing, mopping, vacuuming, glass and window washing, picking up, and airing out. Sounds pretty rough, doesn't it? But try this idea on for size: Not all of this needs to be done every single time you clean the house. Shh, don't let your mother know about this. She may try to persuade you otherwise.

Biannual Cleaning

Let's face it, you just don't have the time to battle the house every day, and you shouldn't have to. You are going to learn how to maintain a plan that requires only two down-and-dirty cleanings a year. Whether you live alone or with a family of ten, you can make this work for you.

First, we are going to take a look at those two cleanings per year. You will want to spread them out, with six months between each. Also, these are going to be pretty arduous, so schedule them for times of the year when you will have some downtime. Don't think you can get this done during Christmas vacation. That is unrealistic and just plain suicidal.

You are going to thoroughly clean your house from top to bottom twice a year. This includes sorting through the junk in the attic, scrubbing the basement floor, and venturing in to remove the "science experiments" growing in your child's room. Every single item in your home will be touched. If you choose to delegate areas of the house to other members of the family or truly loyal friends, make sure they are trustworthy. If you don't do a thorough job with this now, you will have to spend even more time on it later. Depending on the size of your home, this could take you a few hours or a few weeks. Remember to schedule realistically. At the end of each of these cleanings, your home should be immaculate and able to pass the white glove test.

These two cleanings are important because they serve as the foundation for the upkeep of your home. During these two fun-filled times, you will take notes on what needs to be done to maintain the house. For instance, if there is a hole in the wall in one of

Wipe Your Feet!

Use doormats and encourage visitors and family to remove their shoes when entering the house. This will cut down on the amount of dirt, allowing you to clean less often.

your closets, that needs to be written down. Or perhaps the roof leaks slightly in one area of the attic. Every single thing that needs to be fixed should be noted. This doesn't mean they all need to be taken care of right away, just acknowledged.

Once the cleaning is done, you will want to take out your notes on what needs to be fixed around the house. List them in order of importance and urgency. Then use your calendar to find a good time of the year to have them worked on. Don't go overboard and schedule everything within the first month. Some things can wait a bit. Just knowing what needs to be done is half the battle. You will want to do this each time you complete your biannual cleaning. If at all possible, shoot to get everything fixed within the six months— if you can afford it—so next time around you can start fresh.

Once you have finished the grand gala, you can rest easy. Maintenance, and pretty much anything else you will ever do, will seem quite simplistic in comparison. Now comes the easy part.

Dusting

Dusting makes quite the difference between a seemingly spotless house and a dirty one. Because it is all about the surface of items, this is the first thing to be noticed. If you don't have the time to clean your house, but you are expecting company, give it a quick dusting. You'll be amazed at the difference it makes. You don't even have to pull out the spray cleaner, just use a lamb's wool or feather duster and quickly give everything a once over.

You shouldn't have to dust the house more than once a week, unless you live on a dry dirt road and keep the front door open at all times. Limiting the number of times the doors to the outside are opened and closed will make a significant impact on the amount of dust that accumulates in the house. Screens are favored in place of just leaving the windows open. Request that anyone who has been playing or working outside and wants admittance into your home brush themselves off outside before entering.

You will want to use a spray cleaner to dust with every two weeks or once a month, depending on your time schedule. This will help the condition of your furniture and give the house a

One Wastebasket, Two Wastebaskets, Three . . .

You can never have too many wastebaskets. Make sure each room in the house has one. This will encourage visitors and family to dispose of those empty wrappers right away. If they have to get up and walk all the way across the house, who's going to blame them for stuffing them between the couch cushions?

deeper cleaning. Dusting should always be done before vacuuming. If you are going to give the entire house a once over, work your way from the top down.

Dusting shouldn't be a strenuous job that takes up a lot of your time. Don't worry about getting in the cracks every time. Those cracks will be taken care of during the biannual cleanings. It is a superficial task and should be handled as such.

The Floors

After dusting usually come the floors. If at all possible, clean the floors immediately following the dusting. The dust doesn't just magically disappear. If you allow it to get stirred up again, your dusting exercise may have to be repeated too soon. How you handle the floors depends on what type of flooring you have. For instance, dark carpets can go a little longer than light-colored carpets without a cleaning. Plush carpeting is going to take more time to vacuum than a Berber carpet.

Vacuuming can be hard work and time consuming, so you probably want to stay away from it as much as possible. One way to get around vacuuming is to use a nonelectrical carpet sweeper to pick up dirt and other foreign items quickly and conveniently. Of course, this can't take the place of vacuuming altogether. You will still need the sucking power of a vacuum to get rid of the ground-in dirt. However, don't feel it is necessary to move all the furniture each time you vacuum. It may sound like you are cheating, but really now, is anyone going to be on his stomach checking out the floor beneath the couch? Why spend your time on something that isn't going to show?

For tiled floors, mopping is the route to take. You will probably want to get down on your hands and knees and scrub them like Little Orphan Annie during the biannual cleaning, but this shouldn't be done every time. You don't even have to completely mop the whole floor every single time. Use the spot mop technique for quick jobs. Why clean what isn't dirty?

If you have hardwood floors covered by area rugs, these need to be taken outside and shaken and/or beaten. Outside is key here.

The Cleaning Schedule

The next time you clean the house, record the amount of time it takes you to complete each task. For instance, note that it takes you 30 minutes to dust the entire house, or, if you plan to clean in sections, note how long it takes to dust each individual room. This will allow you to schedule realistically in the future.

Don't give yourself extra work to do by shaking them indoors. Leave them outside to air and out of the way while you clean the floors. A dust mop works well on hardwood floors and picks up more than just a regular sweeping. Again, don't feel the need to get under furniture every single time. Waxing and buffing should be done during the biannual cleanings.

Scrubbing

No one likes scrubbing, even professional cleaners. This is why there are several products out on the market devised to keep scrubbing to a minimum. There are shower cleaners you can spray on after each use to cut down on buildup, toilet bowl disks that emit a cleaning solution with every flush, and spray cleaners that work to break down buildup on their own, so you are left with only a wipe-down. Take advantage of these products. They will save you time in the long run. Of course, you can't bypass scrubbing altogether. Do so on an as-needed basis. If you fail to do this, once you get around to it, the buildup may be so terrible that it could take you hours to complete the task.

Glass and Window Washing

This should be done thoroughly twice a year. As for the rest of the time, consider purchasing a wedge-woven rag. These rags need only water and clean glass just as well as a store-bought glass cleaner. All you need to do is run the rag under water, wring it out, and wipe. This saves you the time and energy of spraying the glass down with the cleaner and wiping it dry, trying to keep it free of streaks. These rags also work well on just about any type of surface. Use them all over the house for a quick clean.

Staying Neat

The secret strategy against a messy house is to put away things after each use. Think about how it feels to walk into a house with items slung everywhere. You get that sinking feeling and just know

Quick Cleaning Tip

Use aluminum foil to cover the burner pans on your stovetop. No more scrubbing and scratching involved. When it gets dirty, tear away the aluminum foil and pitch it!

your house desperately needs a good cleaning, even if it really doesn't. On the other hand, if you walk into the house when everything is in its place, you can relax and be comfortable. Don't underestimate the power of perception.

Keeping things in their place will save you time in many ways. Household activities will run smoother, allowing tasks to be done efficiently. You will not spend time searching for lost items. Cleaning will be much easier to accomplish if you don't have to first pick up and put away items that are in the way. The overall peaceful feeling you have when things are not scattered about in the open will lower your stress level, making your use of time easier to keep control of.

The Upkeep Strategy

Cleaning your house should be done on a regular basis. Remember when we talked about routines? This is a good activity to incorporate. Even with all the shortcuts you can find, the cleaning still needs to be done. If you designate certain days to particular chores, such as naming Thursday as dusting and vacuuming day, you will fall into the habit of getting it done and out of the way. Perhaps you would rather clean room by room. So, schedule the living room to be done one day and the kitchen the next. It's up to you, just make sure it complements your time management system.

Also, make use of your delegation skills. If you aren't the only one to live in the house, then you shouldn't be the only one responsible for keeping it clean. Perhaps you are thrilled by the idea of hiring out for the job. If you don't have such an expense budgeted, consider doing it on an irregular basis. Let the professionals handle the tough jobs, and keep the easy upkeep for your own schedule.

Cleaning takes little thought and concentration. Therefore, you can multitask. If there is a radio program you enjoy listening to, turn it on while you clean. The same goes for the television. Schedule the living room to be done when your favorite show is on. Don't torture yourself with house cleaning. Try to make it as

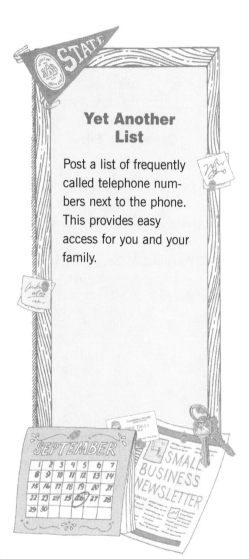

Yet Another List

Post a list of frequently called telephone numbers next to the phone. This provides easy access for you and your family.

enjoyable as possible, and if that means bringing in outside forces, by all means do so.

Furnishing Food

What is one of the first things that comes to mind when you think of the picture-perfect 1950s home life? That fantastic steaming-hot dinner all set out, ready and waiting for you at the table? Is that a regular sight in your home? Probably not. But that doesn't mean you can't have that scene every once in a while, if not every day.

We live in an age of television dinners, frozen entrees, and fast food on the run; that is, if we have time to eat at all. But because your health is vital, and a big chunk of that health relies on good nutrition, it is important for a good time manager such as yourself to learn to make healthy meals within the small allotment of time you have available. If you have children, you are responsible for their nutrition as well. Why not learn to eat well, be healthy, and save time all at once?

In the following pages you'll find ways you can organize your kitchen for the ultimate time efficiency as well as consolidate meals according to preparation time and technique.

Organizing for Convenience

Do a quick walk-through of the kitchen, opening every cabinet and drawer. Then, draw a small model of your kitchen and label where everything is currently located. Now, consider what you use each group of items for. Are they strategically placed throughout the kitchen for convenience? Or have you not given much thought to the layout as long as everything has a place?

If you haven't really considered it before, think now about how much time you spend walking back and forth across the kitchen or sometimes even into a different room retrieving items. Think about how much time you would save if everything you needed was within reach of the area you are working at. For instance, plates, glasses, and silverware could be located close to the kitchen or dining room table. Mixing bowls, measuring cups, rolling pins, and

so forth could be kept in cabinets above or close to the counter. Stovetop condiments such as salt, pepper, and oils could be placed in a cabinet above or next to the stove. Get the picture?

If your kitchen is currently in inconvenient disarray, you may want to use that picture you just sketched out and plan where to place things for more convenience. Having it down on paper is a lot less confusing and a lot less messy—not to mention less time consuming—than pulling everything out of the drawers and cabinets and then trying to figure out where to put everything.

What to Fix?

Now that you are prepared to prepare the meal, what are you going to fix? Assuming you have something healthy in mind, there will be no lecture on that subject. So, we have healthy, all the food groups covered, and as quick as possible. The key to a successful quick meal is timing.

You need to have an idea of how long each dish takes to prepare. People have a tendency to create a meal out of dishes that take either a lot of work to prepare or almost no preparation. Now, how often do you think they are going to fix the no-prep meals? Probably every time. But if you can find a balance between the no-prep and the lot-of-prep, that is ideal. This way, you won't be eating the same no-prep dishes time and time again. You will have coupled those with the dishes that need preparation, yet waste no time.

Consider how much of a hand you play in the preparation. For example, if a dish is comprised mainly of noodles, the length of time it takes for the noodles to cook is part of the prep time, but you really have little to do with that. You aren't busy chopping or mixing, your hands are free. So couple that dish with one that will keep you busy. This way, you can finish one dish while waiting to prepare the other.

Are there any meals you make that will freeze well? Think about making a double batch next time you fix a freezable meal. Certainly you've made a double batch of cookies before. How much more work did it take to make a double as opposed to a single batch? Not a whole lot. The same idea holds true for full

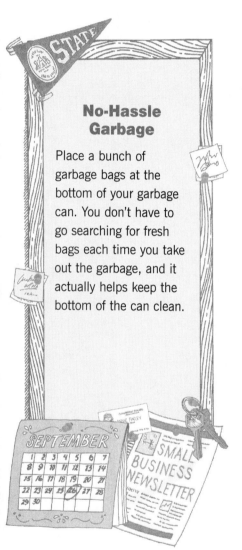

No-Hassle Garbage

Place a bunch of garbage bags at the bottom of your garbage can. You don't have to go searching for fresh bags each time you take out the garbage, and it actually helps keep the bottom of the can clean.

meals as well. You will not add a lot of time making it, yet you will come out with enough food for two meals. Freeze the second half to warm and serve later.

Meal Time!

Schedule time for meals! You are always going to complain you don't have time to eat if you don't make that time. Dinner doesn't have to be a six-course meal. As long as it is healthy and substantial, you can spend as much or as little time as you want. But make this a part of your routine. Give yourself a good-sized allotment of time every single day to make and eat dinner. Make it consistent.

We all know takeout isn't exactly the healthiest choice on a regular basis. But it isn't going to kill you if you give in to it every once in a while. Sometimes you just need that break. If your to-do list is backed up or things got wildly off schedule, order takeout. Let someone else do the work for you. When you get back on track, you can resume your efficient dinner making.

Planning meals ahead of time, having all ingredients available, multitasking with sense, and working within a convenient layout are all good ways to manage your time wisely while making dinner. Since meals are a part of your everyday home life, don't you think you should let your time management system get its claws into this area as well?

Organizing the Home

Organization in the home is important. You want to be able to walk in from a hard day's work to a simple and structured home life. You will do most of your relaxing at home, and it is here that you want an organizational system that allows for that relaxation to come to you with ease.

Earlier in the book, you began thinking about those organizational systems you already have in motion. Now you will expand on

those. How can they apply toward your home life? Is the system based on convenience, simplicity, or what others may consider sheer madness, but to you is a life's structure? Again, it is important for maintenance' sake that you tailor this system to your own individuality and style. You aren't going to be able to force a ready-made system to work if it doesn't have qualities that are similar to your own ideas.

Give Everything a Home

A good way to get started organizing in the home is to find a specific place for everything. This doesn't mean that everything needs to be tucked away and hidden from view. Rather, it simply means that as long as you know exactly where to look for a particular item, you have designated a home for it. Even if your home looks as though items are slung every which way in total disorder, if you know where to find them every time, your home is organized. Looks aren't the key here, organization is.

If you have already thought of this and assigned homes to items, but it just doesn't seem to work, you have most likely overlooked a glitch in your plan. For instance, perhaps not everyone in the house is aware of the assignments. It will do you little good if not every person is cooperating. Or maybe the layout goes against your natural instincts. If you have a place for umbrellas stationed in your bedroom, yet don't concern yourself about whether or not it is raining until you hit the door, chances are the umbrellas are going to find themselves a new home on the foyer floor. Look for any glitches in your plan.

There are a few things you should take into consideration when assigning homes to items. These three considerations might very well take care of some of the hang-ups you come across.

Keep Things Simple

If you are a clutter bug or pack rat, carefully consider why. If you can only relax when your material possessions are surrounding you, then skip this section. The goal here is not to put a dent in your individuality. But if you are a clutter bug because you haven't had the time to dispose of things, or don't know where to begin, you should consider the benefits of a simple lifestyle.

Simplicity can take you a long way with organization. Frankly speaking, the less you have to organize and keep organized, the easier. Take a look around you. Are there items in view that you haven't even noticed for quite a while? Perhaps there are some things you enjoy the sight of but are often in the way. If you want your life to be a simpler one, you need to assign a value in terms of use and importance to those items that surround you.

Get rid of those things you hang on to but don't know why. Surely there is someone else that can put them to use. If not, simply toss them in the garbage. Once you clean your house of these items, it should already begin to reflect a simpler touch.

Next, you will want to think about those items you hold dear but are often in the way or put to little use. By all means, hold on to these. But you don't have to leave them out in the open to disrupt your system of organization. Consider putting them safely away in storage until you either find a use for them or just feel the need to have them out and around you. They aren't gone forever, but they aren't thought of as everyday items. This actually lends an even greater value to these items. If it is something special, you surely want to keep it out of harm's way. Leaving it out in the open will not only place it in potential danger but also give it an ordinary quality.

When you have gone through the entire house and disposed of or stored away those items that are unnecessary, you should get an overall sense of distinctive simplicity. This will make finding homes for the remaining items an easy task to complete.

Designating for Convenience's Sake

Whether you have chosen to simplify your home or not, you should definitely consider assigning homes to items for the sake of convenience. This will save you so much time in the long run, if done correctly. But again, you should not go against your natural instincts. If you do, chances are you will be somewhat stressed by

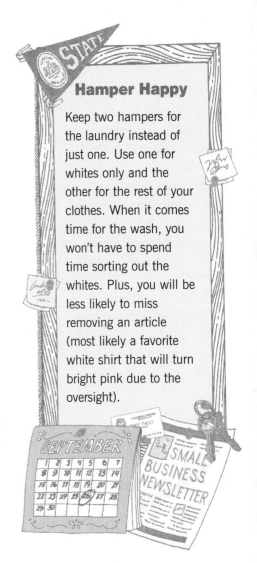

Hamper Happy

Keep two hampers for the laundry instead of just one. Use one for whites only and the other for the rest of your clothes. When it comes time for the wash, you won't have to spend time sorting out the whites. Plus, you will be less likely to miss removing an article (most likely a favorite white shirt that will turn bright pink due to the oversight).

the arrangement and actually spend more time on locating items than you originally would have.

To arrange by convenience you need to match up items with their purpose. For example, the remote control is to be used while you are sitting on the couch so you do not have to get up and manually change the television station. Since this is a popular lost item, it is a good idea to assign it a home and have the entire family agree upon keeping it there. A system of convenience would instruct you to give it a home within arm's reach of the couch. Perhaps you have an end table nearby. Or maybe you could even consider hanging a pouch container off the side of the couch. When you are done with the remote, place it back in its home so you automatically know where to reach the next time it is needed.

This system can be used on all items in all rooms of the house. Think about the items you lose on a regular basis and begin with those. Yes, you know you need to give them a home, but where is it going to be? What is the most convenient location? When you have found a home for the lost souls, move on to other common items.

Use Your Instincts

Establish homes that make sense to you. This is very important and sometimes overlooked. Use your common sense when deciding on where to place items. You know your habits and your thought processes better than anyone. If a convenient location conflicts with what you consider to make sense, definitely go with your sense.

Go back to the umbrella example. Let's say you realize the convenience of having an umbrella stand next to the door. This will save you the hassle of having to carry the umbrella all throughout the house before you are ready to leave. Not to mention the mess you may make dragging a wet umbrella behind you if its home is located anywhere other than next to the door.

However, in your mind it just makes more sense to have the umbrella located in the closet next to your raincoat. It doesn't

The Batteries that Never Quit

A battery recharger is a good investment if you tend to spend hours sorting through that little stockpile that you just know has one good battery, or for the times you are already running late but just can't bear to leave the house without your Walkman. Keep a cycle of freshly charged batteries going. You will always know where they are and can guarantee they will work.

matter why. That is just where you instinctively look for it every time. If you go against these instincts and insist on placing the umbrella next to the door, you will have created a glitch in your system. Sure, you may eventually be able to train your mind to automatically think of the placement of the umbrella, but why go through all that trouble and time? If you already have a home designated, keep it. That is just that much less work you have to do.

Designing an organizational system for your home may prove difficult at times, especially if others live there as well. However, if you start off assigning homes to items, it is easy to get into the groove of things. Once you have this task accomplished, it will seem as though much is already done, and that may very well be the case. But don't stop there; branch out into different ideas of what may or may not work. Create a system that is going to complement, not complicate, your lifestyle, and you will soon find that you look forward to walking into such a relaxed atmosphere after a hard day's work.

The Moving Mess

So you've finally found the house of your dreams. It is in the perfect location, has the perfect layout, and is perfect for your perfect family. While the idea of being settled in your dream home creates a warm and tingly feeling inside you, the moving monster comes to shatter all your happy thoughts. Moving is probably one of the biggest headaches you will ever have to endure in your lifetime. It's right up there with finding a new job and getting a root canal.

However, there are ways to make it more time-efficient and less painstaking, while allowing yourself the luxury of keeping your concentration focused on the dream house.

Even if you aren't planning on moving anytime soon, read this section and keep the information in the back of your mind. It will come in handy sooner or later.

Assuming you've located that perfect house and have everything out of the way but the move, it's time to use those time

One Room at a Time

You may find that it is easier to organize one room at a time instead of hitting random spots throughout the house. This will ensure that your organizational system has not missed any areas. Bear in mind, a weak link can break the chain.

management skills to keep the sanity of everyone involved in the moving experience. Shall we get started?

Now, before you begin packing, you need to make a couple of decisions. First of all, are you prepared to take on superhuman abilities and move yourself? Or would you prefer to hire a moving company and watch someone else take on superhuman abilities while you enjoy your tea? Use your fantastic decision-making skills here.

There are several things you need to take into consideration. For instance, how far away are you moving from your current location? How much stuff do you have to move? How many people are guaranteed to help? How much time can you take off of work to complete the moving process? What is your financial budget? Of course, there are going to be several other questions you need to ask yourself before settling on a decision. Be sure to take your time with this and consider every single factor.

Because time management is our goal here, you need to be very careful estimating the time it will take you to organize, sort, pack, label, transport, unload, unpack, distribute, and reward. This should not be a rush job. Give yourself some cushioning when it comes time to schedule each step of the moving process.

Because every move has the potential to be vastly different from another, this book will hit on the general aspects of the moving process. The following suggestions are designed to help your move to flow smoothly and time efficiently:

- **Create a to-do list.** (Sounds a lot like your time management system, doesn't it?) Pull in the rest of your family for this. Everyone needs to brainstorm to create this list. Keep in mind this will be ongoing, so don't think you've thought of it all right off the bat. From the to-do list you will want to create a schedule. Depending on the size of your home and how much you need to move, this schedule may encompass several weeks before the moving date.
- **Carefully consider everything you own.** If it has no monetary or sentimental value and is kept in storage for

most of its life, you probably want to get rid of it. You should do some serious eliminating during this period. That which you get rid of is going to save you the time of packing, moving, unpacking, and placing it. Think about all the time you are going to save if you have several items that need not go through that process.

- **When you have donated, sold, or otherwise disposed of those items you aren't going to be taking with you, take inventory of those items that are left.** If you are hiring a moving company, separate the inventory into two categories: things the moving company is going to handle, and things you are taking with you.

- **When packing, stay room oriented.** Pack together those items that will find their permanent home together. Don't pack your son's clothes with your daughter's clothes, even though it may be easier to just pull them all out of the dryer and put them straight into a box. The way you pack items will determine whether unpacking is to be a nice and easy process or an all-out disaster.

- **Instead of labeling boxes with generic names, give them numbers.** Keep a set of index cards handy. Each time you pack a box, give that box a number, place that number at the top of an index card, and list all the items that are placed in that box on the index card. Then, when you desperately need an item that has already been packed (and this almost always happens), all you have to do is locate the item on the index card and find the corresponding box. This will save you the time of looking through twelve boxes marked "clothes" for the dress you borrowed and need to return before you move. It is also a good idea to mark an estimated value for each box on the index card.

- **When you are unloading into your new house, set boxes and furniture in their appropriate rooms.** If you leave all of your boxes together and out in the open, stress will take over your life. Instead, place the boxes in their

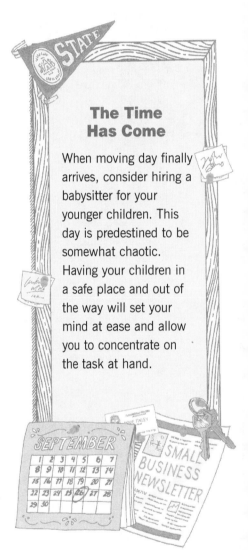

The Time Has Come

When moving day finally arrives, consider hiring a babysitter for your younger children. This day is predestined to be somewhat chaotic. Having your children in a safe place and out of the way will set your mind at ease and allow you to concentrate on the task at hand.

proper rooms. It will be easier to unpack things and place them in their designated areas.

- **Keep one room free of boxes.** Yes, we know, this suggestion somewhat contradicts the previous one. Choose a sitting room or family room that has comfortable furniture. Trust me, you are going to consider that box-free room a little bit of heaven as you go through the tedious process of unpacking. Had enough? Get away from it all and hide in that one room. But don't scatter that room's boxes all throughout the house. Place them as close to the appropriate room as possible without disturbing the peacefulness of it.

- **Create a file or folder for your important moving notes and papers.** Keep your index cards here, as well as receipts, delivery information, inventory sheets, and any other documents you use for the move. Keep this folder in a safe place. This will save you the hassle of trying to find a particular document amid the chaos the moving process creates.

- **If you have children, let them take part in the moving process.** Let them pack, label, and even physically move some of their own items. Not only will they be excited to help out, but you have just delegated some of the work that would otherwise take up your time. Teenagers are quite capable of handling their own stuff. However, if your children are under 13, you may want to keep an eye on what they pack and how. You should take on the responsibility of packing valuable and/or fragile items yourself.

- **Create a box to be unpacked first. Include items you are most likely to need right away.** These may include toilet paper; soap; extra clothes; plastic plates, cups, and utensils; scissors or a knife; beverages; cleaning products; and whatever else you can think of that would come in handy on arrival. This box should be loaded last so it is the first to be unloaded. Getting a good start in unpacking will build momentum and save time.

Hopefully these suggestions will help you save time, energy, and headaches during the moving process. It can be quite tedious and frustrating at times, but this is one area in which you can definitely put your time management skills to the ultimate test.

A Circus of Household Chores

Do you ever feel as though the household chores run your life? They follow you wherever you go, wait loyally for you to return to the house, invade your dreams, and watch over you like an over-protective parent. Laundry, dishes, grocery shopping, paying bills—the list could go on and on. Because your home is your central point where everything comes together at the end of the day, it is also the epicenter for disaster.

When something isn't done, it is usually the first thing to hit you as you walk through the door, already exhausted from a hard day's work. You have come to expect this and sometimes dread going home. Here's a quick list of hints and suggestions to help you get through these miscellaneous chores.

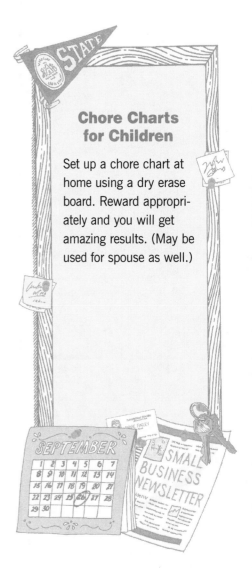

Chore Charts for Children

Set up a chore chart at home using a dry erase board. Reward appropriately and you will get amazing results. (May be used for spouse as well.)

- **Create the ultimate efficient grocery list.** Grocery lists are a staple for most households. These lists will undoubtedly make your trip to the market easier. How often do you find that your list forces you to run all over the market, revisiting certain aisles over and over again? This is a common problem with grocery lists, especially if you have several items to get. To make the most of your grocery list, do a little research. The next time you are at your favorite market, jot down the components of each aisle. Then, when you are ready to compose your next list, you will be able to categorize each item according to its placement in the market. This will save you the time of having to run back and forth with a bulky shopping cart, thus making your trip more efficient and less painstaking.

- **Plan your meals for the entire week.** Add all the ingredients you do not have on supply to your grocery list. Make one trip to the market a week—just one. If you live by yourself you may be able to get away with one trip every two weeks. The point is, do not make a run to the store every

time you fix a meal. This is a huge waste of time. By planning ahead, not only will you have everything available when you need it, but you won't have to spend time worrying about what you are going to fix.

- **Buy items in bulk.** This can save you loads of time in the long run. However, you must have room for these items or your organized masterpiece will turn into a cluttered catastrophe. Some items to consider buying in bulk are paper towels, garbage bags, cat food, toiletries, some food products (those that won't spoil, such as tomato sauce), and so forth. Whatever you know you will use, and have room to store, buy in bulk. It will save you the time of having to make several trips to the store and will save you money as well.

- **Use one set of sheets.** Most people will rotate two sets of sheets for one bed. In other words, when one set gets dirty you take it off the bed and put a fresh set on. When you get around to it, you will wash the dirty set and fold and store it until next round. But it is actually better to just maintain one set of sheets and not rotate. When the sheets are dirty, strip the bed. While you are washing the sheets, the bed has a bit of time to air out. You won't wear out two sets of sheets at once this way, and you won't spend the time it takes to fold, store, and recover the extra sheets.

- **Organize your bills.** What do you do with those bills that pile up every month? If you are like most people, you will toss them aside, preferably out of sight. If you are really ambitious, you will write down the dates they are due in your planner, but when it comes time to pay them, you sometimes have to search and search. Then you begin to ask yourself if you've already paid it, but you know that's just wishful thinking on your part.

So how do you handle bill-paying time efficiently? First, you should have an organizational system set up. Designate a specific area to place your bills as soon as you receive them. Something as simple as a folder will work well for this. Before placing the bills in the folder, open them and write the date they are due on the outside of the envelope. Place a stamp and your return address (use labels if you have them ready-made) on the return envelope. Schedule two days a month—not together, mind you—to pay your bills. You shouldn't have to worry about them any more often than that. When it comes time to pull out the checkbook, you will have all you need right there in front of you. Just write the check, seal the envelope, and be done with it. You may also want to consider setting up a direct deduction payment schedule with a business or service. This will allow the business to automatically withdraw the amount due from your checking account on the day your payment is due, without your having to ever be bothered with sending in payments.

- **File your bills.** If you want to be extremely organized, you can keep a filing system of those companies you shell out your hard-earned money to every month. Give each its own file folder and keep all correspondence and receipts here for future use. You may also want to write the check number on the copy of the bill you keep for your records. This will allow you easy access to payment information should the need arise. Also, you will be able to tell quickly if the bill has been paid.

- **Soak dishes.** If you have a dishwasher, you are blessed. If not, you probably suffer from dishpan hands. But that's quite all right. Even those with dishwashers need to scrub every once in a while. They still have the same mess to clean up after cooking, and they still need to rinse and soak. So unless you have hired or delegated the work to someone else, you have to battle the dishes. An easy way to make cleanup a snap is to keep a sink full of soapy water while you are cooking. When you have finished with a measuring cup or bowl, slide it into the sink. Do this with each utensil and dish you use. When you have finished cooking and the time for cleanup has come, all you need to do is wipe and rinse the dishes. They will have

Mother Taught Me Well

Set out your clothes the night before for the next day. This is especially helpful for those of you who just can't seem to turn on your brain before midmorning. You won't spend time staring at your closet, and you won't have any surprises such as a huge stain or a terribly wrinkled shirt.

been soaking the whole time it took for you to cook. Food will be broken up already and scrubbing won't be much of an issue. Of course, if you are fixing a six-course meal, you may have to keep rotating a cycle of clean soapy water. But for smaller meals, this technique works well to save you time and energy.

- **Get Caller ID.** How many times have you missed a phone call only to miss the message as well? Though you may have well-meaning family members, messages will be lost or forgotten from time to time. This can cost you quite a bit of time and sometimes even embarrassment later on down the line. You could consider investing in a Caller ID feature to let you know who called while you weren't at home, even if someone forgets to tell you. Voice mail and call waiting are also popular features to have. However, you don't always need to acquire all this technology. If you have others in the household, or even if it is just yourself for that matter, keep a pad of paper and pen next to the phone. Connect both to the phone itself if you've tried this before only to find that they both get up and wander off on their own. There will be no excuse to not write down important information. You will save yourself the time it takes to search out writing implements and also the headache of pounding a date or phone number into your memory.

- **Don't underestimate the power of multitasking.** Because household chores can often be mind dulling and monotonous, use this time to overlap another, more energizing activity. It still should be something that isn't going to take up all your concentration, but really, now, how much of your attention needs to be centered on running the vacuum back and forth? If it is a physical activity such as vacuuming that you're undertaking, couple it with a mental activity such as thinking about what to get your sister for

her birthday or outlining in your head that story you've decided to write. Don't go overboard with multitasking. Don't try to iron your best dress while making dinner. Something could easily get burnt.

- **Go with the flow.** The workings of your house have their own rhythm. If you are used to doing things a particular way and it works well for you, don't give it up to try something that may or may not save you a bit of time. Yes, it is important to be time efficient, but you want that comfort to go along with it. If you turn your house upside down, everyone involved is going to have a different reaction, and more likely than not it is going to be a negative one. Don't force change, encourage it. If there is a constant struggle, give it up. You are just going to end up spending even more time and energy on the battle than you would leaving it the old way.

If nothing else, the above suggestions allow your mind to rethink everyday activities. Chances are they will spawn even more handy timesaving tips for the house.

Time Management Maintenance

You have turned your home into a paradise of sorts. You can walk (or run if you prefer) into the house, relax, and make the most of your time at home. All this is possible because of the hard work you put into successfully creating a time management system. You have done a fantastic job thus far, so next on the list is the reward.

Yes, don't forget that vital bit of your time management system! Congratulate yourself on accomplishing what you may have originally thought impossible. This was a big task and don't forget rule 2: "The activity cannot exceed the reward in terms of proportion." So that means that you should treat yourself huge.

Okay, now that we have that out of the way, here comes some disappointing news. You're not finished, nor will you ever be. Yes,

you'll need to be a good time manager for your entire life. But don't fret, you've got the hard part out of the way. Just look at what you've created from scratch!

Now all you need to do is maintain that time management system. Don't worry, it isn't going to be all that difficult. Plus, if you sputter out now, you will just have to start all over once you realize how important your time management system is to your life.

Keeping Control

So what must you do? All you have to do is maintain control. Doesn't sound so bad now, does it? This requires you to stay consistent with your organizational system. If you get off track, make the time to set yourself straight. For the home, this may prove difficult at times if you have others living with you. You may need to become a coach of sorts to encourage them to keep up with the organizational system. As long as everyone does his or her share on a regular basis, the system should run smoothly.

Incorporating Routines

You should also consider creating a routine. This will help you to automatically take care of things that might otherwise hint at procrastination. For instance, consider assigning a particular day to do laundry. If you go through the motions of doing your laundry on a specified day every week, eventually it will become habit. You won't be as inclined to put it off for two reasons. Number one, your body and mind are accustomed to getting it done, and it basically becomes a chore of just going through the motions. Number two, you will realize that by postponing this activity, your schedule will be backed up.

A routine will help with several household chores, not just laundry. Grocery shopping, taking out the trash, ironing, paying bills, and cleaning are other tasks you may consider setting up a routine for. However, don't get so caught up in routines that you become a thoughtless android. You do need a bit of excitement and spontaneity every once in a while. Otherwise, your home life could equal that of a lab rat. No one wants that. So, pick and choose your routine chores carefully.

Priorities and Goals

Keep your priorities in check at all times and refer often to your goals. You need to evaluate your progress and make changes if necessary. Make good use of lists and your schedule. Don't lose interest in these two items; they are essential to gaining control of your time. You may also want to keep a time log from time to time, just to see how well you have improved your use of time or whether you may be slipping behind without even realizing it. Don't allow importants to become urgencies. You simply can't avoid urgencies all the time, but you can cut down on their number by taking care of important matters right away.

Acknowledge the Effects of Your Time Management System

None of these tasks are going to be difficult to complete; it is more a matter of continuance. If your interest begins to fade, reevaluate your time management system and see if you can't spice it up a bit. But don't ever completely give up control. It will be a painstaking process to do over again.

Above all else, give your time management system the recognition it deserves. Acknowledge the effect it has had on your life. This in itself should keep you motivated to maintain management.

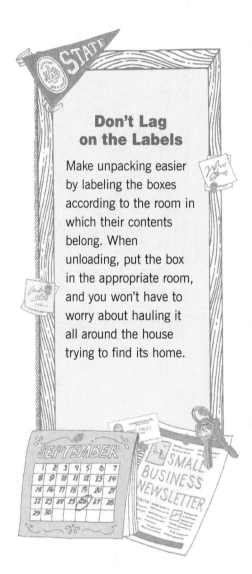

Don't Lag on the Labels

Make unpacking easier by labeling the boxes according to the room in which their contents belong. When unloading, put the box in the appropriate room, and you won't have to worry about hauling it all around the house trying to find its home.

Your Work Space on Your Time

If you are like most people, your work life is a separate entity that has a tendency to crowd its way into the other aspects of your life. You already know by now that you need to create a balance between work and home. This is why it is important to find an effective time management system for your work space. If your work life has a tendency to crowd out your personal life and home life, it is most likely due to poor management of time. This chapter covers how you can create that balance for a happy and well-rounded life.

You've Heard It All Before

Often when people think of time management, their jobs are the first thing to come to mind. This is because work is the place where we feel the most direct pressure on our time. Consider the following statements. You are in constant competition with your coworkers, supervisors, and peers. You feel the need to be busy at all times because that image is equated with success. You have deadlines to meet and people to please. Meetings, lunch dates, phone calls, and paperwork overload you with urgencies. There is a constant stream of people needing your attention right away, and you are bogged down with stress. Does any of this sound familiar to you?

Your work environment can put a strain on you that has the potential to severely affect your home life and personal life. If you don't grab hold of the reins in this aspect of your life, chances are nothing will get accomplished and the work will continue to pile up.

Though you may not think so right now, applying time management to your work space will most likely be easier than applying it to any other area of your life. This is because your work space is going to be more structured. You have assignments, a specific job to do, and particular resources available to you. You work within the confines of your job duties. Because you have these set limitations, it is easier to find ways to work within them. With your home life, however, you have full reign to do as you please. This leaves several options available to you, making the decisions you make broader and requiring much more thought. It is simply much easier to make a decision when there are fewer options to choose from.

With this in mind, the thought of applying time management tactics to your work space should not overwhelm you. In fact, you should be excited and perhaps even feel a sense of relief. This is the easy part, but an important one. So once you conquer this, you will be well on your way to a well-rounded and fulfilling life. Now, let's get started.

Step One

It's all about attitude. The difference between managing your time at work and at home is going to stem from the different attitudes you have about each. You need to first determine your attitude and/or time awareness while at work. This will directly relate to the feelings you have about the work itself. If you take pleasure in your work, you will have a better attitude toward the time you spend there. However, if it is a job you despise, your attitude will reflect those feelings.

Step Two

Once you've determined your attitude, you need to take stock of your priorities. Make a list of what is important to you and then rank the items in terms of life value. Keep in mind that your priorities may differ from those of the company you work for or the overall priorities set by the industry. That's okay. They should reflect your own values, not those of others.

Step Three

Develop a game plan. This is best thought out in terms of goals. Where do you want this job to take you? Where do you see yourself in five years, 10 years, nearing retirement? You need to set goals to achieve these ideals. Figure out the steps you need to take. Will you need to further your education? Perhaps you want to

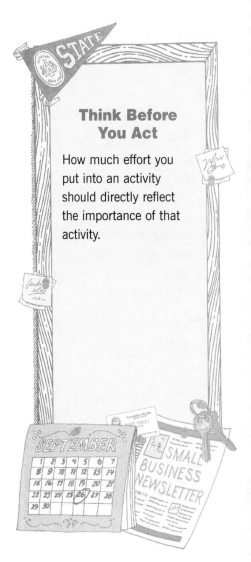

Think Before You Act

How much effort you put into an activity should directly reflect the importance of that activity.

change your function within the company, or change companies altogether. So how are you going to do that? Set time limits on the specific steps and don't be lax.

Step Four

Schedule those activities that will help you achieve your goals. But be realistic. People often get slightly out of control when it comes to their jobs. They have grand ideas and push themselves too hard to make their dreams come true. You want to work your priorities into your schedule, of course, but in a timely fashion. Remember to keep that balance between work and play. Just because you may have some extra time available, don't rush to fill it with work-related activities. Decide first whether you are spending too much, too little, or just the right amount of time on your work. Then work your goals into your schedule. Keep the reins tight. Having an excellent work life doesn't necessarily mean you will have an excellent home life and personal life.

Step Five

Organizing your work space will have a significant impact on the quality of work you do. Having things in their appropriate place and easily accessible will help you to work more efficiently. Arranging your space to fit your needs and comforts will have a tremendous influence on your stress level and self-esteem.

Organization is an important part of time management. Take notice of your daily activities. Are there any hang-ups you come across that could be smothered by better organization? Anything you spend time looking for is a definite yes to this question. What are some others? In just a moment we will give you some specific suggestions on how to organize your work space. However, you need to have your own ideas in mind before you jump on our advice. An organizational system should be tailored to your needs and habits, and what we offer may not work as well as an idea you already have. Use our suggestions to get you started, but personalize the system or it may end up failing you.

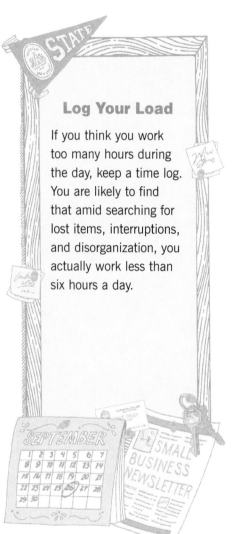

Log Your Load

If you think you work too many hours during the day, keep a time log. You are likely to find that amid searching for lost items, interruptions, and disorganization, you actually work less than six hours a day.

The Foundation Is Set

Your work space is going to differ from mine, but these basics of time management will withstand all variances. Once you have the foundation set, you will be able to move forward with your own time management tactics. Some may be universal; some may work only for you.

Organizing Your Work Space

Whether you work out of a converted barn or a high-rise, city-view office, your work space needs to be organized. Again, just for clarification—organization does not necessarily mean neat and tidy. What could be organized for you may look to another as if it were struck by a tornado. The important thing is to know exactly where to find anything at any given moment and to have some kind of ordered system set up.

There are several ways you can go about this. Of course, if you have a system in mind already, by all means get that geared up to go. Perhaps you can use a similar system to the one you used in your home. The more familiar the system, the easier to stick with it. This is one reason why it is so important to tailor these systems to your individuality. It would be a shameful waste of time to work so hard to incorporate a time management system into your life, only to disregard it a few weeks down the line. If you just don't have the slightest idea as to where to begin, here are a few suggestions.

Paper

You may want to begin with the king of all time management problems: paper. By getting this beast out of the way first, it will seem as though your job is done (of course it isn't, it just looks that way). Paper, as thin as it is, takes up quite a bit of room. It also likes to accumulate and multiply at an amazing rate. Worse than termites on a log cabin, paper can bring your office down in a matter of hours. But you do have the ability to get it under control before permanent damage is done.

Filing

If it is at all possible, handle paper only once. As soon as you get it, figure out what needs to be done with it and get rid of it. Find a place for those papers that you need to hold on to for a while longer. A filing system will work wonders here. Most people will choose to use an alphabetically arranged system. It is convenient and simple. However, if you really want to get down and dirty, you can use a color-coding system within the filing system. As long as everything is clearly labeled and in a location that makes sense, a filing system can become your best defense against the paper problem.

If there are papers you are going to need throughout the course of the day, group the relative papers together. For example, if you have a report to write, bundle all papers with relevant information into one group. Using a specific folder will help keep these papers together and in one place. Be sure to mark the folder clearly for quick access. You can even use rubber bands to keep papers together if you don't have folders readily available. There is no point in having to make several trips to the filing system if you know you are definitely going to be using certain papers during the day.

Paper Trays

Paper trays are excellent organizing tools. They stack well and don't take up a lot of room. You can specify a certain function for each tray. For example, perhaps you have papers that need to be dealt with right away. Place these in the top tray. For those papers that are important, but are of no use to you at the present moment, the second tray is a handy storage area. Perhaps you can use a specific tray for those items that need to be sent out, such as memos or letters. You can even use a tray for items that need to be filed away. (Let's face it, even though handling paper only once is the best route to take, it isn't always the most practical.)

But don't let these trays get too full! Keep them under control. Use them for easy access and practicality, not for procrastination and long-term storage.

Take a look at your office and the current paper situation. Do you already have a system in the works but just don't keep up with it? Or maybe you have never even considered a system. This is the time to get it all under control. Once you have the paper problem by the throat, you will find that the rest of the disorder can be extinguished rather easily.

Convenience

The convenience of the items in your office will directly affect your management of time as well as the constancy of your organization system. Take a look around you. What items do you use the most? Are they within arm's reach or do you have to cross the room to get to them? The inconvenient placement of items can destroy the systems of even the most organized people.

Say, for instance, you repeatedly refer to a series of reference books several times a day. These books are located across the room. Even though you know exactly where they are and are careful to keep them in order, this is still a hindrance to your organizational system. Because you continuously have to stop what you are doing and physically get up and walk across the room each time you need a book, you break your concentration over and over again. This will cost you quite a bit of time in the scheme of things. Perhaps all that physical exertion wears you out. Suddenly, you get grand ideas of laziness and don't return the books to their rightful places each time after use. You justify it with the knowledge that you will eventually use them again, so what is the purpose of wasting time and energy? However, because you don't return the books to their designated area, your desk becomes a heap of clutter. You can't find anything beneath the heavy books. Not all the books will even fit on your desk, so you have some in piles at your feet. Pages are getting torn and covers are getting bent. You have managed to turn your desk into a disaster area.

Seems like you just can't win. Either way you are wasting time, right? So what are you going to do? You are going to nip the problem in the bud. A little rearranging is in order here. If you are panicking at the thought, don't. Be calm and rational. Is there a file cabinet or other mobile object close to your desk that you can switch with the bookcase? (Just make sure that what you decide to

Don't Skimp on Ergonomics

If you spend a lot of time at the computer, invest in a good chair that will help your posture and productivity.

move isn't going to create the exact same problem.) If so, fabulous! Move the items and problem solved. But if you use that file cabinet just as often as you do the bookcase, you have run into a problem. Switching one with the other will do no good, but you can't cram the two into one small space. This is when a little creative thinking on your part will go a long way.

Perhaps you don't need every single book on the case, just those in the reference series. Have you considered hanging a shelf next to your desk? You could place those specific books right within arm's reach without having to worry about moving the entire bookcase. A shelf is attractive and doesn't take up any floor space. If a shelf isn't going to work, consider placing a miniature case or a book rack just big enough for those particular books on the floor next to your desk.

Get creative with your space. Rearrange things for your own convenience. You don't need to copy anyone else's office pattern. When you begin to organize according to your individuality, you will discover a flair that no other office has. It becomes your own, and you will be more comfortable within it, which in turn benefits your overall management of time.

Minor Details

Now that we've got the two big issues under control, it's time to pay attention to the small stuff. I'm sure if your office is anything like the norm, you have lots and lots of small stuff. But remember, you have just won the two major battles, so these little skirmishes shouldn't be a problem. Anything you can do to make your work area comfortable, easily accessible, and less confusing can only aid you, so don't neglect your duties here.

On your desk alone are probably a dozen items that tend to get misplaced or scattered. Pens, pencils, paper clips, staplers, rubber bands, thumbtacks, tape—do you ever spend time looking for these items? Are they readily available for your use? Every item that is used consistently should have its own home. There are a wide variety of products out there that are made specifically for these types of items. If this style of organization suits you, then schedule

Profess a Purpose

Name a legitimate purpose for every item in your work space. If you can't name it, get rid of it.

a trip to your local office supply store and check out the options available. Or you may want to consider designating a particular drawer for these wares. You can divide the drawer into sections with something as simple as cardboard to keep the items from getting jumbled and mixed up together. Just be sure to place the items in a location that makes sense and works well within your system.

You may want to consider incorporating other items into your system. For instance, a bulletin board will allow you to keep important items and lists off your desktop but still within sight. Just make sure you update the bulletin board regularly. You don't want your eyes to take the time to scan items that you no longer have any use for.

A desktop calendar is large enough to pencil in appointments, notes, and any other information you may need at a moment's glance. Plus, you will be able to check the progress of upcoming weeks. It is recommended to get such a calendar that also has the other eleven months in smaller print at the bottom. That way, you won't have to flip back and forth to look ahead or behind.

Keep a small notebook by the phone. When you first sit down at your desk, mark the date on the top line of a clean page. Use this page to make notes of telephone conversations you have. This will come in handy later on when you can't quite remember the details of the information you were given or if someone tries to back out of a deal you made over the phone. Perhaps you are unable to contact a particular person. Write down the name and/or company you are calling and the question you need to ask. It is easy to forget all the phone calls you make in one day. When the call is returned you will only have to glance at the notebook to refresh your memory.

Store similar items together. For instance, you probably have a mélange of stationery products. Letterhead, envelopes, postage-paid return envelopes, even stamps can all be located in one area. Perhaps it is next to your address book, or maybe you would choose to place these items next to the printer. If you keep like items such as these together, you will save yourself the time of running around the office each time you need to mail a letter.

There are several ways you can get the small stuff under control. The best way to start out is to pay attention to what you use the most. Once you have these everyday items settled into an organizational system, the rest will be sure to follow. Organizing your work space allows you more freedom, less stress, and a balance of peace and production.

Multitasking in the Office

Undoubtedly, your workday will have activities that simply don't take much thought or focus on your part for completion. These are the prime candidates for multitasking. All the other important stuff deserves your full attention, so don't let the temptation of multitasking get the better of you. The following are some suggestions that pertain to common work environments.

- **Multitask while on the phone.** Taking telephone calls while engaging in some other activity is a favorite among multitaskers. For the busy individual, it is almost too much to bear staying still while on the phone. Some of the more popular activities to couple with talking on the phone are straightening desktops, filing, scanning e-mail, sorting mail, reevaluating your schedule and/or to-do list, and gathering materials for an upcoming meeting. Of course, you must not forget to gauge the importance of the telephone call before engaging in another task.
- **Do lunch.** Another popular multitasking event is the business lunch. We all need to eat, right? So why not pair up a meeting with a meal? Dining is a favored social pastime and nearly everyone will agree it reflects well on you to acknowledge this. If you think about it, by choosing this, you may be making more sense than you realize. Restaurants are quite a bit more relaxed and casual than offices. Depending on what the meeting concerns, it may be to your benefit to congregate in such an atmosphere.

- **Use a tape recorder.** If you have a lot of busywork on your hands, such as filing or sorting through a waist-high stack of papers, you may want to consider purchasing a tape recorder. You can use it to dictate a letter, practice your sales pitch for an upcoming meeting, or just to make notes to yourself so that whenever something crosses your mind you don't have to stop what you are doing to go write it down.

- **Multitask electronically.** Computers allow multitaskers a lot of freedom. You can keep several applications open at once so you can flip back and forth between them. However, you may want to keep open only those that you are currently working on. Too many open applications can result in confusion and could possibly cause your computer to crash.

- **Move around.** When you take breaks (which you should) to stretch your muscles, consider making that nice little stroll even more worthwhile. If the fax machine is down the hall, wait until your scheduled break to send your documents. However, this works only when the break is purely for physical reasons. If you use this break time to clear your mind and refresh yourself, do not multitask! It defeats the whole purpose behind the break.

Headset Help

Use a headset or speakerphone for telephone calls to keep your hands free for multitasking.

There are probably several other ways in which you personally can multitask. Take a look at the busywork piled in front of you. If you can do a task without having to give it your full concentration, double up with a similar task. You will get more done in half the time when you choose to multitask sensibly.

Delegating in the Workplace

Delegation is a word well known to CEOs, presidents, and high-ranking officials. Do you think it is a coincidence that the people in these positions know how to delegate well? No, it's not. These people have learned to incorporate delegation skills into their time management systems. You should consider doing the same if you want to make the most of your work time.

As you recall, Chapter 4 gives a good rundown of the basics of delegation. Just to refresh your memory, here's a summary of the general steps:

1. Choose the task to be delegated.
2. Choose an appropriate person to complete the task.
3. Give specific instructions.
4. Let go of the task and trust the person chosen to do the job.
5. Set a schedule for measuring progress.
6. Accept the completed task.
7. Praise accordingly.

Chain of Command

When you delegate at work, you must keep in mind that there is an authoritative structure involved. To those you delegate to, you are viewed as an authority figure and maybe nothing other than that. This requires you to have good leadership skills. Do you have the skills you need? Let's take a look at some of the more common leadership skills.

Effective Communication

You must be able to communicate effectively. You simply cannot expect someone to know exactly what you want from him or her if you don't communicate the idea well. Be as detailed and clear as you can. Also, the way you communicate is important. You want to make sure that you don't speak condescendingly toward your workers. Yes, you may be in charge, but you are just as human as they are.

You must also be receptive. Don't allow your workers to be afraid of you. They need to know that they can approach you with a problem or question. Listen to their ideas and respond effectively.

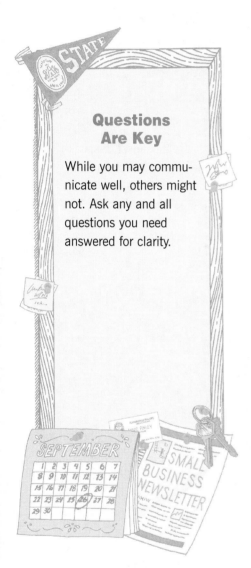

Questions Are Key

While you may communicate well, others might not. Ask any and all questions you need answered for clarity.

It is quite possible that your workers will think of ways to take the project to an even higher level.

Motivation

You may feel as though you don't have the time to concern yourself with the level of motivation your workers are experiencing. But you really don't have the time not to. A good leader will try to keep the overall morale at a high level. This can be accomplished by scheduling progress reports, organizing staff meetings, and rewarding good work on a regular basis. You can also give the workers a bit more freedom. This shows your trust in their abilities, and they will be eager to sustain that trust.

These are just a few of the qualities a leader has. Consider some of the authority figures in your life. What qualities and skills did they possess? Once you have a good idea of what makes a good leader, compare it to yourself. Are there some areas you need to brush up on?

Creating Connections

You know that delegating work to others can make your overall use of time in the workplace much more efficient and effective. But did you know that it will also benefit you by creating a stronger connection to those you work with? If you feel more comfortable with the atmosphere and the work you are doing, your attitude toward time will be shaped for the better, creating a more productive and time-efficient workplace.

How to Make the Most of Your Commute

If you have a long commute to and from work, or even if it is only 10 minutes, that is time that can be put to good use. Don't think because you don't have control over the amount of time you spend on the commute that you don't have control over how you spend

that time. Whether you drive or take public transportation, you can use this time effectively.

Is there anything on your schedule that would coincide nicely with your commute? Are there steps you can take toward your goals that could be accomplished during this time? Use your mind to think creatively. If you think that all you can do is sit there like a vegetable, you haven't yet reached the mindset of a good time manager.

Public Transportation

Taking advantage of public transportation can work exceedingly well in your favor. That is, if it is the practical choice. If you are going to be spending two hours commuting on public transportation compared to a half-hour driving, you are wasting your time. However, if public transportation is an option that is within reason, consider the possibilities.

Public transportation releases you from the stress and responsibility other drivers must assume. You are not in control and, therefore, not obligated to give your full attention to arriving at the destination. This means that you are free to do other things. Your hands aren't tied up, your mind needn't divide its concentration, and your stress level can even out. So what are you going to do with this freedom?

Look at your schedule. Is there some busy work you can get out of the way? Perhaps there is a leftover item from yesterday's to-do list. If you choose to do something directly related to your schedule and/or to-do list, make it something that is not going to need a lot of room to work on and won't require deep thought. You mustn't forget that you will be in the company of several other people. It is not always going to be possible to obtain a seat; sometimes you may have to stand squashed

together like sardines. There is likely to be a lot of noise and a wide variety of potential distractions. Take these factors into consideration when choosing a task to complete.

A way to get around the inevitable distractions is to bring music to listen to. Something you enjoy, but don't get swept away by. It is easier to tune out outside distractions if you are tuned in to a jazzy song. However, you don't want to be too caught up in the music or this just becomes another distraction.

Here are some suggestions on how to make use of your commute time while taking advantage of public transportation:

- **Read the newspaper.** If it is important to you to be knowledgeable about the world around you, use this time to catch up on current events. You can scan headlines and read articles of interest. By the time you reach your destination, you can throw away the paper, satisfied with your enlightenment.

- **Prepare a memo to send out to coworkers or employees.** Memos are supposed to be short and to the point anyway, so you won't need to spend a great deal of thought or time on this. It is easy to scribble down a draft so you don't have to concern yourself with it once you reach the office. Also, you don't need a lot of room for this. You can jot down notes while standing up. You can even use a napkin as paper, if need be.

- **Study your to-do list for the day ahead.** Make any alterations that are needed. Compare it to your schedule. Is everything accounted for? Is your day a good example of how to use time effectively and efficiently? If not, you can make changes now before you are caught up in the heat of the day.

- **Relax.** If you are able to relax in the midst of chaos, this may be an ideal time for you. If you can use this time to mentally prepare yourself to carry you throughout the day, do so. You will be geared up and ready to jump right into things once you make it to work. Those around you will probably need a little alone time with their coffee before getting started. If you have already passed that point, this will only give you a greater advantage.

- **Do something that brings you pleasure.** This is especially true if you aren't happy with the work you do. Perhaps you enjoy reading, so bring that fantastic novel you have been having a hard time putting down. Or maybe you are expecting a child. Start on a list of baby names. If you are involved in a relationship, plan a romantic evening. Whatever it may be that brings a smile to your face, this is a great time to capitalize on it. It will make your workday a little easier to endure if it begins and ends with a bit of happiness.

Driving

Using commute time productively may be a little trickier while driving than if you were using public transportation. While driving, your concentration cannot ever be completely focused on any one thing aside from the traffic around you. You have a responsibility to yourself and those around you to take heed of the rules and regulations that mark safe driving. You don't have the freedom that you have with public transportation, but this doesn't mean you can't use this time effectively.

You need to figure out first what properties you cannot use while driving. For instance, you cannot count on your eyes, hands, and feet to be available for additional tasks while driving. They are accounted for already. So that cuts out reading, writing, and dancing. Your safety is top priority here, so if you feel as though you need to lend your full concentration to driving only, don't think you are wasting your time. Priorities come first, remember? So you are still staying within your time management system.

However, if you are comfortable multitasking while driving and know that you are able to be responsible and careful, by all means consider tasks you can perform while on the road. Think about the

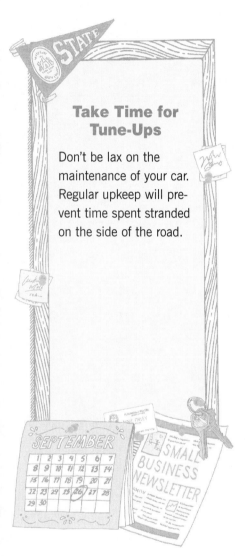

Take Time for Tune-Ups

Don't be lax on the maintenance of your car. Regular upkeep will prevent time spent stranded on the side of the road.

following suggestions and whether or not you can incorporate them into your commute time:

- **Learn a foreign language.** Do you have a tape deck or CD player in your vehicle? If so, you may want to use your driving time to educate yourself. There are hundreds of informative language books on tape and CD that you can listen to while driving.
- **Mentally prepare yourself.** As with public transportation, you can use this time to mentally prepare yourself for the day ahead. Think about the activities you have scheduled and what other tasks you would like to complete. Having these things fresh in your mind when you arrive at work will be just as helpful as a cup of strong coffee to get you going.
- **Practice a speech or presentation you will give in the near future.** Go over the outline in your mind until you are comfortable with it and practice different ways of getting your ideas across. You can practice in the comfort of knowing that no one is going to hear you. Try out different tones of voice, pauses, and inflections to make the speech more interesting. If you practice enough, you will be more confident in presenting.
- **Listen to a news radio show**. You can catch up on current events and what's going on in the world outside your own. If you do this everyday, you may not have any need to get a newspaper, which just cuts back on the paper problem.

Maintain Control of Your Work Space

Now that you have your office in tip-top shape, toned, and perfected to suit your individual needs, you are all done, right? Wrong. Just like cleaning your bedroom, the order and cleanliness

will eventually become disordered and dirty—unless you maintain management.

Reward Yourself

First of all, congratulate yourself on a job well done. Don't forget the importance of rewards! Acknowledge the fact that you put a lot of work and thought into organizing and pulling together an otherwise inept area. You have done the hard part; now you just have to sustain that smoothness.

Keep Control

Maintaining management of your time will not be difficult if you never let go of the reins. This means that you need to be in control at all times.

Again, paper will probably be your biggest problem. All paper must be sorted and disposed of or filed away at least once a week. Magazines, newspapers, and any other literature you receive regularly are included. It is possible you won't have had the time to look over this literature by the time you need to sort. If this is the case, quickly scan the periodical for articles you would like to read. Clip those articles and put them into a file folder for later use. Toss out the rest of the periodical; the bulk will just get in the way.

Mail protocol can take different forms. Some people prefer to leave it until the end of the week when the rest of the paper is sorted. However, others prefer to handle it on a daily basis. Your decision will most likely depend on the amount of mail you receive each day. You may decide that it would take you at least an hour if you sorted only once a week. Not to mention the stacks upon stacks that would accumulate on your desk if left for that long. Or, it could be that all your incoming mail for a week will fit nicely into the mesh basket set out specifically for that purpose, and it would actually take longer to sort every day as opposed to all at once. Regardless of when you choose to sort your mail, always do it next to a trash barrel. Don't even bother opening junk mail (sweepstakes, direct mail offers, etc.). It will only be a waste of your time. For those pieces of mail you do open, you can immediately dispose of any advertisements or other unnecessary additions.

At the end of each day, settle everything into its home. Replace anything you brought in from outside the office. Make your work space look as though it hasn't been touched since your time management skills got hold of it. Take this time to look over your schedule for the following day. Also, check your to-do list once more. Mark off any items you completed but failed to cross off, and transfer any items you did not complete to the following day's to-do list.

Peruse Your Priorities

At the end of each month, take out your list of priorities. Check to see that you are still participating in activities that directly relate. You may find that you would like to change or rearrange some of your priorities. Do that at this time, or even throughout the course of the month—whenever it comes to mind. Also, examine your goals. Have you been meeting the deadlines you set for yourself? Or maybe you are further ahead than you thought. Perhaps you decide a particular goal just isn't worth your time any longer. Whatever changes are to be made can take effect with the beginning of the new month.

Upholding a Balance

Maintaining time management should not be all that difficult at work. Because your job in itself is rather structured, or at least more so than the other areas of your life, routines and order operate well in this atmosphere. Just keep the basics in mind and apply them with your own added style. Also, don't forget to create that all-important balance. If you are working too much, you may be crowding out the other areas of your life. Watch your control; don't let it slip away from you.

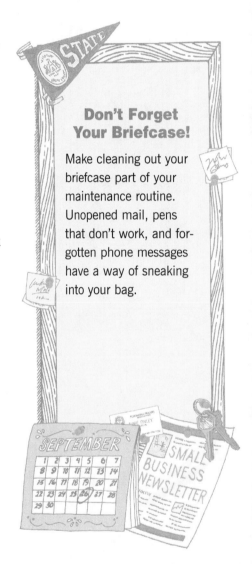

Don't Forget Your Briefcase!

Make cleaning out your briefcase part of your maintenance routine. Unopened mail, pens that don't work, and forgotten phone messages have a way of sneaking into your bag.

Your Personal Life on Your Time

Your personal life will need just as many time management tactics as the rest of your life to make it fulfilling and enjoyable. Don't for a minute think that because you have the rest of your life in order and under control, your personal life can run wild. There must be consistency with time management if it is to work effectively. You don't want a missed date to spill over into your perfected schedule and create chaos for the rest of the areas. Besides, your personal life is supposed to be the most enjoyable time you spend. Why not make the most of it? In this chapter, we will take a look at the possible ways you can apply the time management tactics you have learned to your personal life, making it as satisfying and pleasurable as possible.

Put It into Play

Your venture into personal time management will encounter a medley of various aspects. However, the basics you have learned will be applied in the same manner as they are with your work time and home time.

You may think that managing time in your personal life is a conflict of sorts. Why would you want to stick to a schedule when you are enjoying yourself? Doesn't your awareness of time take away from the pleasures of your personal life? Isn't the whole idea behind having fun essentially allowing yourself freedom from the routine structure? Why bother with time at all? The answer is simple. Time does not stop and start at your whim. How much time you spend on an activity directly reflects on the time allowed for another activity. If you allow disorder in one area of your life, that disorder will spill over into the other areas.

Using your time management skills for your personal life will not take away from your enjoyment of the activity, if used correctly. At the very least, these skills will help you to create more time for pleasurable activities and not allow you to lose sight of your priorities along the way. In the end, your personal life will live in harmony with the other aspects of your life, creating a well-rounded and balanced existence. Shall we begin?

Step One

You have probably evaluated your attitude toward time already and are sick of having to do so. But if you haven't, now is the time. It may be that you have a different attitude toward time when on personal terms than you would if you were concentrating on work. Perhaps you function on internal time only with your personal life, whereas your work space revolves around external time. These differences should be noted and taken into consideration. This means that those skills you applied toward work may require a slight variance when applied to your personal life.

Step Two

Set priorities for your personal life. Since you have already set priorities for your home and work life, those left from the list you created at the beginning are most likely those that deal with your personal life. If you find that you have only a couple left, perhaps you aren't realizing the importance of your personal life. This is a good time for reflection. Are there any other priorities you may have missed the first time around? Outside of work and home, what is important to you? Be as specific as possible. Don't just say, "Having fun." Include details. For instance, "Going to dinner once a week with my best friends" is a clear-cut priority. You will be better able to plan and schedule with detailed priorities.

Step Three

Next up is setting goals. Yes, you should set goals for this area of your life as well.

Because you are human, you are continuously developing. It is important to add structure to that development so your mental, physical, and spiritual states do not get out of control. You most likely already have an ideal of what you want to be. Now, what are the steps you must take to get there? Again, you need to set time frames for your goals or they are just dreams. Take a look at your priorities and use them to help you set goals.

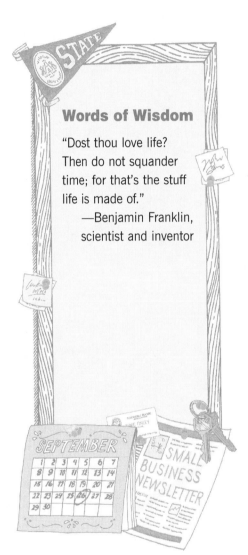

Words of Wisdom

"Dost thou love life? Then do not squander time; for that's the stuff life is made of."

—Benjamin Franklin, scientist and inventor

Step Four

If your schedule is already full, we have a problem. But if you have closely followed the steps as outlined in this book, you should have quite a few slots left to fill. Start fitting together the last pieces of the puzzle. You have set your goals; now you must set the time to fulfill them. Remember to find a balance between work and play. Your schedule should reflect that at this time. If not, a few alterations may be in order.

Step Five

Organizing, though it may not seem so, is also an important part of your personal time management. There are several things in your personal life that may need a bit of simplification, elimination, or organization to get you even further ahead.

For example, most will agree that birthdays, anniversaries, and special occasions should be handled in an organized manner. How many times have you been on the black list because you missed someone's birthday? For some reason, those cute belated birthday cards just don't seem to cut it all the time. These causes for celebration can be entered into your daily planner, or consider keeping a notebook or some other form of reference to refer to once a month when planning your schedule. Another good idea is to categorize your reference guide by month. List all the special occasions that fall under each month instead of listing the occasions by specialty or corresponding person. This will save you the time of searching through each list each month. You shouldn't have to refer to it more than once a month.

For those celebrations that you should acknowledge but that aren't really all that important to you (such as a distant relative's graduation), there are several timesaving tips you can apply. For instance, if you keep a store of general presents, you will save yourself the time of shopping for one particular gift. You will only have to choose from those you have already purchased ahead of time. Yes, this sounds rather impersonal, but for those celebrations that have little meaning to you, the gesture you make is what counts.

Another List

If you find you are overwhelmed with demands for your time, make a list of what you don't have time for in your personal life. This will help you to say no more often.

Having an assortment of greeting cards and wrapping paper on hand is another good timesaver. If you feel you are being a little too indifferent, add a nice handwritten note for a touch of warmth. Mail the package and/or greeting card on your routine trip to the post office. Mailing the package will save you the trip across town for a personal visitation, as well as the time it will take you to "catch up" with Aunt Mary.

Organizing your personal life is just as important as organizing your closet. What it comes down to is a structured and simple system that allows your life to flow smoothly. No one wants hang-ups to drag their personal lives down the drain. With organization, hang-ups are kept to a minimum, if not eliminated entirely.

Step Six

It's time for a reward! Just take a look at what you've done already. By applying those basic time management tactics you have learned thus far, you will be able to make ample time for all the different aspects of your personal life, feel good about the choices you make, and live in relative peace and harmony.

Keep in Touch

Communication is an important aspect of your personal life. Because there are so many lines of communication these days, it is sometimes difficult to decide which is the most appropriate choice and when to use it. Consider keeping all contact information in the same place for each person. For example, let's say you have an address book. For each entry, list not only the name and mailing address, but also the phone number, fax number, work number, e-mail address, and any other possible way to contact them. This will make it easier for you when you decide to make contact. Then you will have specific options to choose from.

Keeping in touch is necessary to maintain relationships with those you value in your personal life. But it often seems as though we don't have the time to do it well, so we don't do it at all. Also,

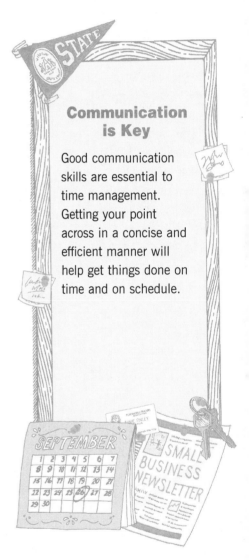

Communication is Key

Good communication skills are essential to time management. Getting your point across in a concise and efficient manner will help get things done on time and on schedule.

Little Secretaries

If you have young children, encourage good message-taking skills by making a game of it. Purchase the professional telephone message pads and let your children pretend they are business professionals.

it may be that urgencies will hold you back from carrying out your good intentions. However, there are ways you can keep in touch without sacrificing a lot of time. For instance, you can always opt to send an e-mail to a friend instead of making that phone call. The telephone allows for instant feedback, which can sometimes carry the conversation far into the wee hours of the morning. However, with e-mail you can send a heartfelt message to let the other person know you are thinking of him or her and then be done with it for the moment. If e-mail just doesn't seem to carry that personal touch, send a letter through snail mail. Handwritten items are always a pleasure to send and receive. You don't have to spend hours composing a letter, just scribble out a short note. Quite often, a short and sweet note will brighten the day of another even more so than a long-winded letter.

You must also take into consideration the other person's schedule. Finding leisure time that corresponds is difficult. Sometimes this can be the hang-up that destroys relationships. You will have your management of time under control, but the other person might not. This is why it is important to be patient and rational. Sometimes it simply won't work to get together. But that doesn't mean you can't communicate. Use the channels mentioned above to keep in touch, and you will eventually be able to work something out. Also keep in mind that the more relaxed your schedule, the easier it will be to come to a compromise with the other's schedule. This isn't to say you should leave a lot of leisure time available (we've discussed the dangers of that), but rather that you should not have such a tightly woven schedule that no alterations can be made.

When you do finally find the time to communicate, how you communicate will make all the difference in the time spent. Clear, concise statements will allow for mutual understanding. If you are vague and distant, you may spend a lot of time just getting to the point, which isn't to say your point will be understood. If the other person is just as vague and distant, you could spend days without getting anywhere. Good communication skills aren't just how well you pronounce your words or the appropriate use of nonverbal signals. It also encompasses your level of self-esteem, the comfort of the situation, your knowledge of the matter, and your stress level. Bear in mind that the better you are at communicating, the better you are at using your time efficiently.

Relationships

Now that we know how to communicate, it seems to make sense to dive right into a popular aspect of personal life: relationships. There are just as many flavors of relationships as there are of ice cream. But one thing holds true for all—for a healthy and satisfying relationship, development and maintenance are important. All are going to require different degrees of these, and it is up to your discretion to determine what is necessary. This means that you must evaluate each relationship you have and rate its value.

Stability

The stability of each relationship must also be taken into account. This is a key factor in determining how much time needs to be spent on its development. You may have people in your life who have excellent self-esteem, an organized life, and a positive outlook. Relationships with these people are likely to require little time and effort on your part to maintain. This isn't to say that you don't want to spend a lot of time with them, but just that they don't need a lot of time. On the other hand, you may have people in your life who have low self-esteem, are chaotic by nature, and focus on the negative. These people will most likely need more time and attention. Depending on the value of the relationship, you may not be willing to invest that much time. That's why it is important to consider the nature of the relationship in regard to time requirements.

In our busy lives, it is sometimes easy to neglect our relationships. We just have so much going on, we take for granted that the relationship will survive. Sadly, this isn't always the case. Consider your own relationships. Does this sound familiar to any of them?

You may need to put a little more time into the maintenance, and sometimes repair, of these relationships.

Communication

We've already established that communication is important, and it is especially so in relationships. For stable relationships, drop a line or two every once in a while to keep in touch and up-to-date. You will most likely have an understanding with the other person as to what is going on in your life at the moment and of those activities that take precedence. If the relationship is healthy, this is all that should be required.

For less stable relationships, quite a bit more time must be involved. Regular meetings and consistent reassurance is often necessary for maintenance. Careful communication is key. The relationship can become more stable with developmental care.

Then, of course, there are the relationships in between, which we can just play by ear. At times they will require more effort, and then sometimes they will stand well on their own. This category makes up the majority of our relationships, which in a way is a little troublesome to our management of time. But remember that your time management skills are designed to help you in the midst of the ever-changing world, so you are going to be able to handle any curveball that gets thrown.

Ways to Strengthen Relationships While Saving Time

Because relationships vary in value and strength, there are several paths you can choose from. For instance, a good way to spend your time developing relationships is to have a gathering of a few close friends. This will save you the time of meeting with each one individually. However, beware of the drawbacks. To avoid disaster, the people involved must get along with each other. Also, this works only for the more stable relationships.

Consider also meeting on a regular basis with someone, such as a Sunday morning breakfast date. This way, the date will be a

Speedy Summons

Make use of that modern-day technology and program the speed dial feature on your telephone. Just don't forget who's name is set to which number, as this could create quite a disaster if you have more than one beau.

consistent item on your schedule and you won't be tempted to push it aside. This will work very well for those somewhat unstable, but important, relationships.

You can even multitask while developing and maintaining relationships. Visualize the classic beauty salon scene where women bond while getting their hair styled. Perhaps you can find a shopping partner or a gym buddy. There are a hundred ways you can accomplish tasks while working on relationships at the same time. Be creative and have fun. Above all else, acknowledge the importance of relationships in your personal life and give them their due.

Education

Work, laundry, cooking, cleaning, organizing, commuting, raising children, meetings—who has time to work on their education? You do. If gaining knowledge appeals to you, then advancing your education is a wise choice to make. Does taking a class on the history of music attract you? There is a wide range of subjects out there just crying out to be studied. Anything from calculus to swing dance (hey, knock out two birds with one stone—education and exercise!), just take your pick. Don't worry about the time issue just yet. Let your mind wander to that forbidden zone of dreams and see if there isn't an urge to learn hiding back there somewhere.

If you have something in mind, try to think of it as a reality. Can you see yourself actually signing up for a class, or maybe even a full semester? Is it important to you? If you have answered yes to any of the previous questions, it is time to let your time management skills work for you.

Of course, you will need to research the institution, course offerings, class times, and so forth. But for our purposes, let's say you already discovered your dream class, but it is offered only in the evening, twice a week. Suddenly you become discouraged and wish you had never done the research.

You believe that there just isn't any possible way you can work it into your already packed schedule. Well, think again. Isn't that

Be Smart and Strengthen a Relationship

Take a class with a friend or family member you need to spend some quality time with.

Ways to Bond

Consider the following suggestions on how to bond and get things done at the same time:

- Form a book group
- Take a class with a friend
- Organize a neighborhood dog walk
- Establish a Sunday tea party
- Have a regular television or movie night with your friends

what your time management skills are good for? You know that your schedule isn't set in stone. If it were, no one would ever be able to live his or her life voluntarily.

Take a look at your schedule. Does it reflect an emphasis on work life and home life over your personal life? If so, great. Something needs to give there anyway to create a balance, and your education will be what fills the void. Look at the time slot that your class would fall into. What is standing in the way? Is it an unimportant item? If so, your job is done—cut and replace it. Chances are, though, you will run into a bit more difficulty than that. So, this item really shouldn't be cut, but it can be moved. Fantastic! All you are going to have to do here is a little reorganizing.

Pull out your handy list of priorities. Match those with the activities on your schedule. Anything left over is up for the cut. Now determining what is to be cut will be a little difficult. Keeping a base in reality is very important here. You will most likely have a couple of urgencies that you simply can't avoid, even though they may not be important. So we'll leave those. Now consider the rest. Are there any items you could possibly delegate to someone else? These will be prime candidates for the axe. Perhaps there are some that could be rescheduled to a later date. There are several possibilities. Don't think that just because you have something else allotted to that specific time frame that all hope is lost.

The same tactic should be applied if you already have the right balance of personal, work, and home life set up. Just concentrate on those items that fall into the personal life category and apply the same deductive time management skills listed above.

If you are still having trouble justifying the class's time expense, think about this: Your education will allow you to gain knowledge. That knowledge will benefit your life on a whole—in every area, not just your personal life. Yes, it may initially just be for fun, but the long-term positive effect should be a justification in itself. If you have the desire to learn more, go for it.

Health

Though your health is a characteristic of every aspect of your life, it is placed in the personal life chapter because of the way it is usually dealt with. There are exceptions, but in many cases, people treat their health as they do their personal lives—placed on the back burner until work and home life are dealt with. Health equates life. So, you are probably asking yourself why on Earth you would want to apply time management skills to something as important as your health? Because in the end, your effective time management skills can lead to a healthier and stronger life.

Procrastination

This is a major time management issue that people face time and time again. Unfortunately, this is the one area in which procrastination can be deadly.

There may be several reasons you procrastinate with your health. Probably the most popular is fear. Let's say you are terrified of the dentist. Of course you would never admit it, so you constantly make excuses (wasting a lot of time) and put off making an appointment. One of your excuses may be that you don't have enough time. Well, let's just put a shot in that one right now. Remember lovely Mr. Parkinson? He said that work expands to fill time. Now, what do you think the chances are that you actually did have enough time to make it to the dentist but subconsciously applied Parkinson's Law to make it seem as though you didn't? Be honest. By now you should be skilled enough as a time manager to have set time aside for your priorities. And your health is a priority.

Let's be realistic. Do you really think that if you have a problem with your teeth it will just go away if you ignore it? We talk our children out of that reasoning, why can't we do it to ourselves? You might argue that you don't have a problem with your teeth. But what if you do and you just don't know about it yet? It makes sense to maintain a schedule of regular checkups so you can discover a problem early on. Would you rather have a cavity filled, or have the decay corrupt your entire tooth, causing it to have to be

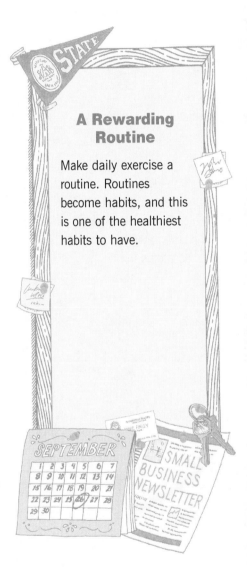

A Rewarding Routine

Make daily exercise a routine. Routines become habits, and this is one of the healthiest habits to have.

pulled? Procrastination has the potential to cause you greater pain. This holds true for your regular physical exams as well. If you are going to take your time management seriously, you must apply it to all aspects of your life, including your health.

Exercise

Regular exercise is another health issue many people disregard. Again, a common excuse is no time. Exercise should be a set part of your schedule that everything else works around. Even if it is only 10 minutes a day, it is still significant.

You can multitask while exercising. For instance, catch up on that hot novel you've been wanting to get to while running the treadmill. It can be done during commercial breaks, while talking on the phone, or even while cooking. You don't have to be a member of a gym. Exercises can be done in the comfort of your own home. Research some exercise programs. There are thousands out there to choose from. The time you spend making excuses for not exercising is the time you could be using to exercise.

Sleep

Everyone knows that sleep is important, but do you really take this information into account in your management of time? Sleep affects everything you do, including how well you manage your time. This is why it is important to understand your natural cycles and sleep patterns. Sleep, like reality, has a hard-core and undeniable impact on your use of time.

First of all, you need to acknowledge that sleep is something you need. It isn't a want or a luxury you can do without. It is essential for your well-being, both physically and mentally.

Next, you will need to discover your body's natural sleep pattern. Just because you go to bed at 11:00 P.M. and wake up at 5:00 A.M. every day doesn't mean that this is your natural sleep pattern. Your natural sleeping pattern will be that which leaves you feeling the most rested and energized for the day to come. If your habit of getting six hours of sleep at night works okay during the week, but you find that on the weekends you need quite a bit more sleep,

Don't Believe Everything You Hear

Don't let your mother's advice of going to bed early and rising early have any effect on you whatsoever.

your pattern is off. While it may be working all right, it is not optimal. To get the most out of your management of time, you will want to find the pattern that works best for your body.

Experts argue over how many hours of sleep our bodies need each night. This argument will continue until the end of time because there is not one right answer. Everyone's chemical makeup is different; therefore, our individual needs are going to be different. Some may require five hours of sleep at night and another two hours during midafternoon. Some will sleep a straight eight hours through the night. It all depends on your body's makeup.

If you are unaware of your body's natural sleep pattern, you may be forcing sleep on your body when it doesn't even need it. Or, on the other hand, you may be depriving your body of sleep when it needs it the most. To find your natural sleep pattern, forget everything you've ever been told about sleep. Disregard the recommended eight hours of sleep at night. Clear your mind of any preconceived notions of sleep.

Once you have done this, let your body tell you when it is ready for sleep. Don't fight the urges. If you begin to get tired around 9:00 P.M., go to sleep then and wake when your body is ready. Spend a weekend getting to know your natural sleep patterns. Don't use alarm clocks or preset guidelines. Let your body tell you when to sleep and when to wake. When you have determined a pattern that allows you to get good, deep sleep and wake refreshed, you have found your natural sleeping pattern.

Now you need to use this knowledge to schedule your sleep times. Apply this pattern every day. Don't fudge on it during the weekends or even during the week when you have several things to do. By finding and taking advantage of your natural sleep pattern, you are going to be able to reach an optimal productive peak during your waking hours.

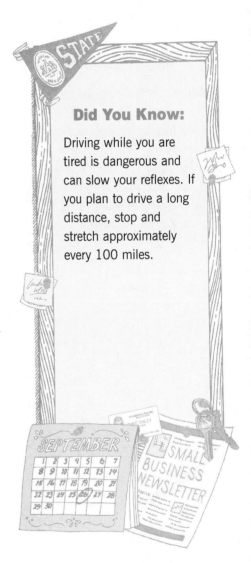

Did You Know:

Driving while you are tired is dangerous and can slow your reflexes. If you plan to drive a long distance, stop and stretch approximately every 100 miles.

Diet

One more health issue and then you're on your own. Your diet. We're not talking about trying to lose weight. We're talking about your eating habits. First of all, are they healthy? Be honest. Do you

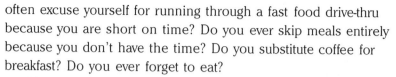

often excuse yourself for running through a fast food drive-thru because you are short on time? Do you ever skip meals entirely because you don't have the time? Do you substitute coffee for breakfast? Do you ever forget to eat?

Use your time management skills to help you eat healthier. Take a look at your schedule—are there time allotments for meals? If you are in the habit of skipping meals, it's time to schedule them. Even if you aren't, schedule them anyway. Use a list for grocery shopping. Carefully plan your meals for a week and get all you need in one trip. Pack your lunch for work. You will save yourself the time of scrambling around town trying to find something appealing to grab on the go. Not to mention the fact that you will save money by not eating out every day. Chances are, you will eat a lot healthier if you bring your own lunch. Write down eating healthy as one of your priorities. Because you will have that master list with you at all times, it is a good way to constantly remind yourself of its importance.

Don't put your health on the back burner. This should definitely hold rank in importance. To put it simply, if you disregard your health, you may not have all that much time left to manage.

Hosting Parties

Unless you are a hermit, social gatherings probably play a role in your personal life. This could be anything from a gossip circle in the ladies' room to a weekly poker game. Whatever your fancy, you will most likely host at least one social gathering in your lifetime. Now this could excite you beyond belief, or it could manifest the most terrifying phobia you've ever known. Regardless, this section shows you how to make the most of your hosting time to create an enjoyable and respectable atmosphere.

If you have ever hosted or witnessed firsthand the hosting of a social gathering, you are aware of the frenzied and disorganized feelings that seem to creep up in even the most reputable host. Now, tell me, who has time for those kinds of feelings? Isn't the social gathering supposed to be pleasant and for the benefit of all involved

Are You Getting Enough Iron?

Take a multivitamin every day. It will take you two seconds to get a healthy dose of nutrients. Plus you won't have to spend time studying the nutritional value chart in the foods you eat to make sure you are getting what you need.

(yes, all)? Once these feelings hit, unless you have a firm grasp on the situation, it is easy to welcome chaos to the front door.

Here are some timesaving tips for hosting a party.

- **Organize a guest list.** Creating the list of guests can always be tricky. You certainly don't want to offend anyone! Use your handy address book. Because we don't like scattered names and numbers, this should be a one-stop shop for all your acquaintances. Simply go through page by page, adding whomever you choose to the list. Definitely keep a list. Don't assume you won't forget to add someone later. Chances are you will.

- **Forget about handwritten invitations.** If your budget can manage it, have the invitations printed by a professional printer or do them on your personal computer. There are software programs that help you create invitations, flyers, and cards in no time. This should be a golden rule if you have more than 10 guests. You simply cannot afford the time it will take to sit down and handwrite the invitations. Yes, I'm sure they would look much nicer and more personal, but you can choose a lovely font and border to give your computer-generated invitations flair. Don't forget to use those return-address labels you have neatly tucked away within your stationery stock.

- **Plan, plan, plan, and plan some more!** Don't makes guesses as to what you will serve, where you will sit people, or what time you will start setting up. This is a disaster waiting to happen. You need to know how many people are going to attend, so add an RSVP request to the invitations. Once you get a number, add a few more. You certainly don't want to run out of anything! When you have a good idea of the quantity you are looking at, you will be able to plan the rest of the evening with little difficulty.

- **Hire professional cleaners to clean the house.** Not only will you get an immaculate house, but you will have

peace of mind as well. This will allow you to free up some time you might not otherwise have. Don't rely on your kids to do the job. They may do it, but there is no guarantee it will be done well.

- **Prepare food beforehand.** If you don't want to dish out even more money and have the soiree catered (which would be a good idea if you don't cook very often), prepare as much food as you can in advance. You could even create your menu based around this idea. Find recipes for foods that will freeze or those that don't take a lot of preparation time. Don't think that if you don't sweat over a hot stove all day long the menu is no good. There are plenty of quick and easy fixes out there that complement a social gathering beautifully.
- **Recruit help.** Surely you have good friends that you can threaten to uninvite if they don't help. Put your delegation skills to the test here. When people ask if they can bring something, say yes! Don't refuse the help of others.

Bear in mind that as long as you are organized, have planned appropriately, and do not leave things until the last minute, your social gathering is sure to be a huge success.

How to Use Your Vacation Wisely

Many working people out there use their vacation time but don't really take vacations. They don't seem to understand that a vacation is the time for relaxation, rest, and pleasure. No headaches, no stress, and definitely no work can come along. For those of you who do know what vacations are for, are you taking advantage of them and using them to their fullest potential? Probably not, if you are having difficulty managing time.

Well, we're going to work on that. This section is in the personal life chapter because vacation time is for personal use only. Home life and work life are restricted from the area. However,

Relax and Have Fun

Never think that hosting a party is too overwhelming for you. All it takes is the application of your basic time management skills.

it will do you no good unless you take a stand and use your vacation time wisely. Remember you want as much time as possible to just relax. Here are some timesaving tips to help you out:

- **Create a to-be-packed list.** The week before you leave, allow your mind to wander along the vacation trail. Keep a small notebook with you all week long. Each time you think of something you need to pack, write it down. Even if it is something you consider common sense, such as underwear, write it down. Then, when it comes time to pack, you will have a prepared list in front of you and won't have to spend time racking your brain to remember everything. Chances are, you won't have forgotten much if your mind has had unpressured time to think of what to bring over the course of an entire week.
- **Plan as far in advance as possible.** As soon as you set the date for your vacation, begin your research. Check out reservations and rentals—prices, availability, and convenience. Use the decision-making process to make the best choice and then leave it alone. Don't keep conducting research thinking you may find a better deal. When your vacation time draws closer, confirm all of your reservations. It will make the transition into peacefulness easier if you have less to worry about. Plus, you won't be spending half your vacation trying to find a place to stay or fighting with the auto rental establishment.
- **Know your route well.** This is especially true for those fantastic road trips. Have your route mapped out long before you get into the driver's seat. Even go so far as to plan an alternate route just in case. You're much better off spending some time figuring out your directions than spending hours lost in the middle of nowhere looking for a gas station.
- **Delegate tasks.** If you are planning to be away from home for a significant period of time, delegate those tasks

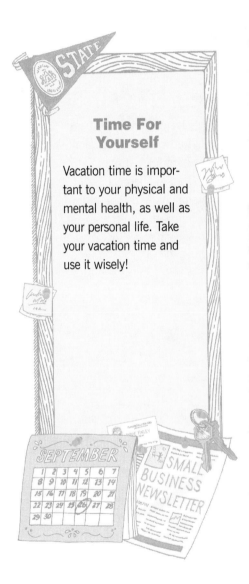

Time For Yourself

Vacation time is important to your physical and mental health, as well as your personal life. Take your vacation time and use it wisely!

that need to be completed while you are away, such as watering the plants or feeding the fish. If you are unclear in your instructions, you are likely to receive a well-meaning, but otherwise bothersome, phone call during your vacation, asking for additional instruction.

Creating Quiet Time

Do you remember way back in the beginning of the book when you figured out why you need time management skills? Taking a wild guess, let's say that one of the answers to this question was that there is always something fighting for your attention. You are pulled in so many different directions, you don't know which way to go first. Well, here's the secret answer: stand still.

The Eye of the Storm

By standing still you are essentially in the eye of the storm. The world around you, the storm, is in pure chaos and is constantly threatening. But you are safe from all the disorder right where you stand, in the eye. The eye represents you; you are the safe haven. Your thoughts and ideas and inner peace are what keep you safe. Would you rather face the storm with or without having a safe place to come back to?

This basically describes a common situation people face when trying to manage their time. They don't realize the importance of creating personal time for themselves. Time when all else is shut out, with only your thoughts and ideas to keep you company. Time to regroup and gather yourself together to face that storm that is raging out there. Instead, people choose to ignore the idea of personal time and drown themselves in the demands of the world. They feel they are obligated to give themselves to others first. This is often because the demands of others are made much louder than the ones we make of ourselves.

If you live your life this way, you probably aren't as happy as you could be. Personal time is very important to your well-being;

Zip It!

Use plastic Ziploc bags for traveling. They are good for just about anything—shampoo, lotions, dirty socks, jewelry—that might spill, smell, or get lost.

it allows you to discover yourself and your potential. You may very easily go through life at the beck and call of others if you do not allow yourself that precious quiet time. It is your chance to escape the storm, sit in front of a nice fire, eat a hearty meal, and rest up for the next engagement.

Making Peace a Priority

Doesn't it sound so nice to be able to find a bit of peace in this hectic world? You will probably agree with the idea, but disagree that it is possible. Well, because this is the ultimate step for a time manager, you are going to learn how to make it possible.

First, get rid of any feelings of selfishness. Yes, you are being selfish, but not in a negative way. So disregard those feelings altogether. Instead, take on an attitude of necessity. Consider your personal time necessary for the quality completion of everything else you have to do. You aren't lying to yourself or making excuses. It is fact, and you'll just have to accept it.

Next, you need to make personal time a priority. This means you need to add it to your master list if it isn't already there. Once it is in writing, it will be easier for you to accept its importance. After you have justified the need for personal time, you can take the step to incorporate it into your life.

Pull out your schedule once more. Where can you place a time slot for personal time that will benefit you the most? What time of the day do you often feel overwhelmed? Perhaps you would like to schedule personal time right in the middle of your day to break up the constant pressure and refresh yourself. Or maybe you would prefer to wait until the end of the day when you know you will best be able to enjoy it. Whatever you choose, schedule it. If it is on your schedule you are more likely to complete it.

Now that you have the time allotted, what are you going to do with it? This is the time when you will disregard all outside distractions and interruptions. The pressures of the outside world do not belong inside the haven. Some people will choose to use this time for meditation or breathing exercises. While that is great, it isn't

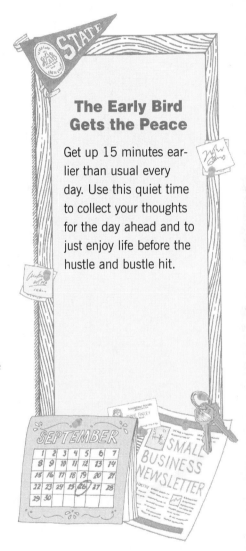

The Early Bird Gets the Peace

Get up 15 minutes earlier than usual every day. Use this quiet time to collect your thoughts for the day ahead and to just enjoy life before the hustle and bustle hit.

necessary. You just need to be quiet with yourself. Let your thoughts wander and don't concentrate on one specific thing. This will probably take some getting used to. It is a difficult thing to accomplish when your mind is constantly chewing on what to do next, the deadline you have to meet, the obstacles you have to face, your family and relationships, and the variety of other concerns and affairs that are such a big part of your life.

You must force yourself to shut all of that out. Focus on yourself. You will never be able to stay dry if you keep all the windows and doors of your haven open to the storm.

To be the ultimate time manager, you need balance and contentment in your life. You can't possibly have these if you do not spend time on yourself.

Keeping Up with Your Personal Life

Priorities and Goals

Constantly updating your priorities and your schedule is a good way to stay on track. Don't falter here; you need to maintain that balance. Every once in a while, check the number of hours you spend on your personal life in comparison to the time spent at work and at home. If you feel as though one area may be taking the lead, check a little more often to keep a close watch on it.

At the beginning of every month, go over your list of anniversaries, birthdays, and so forth, and then schedule accordingly so you are sure to not miss out on something. Do this for any major engagement you have.

Keep an eye on your goals and the progress you have made. Goals will change just as priorities do. This is why it is important to constantly reevaluate yourself and what you are doing. If you don't update your goals, you may find that you are either slipping behind or working hard toward something unimportant.

Healthy Living

Exercise and nutrition are the areas that most people have difficulty maintaining. You may start out gung ho but lose interest and start making excuses. You can't allow this to happen. Find ways to motivate yourself. Perhaps you can set up a chart at a gym and mark your progress. Or you may want to recruit a friend to join you in your quest for perfect health. If you have someone expecting great things from you, you are more likely to stick with it.

Keep Your Chin Up

Try to keep a positive attitude towards all that you do. This is very important for maintenance. Even when things aren't going quite the way you planned (and this will happen), don't give up. You have learned to manage your time effectively, and you have the necessary skills to turn a bad situation into a good one. A positive attitude will go a long way toward helping you achieve what you want. It will help you to stay motivated, to quash all those ingenious excuses, and to maintain good self-esteem.

Time to Yourself

Above all else, do not skimp on your own personal time. Take some time each day for yourself, and you'll find you have substantially more energy and productivity the rest of the time.

Don't Forget the Rewards!

Leading a well-rounded and balanced life should be reward in itself for maintaining management, but most often it is not. Therefore, you need to tap into that determination and drive that is inside you and exploit these resources. What is the point in learning all these time management skills if you aren't going to use them consistently? Obviously you had enough drive to pick up this book; why not allow that drive to carry you through?

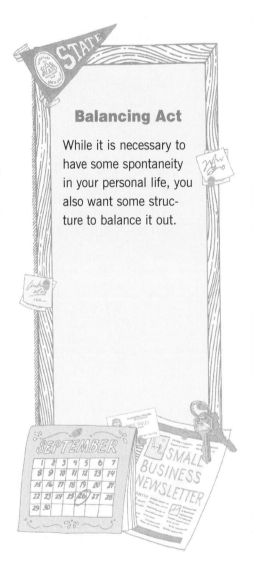

Balancing Act

While it is necessary to have some spontaneity in your personal life, you also want some structure to balance it out.

A

acceptance, of self, 182
accessibility, of to-do list, 35–36
active listening, 77
    criticism and, 186
    guidelines for, 78–79
activity log, 67–68
    stress and, 196–199
anger, 155
assertiveness, lack of, 175
attention span, 29
auction web sites, 114
automobiles. *see* cars

B

bartering, 68
biannual cleaning, 220–221
bills, 236–237
body language, 76, 77
book web sites, 114
bookmarks, on Internet, 100–101
breaks, from work, 129, 132, 253
    momentum and, 132–133
    physical effects of, 133–134
    stress and, 199–200
    types of, 134
business web sites, 122
Buxton, Charles, 131

C

calendar, 55–56
caller ID, 238
cars
    care of, 92
    driving to work, 258–259
    web sites for, 122
catalog web sites, 122
change, fear of, 174

children
    moving and, 234
    teaching about time
        management, 31
choices. *see* decision-making
    process
chores, tips for handling, 235–239
cleaning, 219–220
    biannual, 220–221
    dusting, 221–222
    of floors, 222–223
    picking up, 223–224
    scrubbing, 223
    upkeep and, 224–225
    of windows, 243
clutter
    eliminating, 51–53
    at home, 228–229
    organizing, 50–51
    at work, 250–252
    see also paper
communication
    in personal life, 267–269, 270
    at work, 254–255
commuting, 255–256
    by car, 258–259
    by public transportation, 256–258
competence, 171
competition, 142
concentration, 74
confidence, 171
consumer safety web site, 117
containers, storage, 58
control
    of emotions, 156
    of household chores, 240
    of motivation, 126–128
    at work, 260–261
convenience

    at home, 229–230
    at work, 249–250
correspondence, 51
criticism, 184–185
    defined, 185
    handling, 185–187

D

daily planner, 56–57
daydreaming, 80–81
deadlines
    decision-making and, 164
    large projects and, 151–152
decision-making process, 158–159
    fear and, 164–165
    influences on, 159–160
    self-esteem and, 180
    steps in, 161–162
    time use and, 162–164
delegation, 68
    advantages of, 87–88
    large projects and, 153
    problems with, 90
    process of, 88–89
    self-esteem and, 175, 177
    of vacation tasks, 279–280
    at work, 253–255
    see also help, hiring of
diaries. *see* logs
dictionaries, on Internet, 100
diet, 128, 275–276. *see also* meals
dishes, 237–238
distractions
    eliminating/controlling, 79–81
    from interruptions, 82–84, 87
    from telephone, 84–86
driving time, 258–259
dusting, 221–222

E

e-mail
  advantages of, 101–102, 268
  disadvantages of, 103–104
  resumes and, 118
  uses of, 102–103
education
  on Internet, 112–115
  as priority, 271–272
80/20 rule, 66–68
Einstein, Albert, 4
electronic organizers, 57
elimination
  of clutter, 51–53
  of distractions, 79–86
  before moving, 232–233
emotions, 154–156
  control of, 156
  see also motivation
employees, 92–93
enemy, time as, 10
Engstrom, Ted W., 53
entertainment web sites, 117
escapism, 201
excuses
  made to others, 128–129
  made to self, 129–130
  as time wasters, 128, 130
exercise, 273, 274
  as break from work, 134
  stress and, 200
external time, 5–6

F

failure, fear of, 136–137
faxes, 248
fear, 136
  of change, 174
  of decision-making, 164–165
  of failure, 136–137
  of health issues, 273–274
  of leisure time, 10–11
  of success, 138
  of work time, 11–12
financial web sites, 122
five minutes, using well, 73–74
floor cleaning, 222–223
focus, on what's important, 28–29
food. see meals
forgiveness, of self, 179
Franklin, Benjamin, 265
friends. see relationships

G

gift shopping, 120, 266–267
goals
  defining, 31
  at home, 218, 241
  maintaining, 42
  in personal life, 265–266
  realism about, 32
  rewards and, 144
  schedule and, 37
  self-esteem and, 175, 180
  setting, 29–30, 75
  at work, 245–246
  see also priorities; to-do list
grocery list, 235
guilt, 129

H

health
  diet, 128, 275–276
  exercise, 274
  maintaining good, 200–201, 283
  procrastination about, 273–274
  sleep, 274–275
help, hiring of, 91–93
home. see household management
hooks, 58
housecleaning, 92
household management
  chores and, 235–239
  cleaning and, 219–225
  meals and, 225–227
  moving and, 231–235
  organization of, 58–59, 227–231
  time attitude steps for, 216–219
Hubbard, Elbert, 185
humor
  self-esteem and, 182
  stress and, 200

I

identity, 170
important vs. urgent, 26–28
  to-do list and, 34
independence, 170
intelligence, 171
internal time, 6–8
Internet
  access to, 98
  e-mail on, 101–104
  education on, 112–115
  information resources on, 99–101
  job hunting on, 115–119
  search engine use and, 105–108
  shopping on, 108–109, 114, 117, 120, 121, 122
  travel planning on, 109–112
  wasting time on, 98–99
interruptions, 82–84, 87
intimacy, 170
involvement, 7

J

job searches, on Internet, 115–119

L

lateness, perpetual, 12–13
leisure, 206–208
    fear of, 10–11
    respecting of friends', 268–269
limitations, recognizing and
    respecting, 39–40
listening. *see* active listening
lists, avoiding too many, 53–55.
    see also to-do lists
literature sorters, 58
logs
    of activities, 67–68, 196–199
    of interruptions, 87
    of telephone calls, 84–85
    of time use, 16–18, 217, 246
lunch, 252

M

mail, 260–261
meals
    hiring cook for, 91–92
    importance of, 276
    meeting during, 252
    organizing for, 225–226
    planning for, 235–236
    preparation of, 226–227
    scheduling of, 227
    simplifying of, 51
mistakes
    fear of, 164
    forgiving self for, 141
    self-esteem and, 181
momentum
    large projects and, 150–151

work breaks and, 132–133
motivation
    control and, 126–128
    excuses and, 128–130
    Parkinson's Law and, 131–132
    perfectionism and, 140–142
    procrastination and, 134–140, 142
    rewards and, 127, 142–145
    scheduling and, 71–72
    self-esteem and, 180
    at work, 255
    work breaks and, 128, 129,
        132–134
moving, 231–232
    tips for, 232–235
multitasking, 69
    cleaning and, 224–225
    cons of, 70–71
    at home, 238–239
    pros of, 69–70
    while exercising, 274
    at work, 252–253

N

negative statements, 183
"no," learning to say, 204–206

O

office, organizational tools for,
    59–60. *see also* work
organization
    elimination of clutter, 51–53
    at home, 219, 227–231
    of kitchen, 225–226
    lists and, 53–55
    in personal life, 266–267
    personal nature of, 48–50
    simplification and, 50–51

tools for, 55–60, 106–108
    at work, 246–252

P

package tracking web sites, 122
packing
    to move, 233
    for vacation, 279
paper
    elimination of, 51–52
    handling of, 156–158
    organization of, 58
    at work, 247–249, 260
Pareto, Vilfredo, 66
Parkinson's Law, 131–132
parties. *see* socializing
perfectionism, 140–141
    self-esteem and, 175, 177
    tips for handling, 141–142
personal life
    communication in, 267–269
    control of, 282–283
    education and, 271–272
    health and, 273–276
    quiet time and, 280–282
    relationships in, 269–271
    socializing and, 270–271, 272,
        276–278
    time management steps in,
        264–267
    vacations and, 278–280
personal planner, on Internet,
    106–108
pet web sites, 121
positive attitude, 181, 283
positive self-talk, 182–184
preparation, 77
pride, 171

priorities
    activity values and, 67–68
    delegation and, 88, 90
    evaluating, 26–28
    focus and, 28–29
    at home, 217, 241
    listing, 24–26
    maintaining, 41
    organization and, 51
    in personal life, 265, 282
    quiet time as, 280–281
    rewards and, 144
    to-do list and, 34–35, 218
    at work, 245, 261
    see also goals; to-do list
procrastination, 134–135
    causes of, 135–136
    fear and, 136–138
    health issues and, 273–274
    large projects and, 150
    Parkinson's Law and, 131
    self-esteem and, 175
    tips for handling, 139–140
productivity
    scheduling and, 71–72
    telephone and, 86
projects. *see* tasks
public transportation, 256–258

Q

quiet time, 280–281

R

realism
    about goals, 32
    about time management, 18–19
    about to-do list, 35

relationships
    communication about,
        267–269, 270
    stability in, 269–270
    strengthening, 270–271
responsibility, excepting, 139
resumes, electronic, 116–119
    pros and cons of, 119
    sample, 117
rewards, 142–143
    guidelines for, 143–144
    at home, 219
    motivation and, 127
    in personal life, 267, 283
    procrastination and, 140
    self-esteem and, 180
    stress and, 201
    system for, 144–145
    at work, 260
risks, 142, 181
routines, 201
    bad, 204
    cons of, 203
    good, 203–204
    pros of, 202
Ruskin, John, 177

S

schedules/scheduling, 36–39
    around productive times, 71–72
    at home, 218–219
    of large projects, 152
    maintaining, 42
    of meals, 227
    of necessities, 36–37, 38
    in personal life, 266
    routine and, 202–203
    trade-offs and, 152–154
    of work, 246

scrubbing, 223
search engines (Internet)
    customizing of, 105–106
    personal planner and, 106–108
self-esteem
    criticism and, 184–187
    decision-making and, 160
    defined, 170–172
    fear of success and, 138
    good, 178
    high, 176–178
    improving, 178–182
    low, 173–176
    routine and, 203
    self-talk and, 182–184
    test about, 172–173
self-talk, positive, 182–184
sensory overload, 165–167
    decisions and, 158–164
    emotions and, 154–156
    large projects and, 150–152
    paper and, 156–158
    self-esteem and, 174
    trade-offs and, 152–154
    see also stress
setbacks, to time management,
    14–15
sheets, 236
shelving, 58–59
shopping
    for gifts, 266–267
    on Internet, 108–109, 114, 117,
        120, 121, 122
simplicity/simplification, 50–51
    organization and, 48
    of to-do list, 35
    of household organization,
        228–229

sleep
  importance of, 200
  naps, 128, 129
  patterns of, 274–275
Smiles, Samuel, 14
socializing, 270–271, 272
  party planning and, 276–278
speed reading, 74
stress
  healthy lifestyle and, 193,
    200–201
  identifying sources of, 193,
    196–199
  leisure and, 206–208
  routine and, 201–204
  saying "no" and, 204–206
  side effects of, 193–194
  test about, 195–196
success, fear of, 138

T

talents, 171
tape recorder, 253
tardiness, 12–13
tasks
  doing right the first time, 75–77
  hiring help for, 91–93
  at home, 217
  multitasking, 69–71
  scheduling around productive
    times, 71–72
  sticking to one at a time, 74–75
  tackling of large, 150–152
  trading off, 152–154
  using short time periods for,
    73–74
telephone
  caller ID and, 238
  headset for, 253

multitasking and, 69, 252, 253
  simplifying use of, 51
  wise use of, 84–86
time
  attitude toward, 4–5, 9–16, 20–22
  external, 5–6
  home, 216
  internal, 6–8
  keeping track of, 16–19
  lack of regard for, 13
  money not equal to, xi
  personal, 265
  work, 244–245
time limits, 31
time log
  of home activities, 217
  keeping, 16–18
  sample, 17–18
  of work, 246
time management
  defined, 19
  maintaining system of, 41–42,
    214, 239–241, 244–247, 264–267
to-do list, 32
  about moving, 232
  benefits of, 32–33
  consequences of poor, 33–34
  creating, 34–36
  of household chores, 218,
    240–241
  procrastination and, 139
  rewards and, 143, 144
  schedule and, 72
  small tasks on, 73–74
tools, organizational, 55
  basic, 55–57
  electronic, 57
  for home, 58–59
  for office, 59–60

trade-offs, 152–154
travel
  planning of, 109–112
  web sites for, 110, 111, 112
trust
  in others, 170–171
  in self, 179

U

urgent vs. important, 26–28
  to-do list and, 34

V

vacation, 278–280
  planning on Internet, 109–112
value scale. *see* priorities

W

window washing, 243
work
  commuting to, 255–259
  delegating at, 253–255
  fear of time and, 11–12
  maintaining control of, 259–261
  multitasking at, 252–253
  organizing space at, 246–252
  time management steps for,
    244–247
  see also tasks
World Wide Web. *see* Internet
worry, 51, 201

Y

yard work, 91
"yes," saying, 204–205

We Have EVERYTHING!

Everything® **After College Book**
$12.95, 1-55850-847-3

Everything® **American History Book**
$12.95, 1-58062-531-2

Everything® **Angels Book**
$12.95, 1-58062-398-0

Everything® **Anti-Aging Book**
$12.95, 1-58062-565-7

Everything® **Astrology Book**
$12.95, 1-58062-062-0

Everything® **Baby Names Book**
$12.95, 1-55850-655-1

Everything® **Baby Shower Book**
$12.95, 1-58062-305-0

Everything® **Baby's First Food Book**
$12.95, 1-58062-512-6

Everything® **Baby's First Year Book**
$12.95, 1-58062-581-9

Everything® **Barbeque Cookbook**
$12.95, 1-58062-316-6

Everything® **Bartender's Book**
$9.95, 1-55850-536-9

Everything® **Bedtime Story Book**
$12.95, 1-58062-147-3

Everything® **Bicycle Book**
$12.00, 1-55850-706-X

Everything® **Build Your Own Home Page**
$12.95, 1-58062-339-5

Everything® **Business Planning Book**
$12.95, 1-58062-491-X

Everything® **Casino Gambling Book**
$12.95, 1-55850-762-0

Everything® **Cat Book**
$12.95, 1-55850-710-8

Everything® **Chocolate Cookbook**
$12.95, 1-58062-405-7

Everything® **Christmas Book**
$15.00, 1-55850-697-7

Everything® **Civil War Book**
$12.95, 1-58062-366-2

Everything® **College Survival Book**
$12.95, 1-55850-720-5

Everything® **Computer Book**
$12.95, 1-58062-401-4

Everything® **Cookbook**
$14.95, 1-58062-400-6

Everything® **Cover Letter Book**
$12.95, 1-58062-312-3

Everything® **Crossword and Puzzle Book**
$12.95, 1-55850-764-7

Everything® **Dating Book**
$12.95, 1-58062-185-6

Everything® **Dessert Book**
$12.95, 1-55850-717-5

Everything® **Digital Photography Book**
$12.95, 1-58062-574-6

Everything® **Dog Book**
$12.95, 1-58062-144-9

Everything® **Dreams Book**
$12.95, 1-55850-806-6

Everything® **Etiquette Book**
$12.95, 1-55850-807-4

Everything® **Fairy Tales Book**
$12.95, 1-58062-546-0

Everything® **Family Tree Book**
$12.95, 1-55850-763-9

Everything® **Fly-Fishing Book**
$12.95, 1-58062-148-1

Everything® **Games Book**
$12.95, 1-55850-643-8

Everything® **Get-A-Job Book**
$12.95, 1-58062-223-2

Everything® **Get Published Book**
$12.95, 1-58062-315-8

Everything® **Get Ready for Baby Book**
$12.95, 1-55850-844-9

Everything® **Ghost Book**
$12.95, 1-58062-533-9

Everything® **Golf Book**
$12.95, 1-55850-814-7

Everything® **Grammar and Style Book**
$12.95, 1-58062-573-8

Everything® **Guide to Las Vegas**
$12.95, 1-58062-438-3

Everything® **Guide to New York City**
$12.95, 1-58062-314-X

Everything® **Guide to Walt Disney World®,**
Universal Studios®, and
Greater Orlando, 2nd Edition
$12.95, 1-58062-404-9

Everything® **Guide to Washington, D.C.**
$12.95, 1-58062-313-1

Everything® **Guitar Book**
$12.95, 1-58062-555-X

Everything® **Herbal Remedies Book**
$12.95, 1-58062-331-X

Everything® **Home-Based Business Book**
$12.95, 1-58062-364-6

Everything® **Homebuying Book**
$12.95, 1-58062-074-4

Everything® **Homeselling Book**
$12.95, 1-58062-304-2

For more information, or to order, call 800-872-5627
or visit everything.com
Adams Media Corporation, 57 Littlefield Street, Avon, MA 02322

Available wherever books are sold!
Visit us at everything.com

Everything® **Home Improvement Book**
$12.95, 1-55850-718-3

Everything® **Horse Book**
$12.95, 1-58062-564-9

Everything® **Hot Careers Book**
$12.95, 1-58062-486-3

Everything® **Internet Book**
$12.95, 1-58062-073-6

Everything® **Investing Book**
$12.95, 1-58062-149-X

Everything® **Jewish Wedding Book**
$12.95, 1-55850-801-5

Everything® **Job Interviews Book**
$12.95, 1-58062-493-6

Everything® **Lawn Care Book**
$12.95, 1-58062-487-1

Everything® **Leadership Book**
$12.95, 1-58062-513-4

Everything® **Learning Spanish Book**
$12.95, 1-58062-575-4

Everything® **Low-Fat High-Flavor Cookbook**
$12.95, 1-55850-802-3

Everything® **Magic Book**
$12.95, 1-58062-418-9

Everything® **Managing People Book**
$12.95, 1-58062-577-0

Everything® **Microsoft® Word 2000 Book**
$12.95, 1-58062-306-9

Everything® **Money Book**
$12.95, 1-58062-145-7

Everything® **Mother Goose Book**
$12.95, 1-58062-490-1

Everything® **Mutual Funds Book**
$12.95, 1-58062-419-7

Everything® **One-Pot Cookbook**
$12.95, 1-58062-186-4

Everything® **Online Business Book**
$12.95, 1-58062-320-4

Everything® **Online Genealogy Book**
$12.95, 1-58062-402-2

Everything® **Online Investing Book**
$12.95, 1-58062-338-7

Everything® **Online Job Search Book**
$12.95, 1-58062-365-4

Everything® **Pasta Book**
$12.95, 1-55850-719-1

Everything® **Pregnancy Book**
$12.95, 1-58062-146-5

Everything® **Pregnancy Organizer**
$15.00, 1-58062-336-0

Everything® **Project Management Book**
$12.95, 1-58062-583-5

Everything® **Puppy Book**
$12.95, 1-58062-576-2

Everything® **Quick Meals Cookbook**
$12.95, 1-58062-488-X

Everything® **Resume Book**
$12.95, 1-58062-311-5

Everything® **Romance Book**
$12.95, 1-58062-566-5

Everything® **Sailing Book**
$12.95, 1-58062-187-2

Everything® **Saints Book**
$12.95, 1-58062-534-7

Everything® **Selling Book**
$12.95, 1-58062-319-0

Everything® **Spells and Charms Book**
$12.95, 1-58062-532-0

Everything® **Stress Management Book**
$12.95, 1-58062-578-9

Everything® **Study Book**
$12.95, 1-55850-615-2

Everything® **Tall Tales, Legends, and Outrageous Lies Book**
$12.95, 1-58062-514-2

Everything® **Tarot Book**
$12.95, 1-58062-191-0

Everything® **Time Management Book**
$12.95, 1-58062-492-8

Everything® **Toasts Book**
$12.95, 1-58062-189-9

Everything® **Total Fitness Book**
$12.95, 1-58062-318-2

Everything® **Trivia Book**
$12.95, 1-58062-143-0

Everything® **Tropical Fish Book**
$12.95, 1-58062-343-3

Everything® **Vitamins, Minerals, and Nutritional Supplements Book**
$12.95, 1-58062-496-0

Everything® **Wedding Book, 2nd Edition**
$12.95, 1-58062-190-2

Everything® **Wedding Checklist**
$7.95, 1-58062-456-1

Everything® **Wedding Etiquette Book**
$7.95, 1-58062-454-5

Everything® **Wedding Organizer**
$15.00, 1-55850-828-7

Everything® **Wedding Shower Book**
$7.95, 1-58062-188-0

Everything® **Wedding Vows Book**
$7.95, 1-58062-455-3

Everything® **Wine Book**
$12.95, 1-55850-808-2

Everything® **World War II Book**
$12.95, 1-58062-572-X

Everything® is a registered trademark of Adams Media Corporation.

For more information, or to order, call 800-872-5627
or visit everything.com
Adams Media Corporation, 57 Littlefield Street, Avon, MA 02322

We Have

EVERYTHING KIDS'!

Everything® Kids' Baseball Book
$9.95, 1-58062-489-8

Everything® Kids' Joke Book
$9.95, 1-58062-495-2

Everything® Kids' Mazes Book
$6.95, 1-58062-558-4

Everything® Kids' Money Book
$9.95, 1-58062-322-0

Everything® Kids' Nature Book
$9.95, 1-58062-321-2

Everything® Kids' Online Book
$9.95, 1-58062-394-8

Everything® Kids' Puzzle Book
$9.95, 1-58062-323-9

Everything® Kids' Science Experiments Book
$6.95, 1-58062-557-6

Everything® Kids' Space Book
$9.95, 1-58062-395-6

Everything® Kids' Witches and Wizards Book
$9.95, 1-58062-396-4

Available wherever books are sold!

For more information, or to order,
call 800-872-5627 or visit everything.com

Adams Media Corporation, 57 Littlefield Street, Avon, MA 02322

Everything® is a registered trademark of Adams Media Corporation.